Xaviera Goes Wild

By

Xaviera Hollander

WARNER
PAPERBACK
LIBRARY

A Warner Communications Company

WARNER PAPERBACK LIBRARY EDITION
First Printing: July, 1974

Copyright © 1974 by Artistae-Stiftung
All rights reserved

Front cover photograph by George H. Rabovsky
Back cover photograph by Derek Case

Warner Paperback Library is a division of Warner Books, Inc.,
75 Rockefeller Plaza, New York, N.Y. 10019.

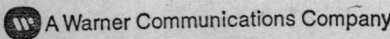 A Warner Communications Company

Printed in the United States of America

XAVIERA GOES...
WILD
WILDER
WILDEST!

Around the world with the least-inhibited girl guide you're likely to meet in a month of X-rated fantasies:

★ Meet Leo and Marika, Europe's super-swingers and the Amsterdamsels.

★ That first tango in Paris—even Marlon Brando would be jealous!

★ The French Connections, or how green was my daisy chain!

★ Freda's Plastic Fantastic Lover—"Thanks, she needed that!"

★ Morrocan on the rocks—hits the spot, says Xaviera.

★ Sex, without a hitch, is good for several uncomplicated orgasms.

★ Hot buttered rump is kinky with a capital 'E'! (for Englishmen)

★ The Sensuous Drill—different strokes do different folks (jest fine!)

★ Happy Hooker's Hot Seat—and she asked for it!

And here's what YOU'VE asked for—The further adventures of the world's wildest woman!

Love is like linen often chang'd, the sweeter.
—Phineas Fletcher
(1582-1650)

Women hate men who manage to talk them into bed . . . and loathe men who can't.
—Ray Canale
playwright

I had rather wear out than rust out.
—George Whitefield
(1714-1770)

AUTHOR'S NOTE: The people, places and events in this book are real. With the exception of established entertainers and public figures, all names have been changed, and we genuinely regret any inadvertent similarity between these pseudonyms and the names of real persons. Physical descriptions matching the names of real persons are pure coincidence and unintentional. To protect their privacy, certain locations may have been purposely obscured. But the stories, the characters and the events are very, very real!

EDITOR'S NOTE: Just in case you're not certain, Xaviera's name is pronounced *zahv-yair-ah*.

PROLOGUE

As the back cover of this book says, I've been around the world . . . or at least I've done a considerable amount of traveling since I took down my shingle as New York's Happy Hooker. And the trips I've taken are definitely not in the same league as your packaged European charter.

Though I grew up in Europe, and traveled throughout it with my parents as a child and teenager, I had long forgotten the aroma of a fresh croissant with marmalade in a Paris sidewalk cafe; the vinegar-and-newsprint taste of chips from a London fish-and-chips shop, crisp Danish bacon snuggling up against a pair of country-fresh cackleberries in Copenhagen, or real tutti-frutti ice cream in an Italian street.

And it wasn't just the flavor of European food I'd forgotten. I'd missed the old world sights and sounds, too. No wonder I frolicked around like a child as soon as I set foot on European soil again, trying to make up for lost time and tastes.

And finally, I could live and write without pressure from police, the press, and the Internal Revenue Service. I truly felt free as a bird again, fluttering hither and thither, doing whatever—and whomever—I pleased.

Europe's sexual maturity was an amazing change, too . . . after all, the Greeks and Romans were doing things two thousand years ago that still make the average American uptight today.

In Italy I actually overheard a Roman giving this witty put-down to an Englishman. "My dear man," he said, "when your ancestors were still living in caves, mine had been homosexual for a thousand years!"

I think you'll find my European coadventurers refreshingly different—more liberated and fun-filled, less hung-up and guilt-ridden than those in *The Happy Hooker*.

Incidentally, while this, like all my books, is in the nonfiction category, my honesty has led me into trouble. Because my books are interpreted as public admissions of criminal acts (being a madam is criminal), some governments therefore consider me a self-confessed criminal and thus I'm not eligible for immigration status. So if it's all right with you, dear reader, I'm going to say that certain events and actions in this book never happened. I made them up. I'm just a quiet little Dutch girl with a vivid imagination, okay? (That's what is known in the trade as a disclaimer.)

I wanted to call this book "Around the World in 69 Ways," but my publishers thought that some stores might refuse to sell such a saucily titled book. My editor suggested "If this is Tuesday, it must be Fellatio," and a friend suggested "Europe on Five Inches a Day." But finally, when everyone read the manuscript, they agreed there was only one thing to do—tell it like it is. Hence: "Xaviera Goes Wild."

And I hope that wherever you are, and whenever it is that you read this book, you'll bear in mind that healthy adults don't have to sleep alone. Sex, European-style, is a healthy, necessary and refreshing aspect of life, something beautiful to be fully enjoyed and enthusiastically pursued, with no implications of sin.

So come with me, around the world, and let's go wild. . . .

XAVIERA STARTS WILD

In the old days, as a madam in New York, I often found myself in the middle of some incredible situations. And, like the working girl that I was, I'd just shrug my shoulders, think, "Oh, well, it's a living" . . . and get on with the job.

But now that's all behind me.

It's all for fun these days, and while I'm doing it less, I'm enjoying it more.

And the more I enjoy it, the wilder it gets.

I still get all juicy thinking about that night in Paris. . . .

Leo and I were at an elegant, exclusive swingers' club —I'll call it Le Chateau Roger—near the Bois de Boulogne. The lighting was low and intimate, the music was solid and irresistible. The scene was totally sensual.

As the music pounded away (it was the Rolling Stones' "Brown Sugar") with its seductive, insistent beat, the soft colored lights dimmed and glowed, in tune to the driving rhythm. The air was supercharged with lust.

Leo and I were dancing tightly together, wrapped around each other, completely under the mood's magic spell. His hands were firmly around my hips and mine held his shoulders. I could feel the hard warmth of his aroused cock.

And I could also feel a cool pair of hands exploring my thighs. They lightly caressed my legs, reached between them, and slipped into my panties.

"Leo," I whispered, "what's going on?"

"I don't know," he answered. "I can't feel a thing!"

"I can."

"I know. It's a swinging club . . . the guy digs you. Just let it happen. You're not afraid of sex, are you?"

"Xaviera afraid of sex?! Is a whale afraid of water?"

My phantom feeler was getting friendlier . . . and I was slowly getting stripped. He had my underpants down around my knees, which is no way to dance. So without missing a beat, I stepped out of them.

Leo took his hands off my hips and hugged me. The scene was exciting him tremendously, and his hard-on was getting harder.

The mystery molester reached up under my dress and soon lifted it above my waist. He was close against my back, and my bottom could feel his stiff prick throbbing through his pants. I had hard-ons coming and going!

I was almost in a trance. Then the man behind me began to fondle my breasts. As he opened the top of my dress, it slipped down and in moments I'd shed it.

The music changed, and it was the Beatles' *Abbey Road* album. John Lennon's voice filled the air with "Come Together" (it was that kind of club), and as I swayed to the sound, the man behind—whom I hadn't seen yet— finger-flirted with my damp pussy. And then I had the unmistakable feeling of a hot cock pushing through my legs. I was so moist and receptive that it slipped easily into my vagina.

I was holding on to Leo for dear life now, and he was my support as I leaned slightly forward. The stereo tracked into "something in the way she moves . . ." and the strong stranger behind moved into me, slowly thrusting his meaty prick, his hips and mine both responding to the sexy *son et lumiere*.

Then . . . oooohhhhh! The tempo picked up and with my arms still around Leo's neck, I wiggled up and down with pure pleasure.

"Leo," I whispered. "I'm getting a fabulous fuck . . . oohhh, fabulous."

"Good," he smiled. "For a while I thought it was just a new dance."

The craziness of the situation must have gotten to me, because I found this fantastically funny. I started giggling and Leo giggled back and I was soon shaking so much with laughter that my phantom fucker nearly slipped out of me. . . .

But not for long.

He was back in with renewed energy, and my shaking had turned him on even more.

"Oh Darlin'" was beginning to pump out of the speakers, and "That Old Feeling" was beginning to pump into me. With heaves and jerks that made me scream with ecstasy, the rear rapist grabbed my hips and thrashed into a frenetic climax, coming and coming, flooding me with hot sensations. One more great shuddering spasm, and it was over. With a sigh and a moan he covered my shoulders and back with kisses; then, without a word and without even waiting for the record to finish, he backed away and was gone.

Talk about fancy dancing!

Leo held me strongly and said with a smile, "I think he's finished!"

I was still burning with sensation and squeezed my legs tight for another thrilling moment. "I *know* he's finished," I replied!

We both got the giggles again, and then it struck me.

"Leo?"

"Yes, Xaviera?"

"Can you tell me something? Please?"

"Sure."

"Was he good-looking?"

We both realized how outrageous this sounded, and collapsed, heaving with laughter, into each other's arms. It was wild and wonderful, and I hadn't even seen him!

That's what I call an out-of-sight fuck!

LEO AND MARIKA

Just a few days earlier I'd been in Amsterdam, bored out of my mind as compared to my recent situation—which was being bored from beyond. How had I made this happy transition in boredoms? How had I stepped into this brand new dance of love?

Well, it's all because of a happily married couple I'd met in Amsterdam.

Riddle: Many people have married lovers.

Many people have two married lovers.

But who do you know who had two lovers who are married to each other?

Answer: Me. (Surprised, huh?) And their names were Leo and Marika.

I'd met them just a few days after returning to Holland from the United States and they were as welcome as nookie night to a sailor on leave. A friend I'd known in the States, an architect named Ned, was now living in Amsterdam and he called me and invited me to have a drink with him. When I met him at the bar we'd chosen, there was another man with him, his good friend Leo Hoffman. For reasons I'm still not certain about, I liked Leo instantly. He looked like a cross between Toulouse Lautrec and Vincent Van Gogh (no, *not* a midget with one ear missing!). My guess was that he was in his mid-forties, though a bit later on I learned that he was actually fifty-one—he had an extremely youngish round face with short blond hair that was thinning but well styled to make him look younger than his years. His goatee beard and moustache looked very aristocratic and he was in excellent physical condition . . . as you'll find out later.

After the introductions I said to Leo: "Your name is very familiar. Is your wife's name Marika?"

"Yes," said Leo. "Are we getting an international reputation?"

"Sort of. By coincidence I'd been given your number by someone I know. And I'd planned to phone you in a few days anyway."

Leo told me that he'd heard a lot about me, too, and that he and his wife, Marika, had not only read my book but often read it to each other as a turn-on. He invited me to come along to their house the following night for dinner and gave me their address—a big old *grachtenhuis,* or canal house, on one of the city's famous waterways.

Ned later took me aside to warn me about Leo and Marika. The reason for his warning: they were swingers. I laughed out loud.

"What the hell do you think I am?" I replied, with more than a little edge in my voice.

"Don't be surprised to find twenty people in the house, and you're expected to fuck each and every one of them," he said.

"That's like warning the Pope away from church."

Ned seemed to have a double standard. I confirmed this later when he and his girl, Anne, took me to dinner that evening. She was considerably younger than he, and at twenty-one she was one of Holland's most famous models. She had read my book and was very excited about meeting me. However, although she was charming, there was something cool and aloof about her, possibly because Ned was watching her like a hawk. He must have known from my book that I liked women as well as men.

He needn't have worried. Yes, she was a beautiful girl and I quite liked her, but I wasn't physically attracted to her. I must say models are not usually my cup of tea, as most of them are too selfish to give themselves freely to another. You can always tell a model's room by her lipstick marks on the mirror.

Yet despite the fact that he had no cause to fear that I'd try to steal his girl, Ned became more and more uptight. In fact, right after dinner he dropped me off at home and since then I've only spoken to Ned once, and that was on the telephone. However, I'm grateful to him for introducing me to two of the most sexually interesting people I've ever met, Leo and Marika.

I was certainly looking forward to their dinner party. I hadn't had sex in a few days and was pretty horny. I like to swing, and hadn't done much since retiring as the doyenne of New York's madams. Whether it was just the two of them or a cast of twenty, I was more than ready.

When I visited them the next evening I was immediately impressed by the way they had furnished their one big floor in the *grachtenhuis*. In the huge living room there was a number of handsome couches, thick, furry carpets, huge floor pillows, and comfy leather chairs . . . plus a great bar.

The walls were covered with modern paintings, and there were erotic sculptures all over the room, adding just the right sensual feel to the high-ceilinged, timber-beamed pleasure chamber.

One of the paintings was by Betty Dodson. I'd met her several times in New York while doing television interviews on sexuality and we had also lectured together on sex in the media. Although I had never gotten to know her well, I think I could have really dug her; I'd heard that she had become something of a legend in artistic swinging circles in Manhattan.

Her painting here, a large one in just black and white, showed a couple making love and while it wasn't explicit it was certainly obvious that they were copulating. Yet it was very tasteful, a very sensitive portrait, and I couldn't help but tune in to the beautiful emotions, the love, the eroticism that radiated from it. It was one of the legion of things in the house which contributed to the sensual ambience.

Leo greeted me warmly and introduced me proudly to his beautiful wife, Marika, who absolutely complemented the mood of the room. She was tall—about five feet nine —in fact a few inches taller than Leo, and with her long legs could easily have been a fashion model, even though she was in her mid-thirties. Her hair was reddish blond, very close to my favorite color in women: red. Her eyes were big and blue and her complexion was pale and lightly freckled. Her breasts seemed to be about my size (36-B), with a nice, firm shape.

"I was delighted when Leo told me he'd invited you here," she said.

"My pleasure . . . I hope," I said, with a meaningful look.

She laughed and said that's what her house was for.

We sat down and started to get to know each other, those early tentative steps which are the first stage in a great relationship . . . which this was to become.

As we chatted I thought how nice it would be to swing with them because they were obviously people who led interesting lives. Marika had flown with KLM as a stewardess for a number of years. She had lived in Rio de Janeiro with a young South American man for about a year and had even lived in the States—oddly enough, with a friend of Leo's, even while chasing Leo all the time. But Leo was living there with a girl named Melanie. Leo quickly produced some photographs showing a lovely blond with a sexy, beautiful body.

Leo told me all about her:

"She was pretty kinky. She loved leather, bondage, and was a masochist. She often begged me to tie her up and beat her, and dress her in leather things. I liked it a bit at first, but I just couldn't bring myself to hurt her badly."

He told me it wasn't his bag to beat girls or burn their skin or tie them down or mark them. Apparently Melanie would beg him to put hot wax on her and extinguish his cigarettes on her breasts.

"Eventually," he continued, "she left when she met an English producer of pornographic movies. He was a sadist and she was his perfect masochist victim. They're married now and she's his complete slave and will do anything he wants."

"That sounds like a fair description of most marriages," I said with a laugh, hoping to lighten the mood a little.

"Not ours," Marika quickly interjected. "A little sado-maso fun is okay every now and then. But a little goes a long way. Give me fucking and sucking any day. Or night."

"As soon as Melanie had left Leo," continued Marika, "I chased after him. We'd once spent a night together and he just about drove me out of my mind."

They found they were very comfortable with each other and decided to get married.

Leo is a fascinating man and in a way I envy Marika. They're complete opposites. He has a bubbling personality. He prides himself on his taste and his expert knowledge of art and music. He's composed songs and has made several records and some of his songs are played and sung by famous artists all around the world.

"In fact," he told me, "if I hadn't become a manufacturer of bicycles I think I would have become a pianist."

And later, when we were discussing marriage and money, he remarked, "Money is as important to me as the man in the moon. If Marika wanted to divorce me some day, or if I wanted to divorce her and she wanted all my money, she could have it. I can always make a living playing piano in a bar."

Marika has a more moody personality. She's a typical Pisces, stubborn and cool though outwardly friendly. She has very set ideas and it's hard to argue with her. As I got to know them better, Marika laid down the ground rules of swinging, which were:

"If you want to fuck my husband, fuck him while I'm there. But don't fuck him behind my back. If you want to have an honest relationship, have it with the two of us."

Leo was an easygoing man who liked his freedom, like I do. He had tremendous energy and stamina and even though he worked long hours he was still brimming with life when he got home.

"He's always full of new ideas," Marika told me. "On the phone all the time, arranging swings, parties, and even doing some amateur pimping for his friends."

For instance, friends like Ned would call him and say, "I want a girl between three and six this afternoon while my girlfriend's at the hairdresser."

And Leo, being the good-natured guy that he is, would call up some girl and arrange for her to fuck Ned in the afternoon.

Leo and Marika both liked Ned's girlfriend, Anne, and couldn't quite cope with his double standards. Ned would never let her fool around or participate in a swing. But if *he* was horny for strange tail, it was always good old Leo who laid it on, and with never a word to Anne.

True swingers have a moral code: You don't try to steal someone's partner just because you get to screw them during a swing. Couples who go to a swing will usually arrive together and leave together (and in between they'll come with as many other people as they can!); there won't be any emotional attachment with other people. It's just spontaneous physical pleasure, an act of sharing and enjoying others.

However, that was precisely the kind of situation that Ned couldn't tolerate, so Leo now told him that he didn't know any girls who were available for those short, lunchtime freebees. If she was a hooker and got paid for it, fine. But no straight girl likes to be squeezed into a schedule for just a couple of hours, no matter how free and liberal she is, and especially not to satisfy a man who has to run back to his girlfriend. After all, Ned wasn't all that groovy or generous. He was a nice guy, with a good sense of humor, but hardly a sexual Adonis.

"Have you seen this?" asked Leo, changing the subject. He handed me a large piece of plaster which was unmistakably a proud, pretty penis.

"Does Marika keep this for when you're away on business trips?" I laughed.

"Why not? It's mine!"

"Yours?"

"Sure. Where do you think we got the mold? I got it done in New York by one of those crazy chicks in Greenwich Village—groupies, I think they call them."

Groupies, as you may recall, were girls (and the occasional boys) who liked to fuck famous entertainers. Mostly musicians, though . . . I don't think they ever got around to Sir Laurence Olivier. Many of the girls were also known as plaster-casters because of their crazy hobby of casting illustrious cocks in plaster. Plaster casting was to rock and cock what the sidewalk outside Graumann's is to film and feet.

Leo explained how his claim to immortality was accomplished.

"Marika had to come along with me," he said, "and suck my cock to get it good and hard. Then, when it was nice and big, the girl quickly coated it with a warm wax while fondling my balls to keep me up while it hardened . . . the wax, that is."

Apparently once the wax hardened, the prick softened

and slipped out and the mold was then filled with plaster. The result is a perfect reproduction right down to the smiling tumescent tip.

Depending on your inclinations, it could be used as a doorstop, a tasteful lamp pole, or as a conversation piece, an objet d'art on the coffee table . . . right next to the copy of *Reader's Digest*.

Leo's plaster penis was functioning here as a *presse papier* to hold down his letters. See how handy it is to have a spare cock around the house?

The more I looked around their living room, the more curious erotica I noticed. The bookshelves, the coffee tables, all were decorated with stunning phallic figurines from all over the world, obviously the gifts of international swingers who made the Hoffman home their European headquarters. (Pun intended.)

Now it was time for dinner and for an hour or so there was actually no talk about sex. After dinner, however, Leo and Marika began to show me pictures of themselves in the nude, together with other swingers they had met while vacationing on Ile du Levant, a nudist island in the South of France.

One unusual photo showed three young girls, their cunts completely shaven. Upon closer examination I noticed that there were small rings through their nipples and their vaginal lips, sealing off their pussies like a chastity belt. It took very little coaxing to persuade Leo to show me stag movies of the same girls performing sex.

In one film, one of the girls took a bunch of keys from a chain which hung from her cunt ring and handed them to a man so he could open the locks on the chains on the other girls' cunts. From there they went through various routines showing how the stud could pull on the chains, the keys, and the rings without hurting the girls, providing he didn't do it too roughly.

To me it wasn't very sexy, but Leo and Marika felt it was super. They said it was one of the most beautiful, most exciting things they'd ever seen.

Leo told me about a funny incident involving the girls in a St. Tropez restaurant, which he had witnessed. The girls were wearing the shortest miniskirts imaginable and one of them actually had little tinkling bells attached to her cunt ring. When the rather naive waiter brought their order, the girl just spread her legs, and ding-a-ling-a-ling!

Wondering where the noise was coming from, the waiter looked down to find himself eye to eye with a bald, bold, belled box. His tray hit the floor with a crash, and within a second he had dropped to his knees and was pretending to pick up the pieces while eyeing the horniest belfry he'd ever seen!

Marika said that all those girls wanted to do was fuck and suck, and make love to each other. They stopped at nothing.

"This was nice for a day or two," said Marika, "but then it got a bit boring because they had nothing else to offer except sex. We certainly don't mind sex, but we want something more than just bodies. We like people with imagination and taste who realize that the mind is just as important as the body."

We were back to the photographs now and Leo's next photo was of a beautiful, exquisitely built blond girl. He said that all of her life had revolved around sex and that she had enjoyed posing in the nude for magazines and movies. Then she'd fallen in love with an incredible sadist and her life became a replica of *The Story of O,* the famous French novel of bizarre bondage. She became this man's slave and all she wanted was to be tied down, spanked, whipped, to wear chains and heavy leather belts, and be continually humiliated.

This was sad enough, but recently this woman and her master were driving along the Cote d'Azur at a high speed, while having a vicious argument. He threatened to expel her from his life and never see her again. She became so desperate that she threw open the car door and tried to commit suicide. But instead of dying she lost her arm in the accident. Suddenly, from having been so fully involved with exposing the beauty and perfection of her body, she ended up disfigured . . . not in the minor way her kinky sex demanded, but permanently, irrevocably.

Before we knew it, it was after midnight and while I wanted to spend the night with Leo and Marika, I realized that this was the beginning of a relationship which had fantastic possibilities but couldn't be rushed. I had made up my mind that I would try to be a good friend to them, and I'd gotten the message from Marika that I should not attempt any intrigues, or a separate affair, with Leo. Still and all, it was difficult not to flirt with him a little because he can be quite a tease.

That night, the minute I slipped into bed, I fell into a deep sleep—the kind which comes from sheer contentment and the knowledge that two wonderful people had come into my life. And I into theirs.

I was so looking forward to another evening with Leo and Marika that the day just dragged by. But finally it was six o'clock and I arrived—with great expectations (no, of course I wasn't pregnant!)—at the door of their *grachtenhuis*. Marika welcomed me with a friendly kiss, and Leo welcomed me with an even friendlier one. We relaxed in their comfortable living room and chatted about their far-out, free-wheeling lifestyle.

Without any false modesty, they admitted that the orgies they had organized had become the talk of Europe. If uptight American society ever gets it together sexually, I can just imagine Leo and Marika welcoming charter flights at Amsterdam airport for the F&S package tour: two weeks of fucking and sucking, complete with organized orgies, all the cock 'n cunt you can eat, plus color slides to show the folks back home in Dubuque. It could cover Amsterdam and Paris, and they could call it "The Tail of Two Cities"!

As an example of just how good it could be, they told me about the time a well-known American TV performer had come over to Amsterdam for the Wet Dream Film Festival—the Cannes of porno movies. Each day she acted as the leader of the group that gathered daily at Leo and Marika's home. After the food, drinks, and music, it was Naked Lunch time—the living room scattered with clothes, looking like a plush coed locker room before a ball game. Leo and Marika had imported two huge king-size beds from the States, together with matching mirrors for the ceilings. Closed-circuit video cameras were focused on each bed and the reproduction equipment (if you'll pardon the expression) was installed in one of the guest rooms. This equipment had been previously used by the Kronhausens (Phyllis and Eberhard Kronhausen, who are sex researchers and psychologists) when they made one of their films in the Hoffmans' house—part of a two-film documentary on sexual behavior in Europe. Leo and spouse had gone so far as to participate in one of their scenes, and gave an outstanding performance of copulation, Dutch-style. If the Academy Awards ever include a Best Orgasm category, my swinging friends may pick up an Oscar.

Both my hosts raved about the American TV actress, who, they said, came on like a butch lesbian, but was in fact a highly intelligent woman with very distinctive ideas on sex—with both men and women. To her, it was the basic form of communication. And she may be right. Oddly enough, I've checked my dictionary, and the first two definitions for the word *conversation* are: 1, talk; interchange of thoughts and words; 2, sexual intercourse. So next time somebody says they'd like to have a conversation with you, find out exactly what they mean!

Their actress friend so believed in this principle that she refused to discriminate between the good or bad, the old or young, the ugly or pretty—she'd bang them all. Often, I understand, she would fuck every single man at a party. And the married ones, too, I guess! Now *that's* conversation in any language! What you might call "the gift of tongues."

On the other hand, Leo remarked, he knew a famous arch-feminist who was a "closet banger." Shortly after her first book had come out, she turned up at one of their orgies, and everyone had expected her to swing like a pendulum. Or failing that, they expected her to go to the other extreme, and refuse everyone. But, in fact, she proved to be somewhere in between, locking herself away in a big bedroom with the man of her choice, and fucking away in privacy.

This didn't make her too popular with the other guests since she didn't come out till dawn, and had tied up half the king-size bed supply all through the night. Leo and Marika thought this rather unsociable of her, since it forced everyone else to fuck on the rugs, carpets, and chairs, with the one king-size bed having to be reserved hours in advance—like the town whore at a truckdrivers' convention.

On the other hand, this actress from America truly practiced what she preached. She had even assured Marika, who had a taste for masturbating, that it was perfectly healthy. This artist of sexuality, it turns out, had taught her mother—at the age of seventy-two!—how to masturbate and use a vibrator, and now it seems that the dear old lady is getting her rocks off regularly, twice a week. Who knows? Maybe that explains the satisfied smile on the face of Whistler's Mother!

Marika had been so impressed by this philosophy that she now read aloud from an interview in *Evergreen Review*, in which the painter Betty Dodson expressed similar views:

> "I recommend masturbation across the board," Miss Dodson stated. "Masturbation is our first sexual lifestyle, naturally. It is the way we learn to relate to ourselves as sexual beings and to learn about our sexual responses. It gets sabotaged by parents, religion, and society. That's the first and most effective negative sex conditioning we confront—the repression of masturbation. It has permanently sexually crippled many people for life. . . .
>
> "In this sexist society there are many people who cannot connect with other human beings, and masturbation is for them their only outlet. There are people who are institutionalized, confined to homes. They're old people and other sexual minorities. We've got to understand that it's very important that they have masturbation available for them completely, without a feeling of guilt or shame.
>
> "Masturbation is the only way a lot of women reach orgasms in or out of marriage. I secretly masturbated when I was married because we were gradually giving up on sex. I masturbate now because I know that it's an integral and essential part of total human sexuality."

Betty Dodson's views on the subject prompted the three of us to exchange *our* views on solo sex.

"I myself don't enjoy masturbating," I confessed, "and to tell you the truth I'm very bad at it. I prefer the real thing."

"But, Xaviera, what if you're lying in bed with a man," asked Leo, "and he's pulling himself—wouldn't you enjoy masturbating, too, at the same time?"

"Ah, that's different," I answered. "I can dig masturbating if I can feel a man's body close to me. But I've got to touch his balls, or hold his hand while he's jerking off. And sometimes I tremendously enjoy giving him a hand, or while I'm eating him, letting him help me finish him off."

They both smiled understandingly when I mentioned how I loved to see the expression on a man's face the moment he comes, and the jism shoots out.

"I usually keep my eyes shut when making love," I said, "and so does the man, but it's beautiful to lay halfway hunched over a man and play with him, feel his body shake and tremble, then the furious climax—his sperm splashing all over the place, juicing up his stomach, or else juicing up my mouth or my breasts or my hair or my face."

Talking of masturbation, though, I don't want to give you the impression that I never indulge in the solitary sport. It's simply that I've always been a better baller than masturbator! But during those occasional "dry spells" when my sex life isn't too busy, I do enjoy fantasizing and bringing myself off, though rarely with my hand.

One pleasurable way is in the bathtub. During this sexless week in Holland, I was bathing one day and maneuvered my vagina under the faucet, hanging my legs over the edge of the tub. I let the gushing water play on my pussy, and soon the warm, concentrated jet was having a delicious effect on my clitoris. Just as I began to have a delightful, tingly orgasm, my mother happened to open the bathroom door and look in, and I felt like a teenager caught with my pants down!

Other times, I must confess, I've been known to use the vibrating tip of my automatic toothbrush as an autoerotic aid. So while I prefer the real thing, I do confess, in Leonard Cohen's words, to occasionally "making a pass at myself"!

In any case, this conversation was reminding me that masturbation is fine as long as it's part of a varied sex life, but all pull and no pussy isn't healthy for a growing boy, so I asked Leo and Marika if they wanted to hear about one of my experiences as madam therapist in New York. "Yes!" they said in unison.

"Oh, well," I said, "if you insist." Leo and Marika sat back on the couch and I began my story of Rollo, the horny-handed young man who had been brought up by a very strict Catholic mother. Instead of learning the facts of life from his father, he got the myths of life from his mother, who, despite having had one child, still didn't know the facts of life herself.

In brief, what she'd told him was that handling his peepee would cause him to go blind and that making love to a woman would cause an instant case of pregnancy. Little wonder that the poor kid was 1, afraid of women; 2, responding to his mother's admonitions about the female sex by displaying a marked interest in his own sex; 3, best of all the good done him by bigoted Mama, he was interested most of all in his very own private personal sex—since the age of fifteen, he'd been jerking off four or five times a day.

He'd wake up in the morning and pull his pudding first thing—as an eye-opener. At lunchtime he'd get into his car for a quick solo nooner, and on and on like that. Only he wasn't having any fun—each orgasm was accompanied by some good feelings and a lot more guilt. Well, at least he hadn't gone blind—he didn't even wear contact lenses!

I'd learned all this from a psychiatrist I knew, who was liberated and hip enough to refer patients to me when he felt he wasn't making any progress with them—even at a hundred dollars a session!

"Xaviera," he said to me, "this kid is in desperate need of getting laid—he lives in an entire fantasy world with his girlie magazines."

"Oh, have I got a girlie for him!" I quipped.

"No, seriously, will you see him and do your specialty?"

"You mean my open-hearted surgery?"

"No," he laughed, "I mean your cherry-popping pundendum."

Well, despite the kidding around, I wanted to make clear to Leo and Marika that I was quite serious about wanting to get this young man out of hand and into a more suitable orifice.

"What did he look like?" Marika wanted to know. "Was he a pleasant-looking young man, or what?"

"When he wasn't being nervous—which was most of the time—he was quite an attractive kid," I responded. "About six feet tall, nice trim body, dark hair and green eyes and, I later learned, a good long cock."

Marika applauded and Leo laughed at her enthusiasm for good long cocks.

I knew they expected me to weave this terrific tale of how I seduced this kid out of his virginal unhappiness, but no, I had to admit that nothing I did for him—and he got some of the finest oral aid a human being can endure without coming up for firsts, much less seconds—did the job.

"He would get hard, then fall down on the job—no matter what I did for him," I told my two friends. "That poor kid couldn't keep it up if his life depended on it."

"I'm glad *your* life didn't depend on it," kidded Leo.

"Hush, Leo," Marika said, impatient to hear the climax of my story. "Let Xaviera tell us what happened."

"Nothing happened," I said.

"Booooo," said Leo.

"No, *really* . . ." said Marika.

"What really happened," I told her, "is nothing—the poor kid wanted to make love to me, and at times his penis seemed quite willing, but somewhere between his head and the head of his penis, communication kept breaking down."

"So what'd you finally do?" Marika asked, still expecting a happy ending to this story.

"I sent him home," I answered her, "with strict instructions to stay off the beat, not to touch his penis—except when taking a leak—for two solid weeks. It was Meatless Sunday, Monday, and Tuesday for him, and if he pulled his pork, I told him, don't bother calling me at all. I wouldn't see him. I didn't care to compete with his favorite girlfriend, Felicia Five-Fingers."

"I can't believe the kid kept his hands off his dork after a solid decade of deliciously guilty self-abuse," Leo said, rather jocularly. "Hell, he probably got off on the guilt alone."

"Stop interrupting Xaviera," said Marika. "I want to hear the rest of the story."

"Me, too," Leo said. "I like this story—I may set it to music. It's already got a good beat."

We all laughed. It was a very funny notion.

"Well," I said, "two weeks, almost to the minute, went by, and my phone rang. It was him.

" 'Hello, Xaviera, it's Rollo. Remember me?' he asked.

" 'Of course I do. How *are* you?'

" 'Can I come tomorrow afternoon at two?' he wanted to know.

" 'That depends on you,' I said with a smile. 'Did you follow my instructions?'

" 'I swear I did. I even tried not to touch it when I peed,' he said, trying to sound casual and friendly. I believed him.

"Next day, the doorbell rang right on the stroke of two. What a different Rollo this was! He was wearing tight blue slacks and a blue sweater, and I could sense he was eager. He swept into the room, brushing past me, like a horny billy goat. He seemed confident, and with barely a 'hello' to me, he was out of his clothes in ten seconds flat. Only he wasn't flat.

" 'Hey, take it easy,' I told him. 'Let's build a little excitement here first.'

" 'Excitement! Excitement? What the hell do you think this is? I've been climbing walls for two weeks. If only you knew how hard it was to keep my hands off it. . . . And probably for nothing, too,' he added petulantly.

" 'What do you mean?' I asked him.

" 'The psychiatrist told me it isn't going to work,' he pouted. 'After I told him how I'd failed last time, after an hour of trying, he said I'd never be able to come inside you.'

" 'Look, Rollo, let's not talk. Let's just do things.'

"I took off my clothes, walked over to him, and checked his cock. It was even bigger than last time. I made a quick decision not to lay a hand on it. I just touched it lightly with my tongue and slipped it into my mouth. It was like sucking on a hot sausage. I could feel the vibrations, and at that moment I knew I was going to win. That shrink may have been great with heads, but I was the tail expert.

"Rollo was too horny for any subtleties so I just stroked him swiftly on the belly, and suddenly squatted on his cock. This time, I could feel it had no plans to come down. Once, twice, three times I pumped him, and I could feel him shake and tremble as he came to the edge of orgasm. Then I laid my body flat out on top of him and stretched out my legs so that I could control him completely, hugging his shoulders close to my body and kissing his mouth. His eyelids were trembling and I could feel a great movement starting inside him."

"I think I can feel a great movement starting deep inside *me*," Leo said.

"Shhh—Rollo's just about to come," I said.

"Thank God," Leo exclaimed.

"I'm really glad for him," said Marika, looking almost schoolgirlish as she spoke.

"Rollo was really cute," I said.

" 'Congratulate me,' he roared.

" 'Congratulations,' I whispered.

" 'After twenty-five years, I've become a man. A quarter of a fucking century. And you know the first thing I'm gonna do?'

" 'What?'

" 'I'm gonna go tell that goddamn psychiatrist he can go put on his Freudian slip and fuck himself!' "

Leo and Marika curled up on the couch in laughter at this outburst—I'd done a pantomime of Rollo's triumphant moment—and I was glad that my story (at last!) had a happy fucking ending. Or was that a fucking happy ending?

Leo and Marika began fooling around with each other on the couch, and I thought this might be the moment for the start of a more intimate relationship between the three of us, but no, they sat up after a minute or so of tickling each other—like two kids, really—and instead of starting to swing, we continued talking well into the night.

I was horny, but there are all kinds of intimacy—and this growing friendship of ours was gratification enough for the present. But . . . thank goodness for the bathtub spigot! (Of course, goodness had nothing to do with it!)

AMSTERDAMSELS

Despite my continuing case of sexual malnutrition, the way Leo and Marika had accepted me into their ménage was a real turn-on. In fact, everything about the Hoffmans and their friends was an entirely new scene to me; they were swinging to a different drummer, for their philosophy of living and loving was completely opposite to the hard, money-oriented realities I'd known in New York. There was no prostitution and no money involved, just free sex, free loving, and warm, caring friendships—without jealousies, hang-ups, or arguments.

Of course my old lifestyle was behind me, but now I not only wasn't selling sex, I wasn't getting any either. I'd been celibate since arriving in Amsterdam, and half out of my mind from desire—a condition which wasn't helped by a visit to Amsterdam's red light district with Leo and Marika. I won't say that it was a turn-on, but it sure kept my mind on sex.

The girls were a bizarre mixture ranging from the cute young things to the old and ugly, all of them sitting in street-level picture windows like department-store mannequins. And behind each girl, the setting was identical: a neatly made-up double bed, topped with a towel, a sink with a roll of toilet paper and a side table holding a package of condoms.

When a man goes in, the girl closes the curtains and they quickly work out the price for what he wants. And the girl has his money in her hand before any action begins.

Then she leads him off to the bathroom and makes him take a leak before squeezing his penis for telltale signs of venereal disease.

It's like a safety check in a factory, and about as romantic. But the girls are experts. Any john who complains gets a rubber put on his cock, whether he wants it or not. And what's more, he doesn't even know it's on.

How do they do it?

Well, when the girl gets down on her knees and starts sucking her man's cock—a service, incidentally, which is more expensive than straight fucking—she's already hidden a rubber in her mouth, which she then expertly slips over the head of his prick. With the assistance of playful fingers, which the john thinks are being used to excite him, she rolls the rubber down his erection.

Then, before he knows what's happening, she's up and on him. And it's only afterward, as he stares down at his flaccid member, that he realizes he's been conned into a condom.

The girls must average one john every ten to fifteen minutes, and if a stud stays too long, there's a polite knock on the door. Three minutes later, if he still hasn't left, it's replaced by a heavy knock and an impolite shout. If five minutes go by, he gets thrown out the door, bare-assed, by the girl's pimp or his stand-in, who is sometimes a very large female-type person who doesn't care very much for men.

Many of the girls are also expert pickpockets, and many a G.I. or American sailor has been picked clean during a furlough in Amsterdam.

The girls are known for their wit but they can also be very, very mean. I stopped in front of one window with Leo and Marika and pointed at an older woman sitting with a very young lovely girl. Teasingly I said, "Which one do you think is the mother, and which one the daughter?" About two minutes later, when we went past them again, the older woman dashed out and screamed, "You want to find out who's the mother and who's the daughter? Well, get your ass over here so we can throw this bucket of rubbers over your head!"

We got the hell away from there, as she continued screaming and yelling like the old shrew that she was. If there's one thing to avoid on the canals, it's a fight, especially if the pimps start taking an interest.

In the years I'd been away, there had been an influx of young Surinam girls—blacks, from the Dutch colonies, who are citizens of Holland. They are nearly always handled by black guys, also from Surinam, who all seem to go the same route. These "poor natives" are the ones you'll find at night, hanging around the canals and the hooker bars where their so-called wives are sitting in windows looking for tricks.

They've also been known to pull a gun or knife on rich-looking tourists and say *betalen,* which means "you pay or you die!" And they're not bluffing. They'd have no qualms about taking a wallet from your dead body.

The Amsterdam red light district also caters to the kinky. The picture-window prostitute, in this case, is usually an older hooker with a mean streak showing in her face. Behind her, through the window, can be seen swords, whips, handcuffs, cat-o'-nine-tails, and leg irons—the latter presumably for that rare bird, the masochistic foot fetishist!

These Madames de Sade are tightly corsetted in leather outfits and wear high, sharp boots. Their black leather bras push out their nipples like pistols. Not your cup of titillation, eh? Well, they do terrific business.

Peak business hours for the red light district are between seven and eleven P.M. The sex book shops, with publications much more explicit than any you'll find in most North American cities, are always packed during these hours, and the counters displaying sex toys and devices are lined with customers all looking for a new way to get a bigger bang for their buck.

These stores stand along the canals side by side with live sex shows which, to be honest, are awful—unattractive performers in sleazy theaters going through sexual numbers with all the enthusiasm of an unplugged computer. There are also peep shows to warm up the customers about to enter the brothels for a quick lay.

Also roaming along these streets are the freelancers, groups of attractive young girls looking for a quick way out of the mundane poverty of office work.

These girls may have some fun 'n gain if they don't fall into the hands of a pimp, but here and there I noticed a girl with heavy black marks on her arms or legs or perhaps a black eye covered with heavy makeup. But they seemed happy, and trade was boffo at the box office, as they say in show biz!

I also noticed some girls turning down a trick for no apparent reason, while others would whistle and call after the ugliest and dirtiest kind of man—the kind who looked as if he never washed, and didn't have a penny in his pocket.

Maybe it's because the fees are so low, averaging twenty-five to fifty guilders—about eight to fifteen dollars. These rates have been the same ever since I first realized that there was prostitution in Amsterdam, and I feel sorry for the poor Dutch hookers who have to literally work their asses off to keep up with inflation.

The city's cab drivers are also plugged into the hooker network, and make a good dollar taking customers to various high-class brothels sprinkled across the town. They also hand out the girls' business cards, and get no hassles from the police.

On the whole, this legalized prostitution is really a good thing. While perhaps the fact that it's so open cuts out some of the excitement that many people derive from an illicit sport, business is booming. Or should I say *banging*?

As I drove back from the bordello district with Leo and Marika my mind began estimating just how much fucking and sucking was going on around me at that very moment. Here I was, one of the world's most famous pleasure ladies, surrounded by humping and bumping, but not getting any of it.

Leo must have sensed my thoughts.

"Tomorrow, Xaviera," he said softly, "the three of us leave for Paris."

Paris! The city of lights and love. What better place to surrender my week-long virginity!

FIRST TANGO IN PARIS

Paris! Ernest Hemingway's "moveable feast"—it's such a wonderful, elegant setting for loving and laughing.

Marika and I arrived there without Leo—he had some business to complete, and would join us later in the day. It was lovely and sunny, much brighter than Amsterdam had been when we'd left, and I was so happy to be in this magnificent city which really does look like it does in movies. I hadn't been here since I was a young girl, so I really was anticipating a good time.

We soon arrived at our hotel, in the Saint Germain des Près *quartier* of Paris. The area was largely developed in the early eighteenth century, though its origins date back to the sixth. It's on the Left Bank, and its streets are filled with magnificent old houses, elegant antique stores, and, of course, superb restaurants.

Marika and I were received rather coolly at first by the staff at the stately hotel where Leo had made reservations. The staff, of course, didn't know us, although Leo was well known there as a big swinger and a big spender. Marika told me not to worry.

"That's the way the French are," she reminded me. "They tend to be a bit rude and rather reserved, but once they get to know us—especially once Leo is here—you'll see how they turn around."

She told me that Leo had once held a swing there, with about twenty people in his single hotel room, and no one complained; in fact, the entire hotel staff knew what was happening and went around smiling, as if they were conspirators.

Marika and I went to our respective rooms—hers on the

sixth floor, mine on the third—to freshen up. Leo would be arriving at eight o'clock, and we'd planned dinner for nine P.M.—the three of us, plus Leo's associate, Joop. I'd already been warned that Joop was square and I was to behave myself!

It was soon dinnertime, and the four of us met in the lobby. Joop was indeed as square as advertised—a typical Dutch guy, though he did have a good sense of humor. So while I didn't try to shock him, I gave him a few double entendres here and there. But otherwise I was the perfect lady, and we had a very sedate dinner at a nearby restaurant.

When we returned to our hotel, Joop found some excuse to remain in the lobby, arranging something at the front desk, since he was to leave the following day. I rather suspect he did it out of fear that I might try to seduce him in the elevator, between floors.

Anyway, the Hoffmans and I went up to our rooms without him. Remember, I had never slept with them yet, and I was getting anxious to see who would make the first move.

It was Leo. Just as I was stepping out of the elevator, he casually said, "Why don't you come up and have a little party with us, when you've undressed and freshened up."

Marika suppressed a little yawn and said, "But it's late already, and I'm tired. I want to be up early tomorrow and do some shopping."

So I said, "Leo, I don't really think Marika feels like it."

"Don't worry about Marika," he said flatly. "If you feel like it, come up." And I sensed then that this was how they worked: Marika was often the submissive one, allowing him to make the decisions.

About fifteen minutes later, after a quick bath and douche, I felt rather awkward when I tapped at their door. But I needn't have worried. Leo called out, "Come in," and as I opened the door I could see Marika in bed, completely naked, covered just by the sheet. Leo was standing with a towel around his middle and a tie around his neck. He was obviously the master of ceremonies.

I was wearing a beach gown—the back was completely bare and the front had a low decolletage—and it was the type you could just slip out of in a second. Marika looked at me questioningly, so I did just that: I slipped out of my dress and pulled back the sheet that was lightly covering her.

Until now I'd never seen either of them in the nude, except in photographs, and of course I'd admired Leo's plaster-cast cock.

Marika in the nude was a bit of a shock to me, because she seemed to have no hair at all on her cunt. I prefer short, trimmed beaver, but not completely shaved. I soon discovered, though, that she hadn't shaved it. Her hair was a light shade anyway, and she'd trimmed it very short with scissors. So when I went down on her a few minutes later, she didn't tickle my chin with shaved stubble. Oh no, it was nice and soft, and made it very easy for me to find her terrific clit. Marika must have really masturbated a great deal, because her vaginal lips were far more developed than those of women who don't pet their own pussies.

While I was giving head to Marika, Leo let the towel slip off his body and soon we were in a daisy chain. He was eating me, I was eating Marika, and she was eating Leo. Then we switched, and I sucked Leo while he tongue-fucked Marika, and she went down on me. But I wasn't too comfortable with that arrangement. I always prefer to give head to the other woman, not vice versa. Marika was a bit upset that I wanted to do her, but didn't want to be done by her, so, wanting to placate and soothe her, we rearranged positions and I resumed eating her out, sucking her tits, and blowing kisses in her ears while Leo, too, was playing with her. I liked her, but wasn't emotionally turned on to her, so it was difficult for me to reach a climax. But she, meanwhile, was enjoying every bit of it, moaning and groaning and carrying on, and knowing that I was doing a good job turned me on, too.

Then Leo got hold of me. His penis was as rigid as a steel ruler, and I made up my mind that after Marika had sucked him for a while, I'd really show him just what a quick tongue could do for him.

I began gobbling his cock, starting with teasing, circular tongue-touches at its head, then quickly flicking at the sensitive area just under the head, then sucking all the way down to the base, and back to the tip again. While I was blowing her husband, Marika watched with pleasure and played with herself. In contrast to all the laughing and talking we'd done together during the previous week, none of us spoke now. We were all quietly adoring each other, wordlessly fulfilling ourselves in mutual abandon.

Marika was still masturbating, though without really reaching an orgasm—just hanging on to the edge of a climax. As for Leo, he was demonstrating some dazzling control. After about fifteen minutes of my performing fellatio on him, he was easily holding back, and in fact decided to please me as well. We shifted into the 69 position, and he moved in on my moist snatch with his little moustache and goatee. It tickled at first, but as I got used to it, it become pretty exciting. As they say in Dutch, "A kiss without a moustache is like an egg without salt."

Leo did his utmost, but had some difficulty hitting my clitoris at just the right spot. With Marika, I'd known just where to turn her on immediately; women usually know best how to stimulate one another. With men, I find it takes a little time before we work really well together. But Leo was really trying hard and, although he wasn't bringing me close to a climax, I was utterly enjoying it.

Only when he finally moved on top of me and deeply penetrated me with his thick, clean-cut cock did I really get aroused. The feeling of his strong body on top of mine, his soft breathing and kissing on my neck, and his beautiful gentle manner all combined to arouse me tremendously and bring me to the orgasm I'd been working toward for so long.

When I began to come, it was violent. Suddenly, almost as if cramped, my whole body began to shake and shudder with passion. I grabbed Leo's broad shoulders, and I'm sure he must have had scratches on his back from my fingernails. I was having a fantastic come, arching my body again and again, feeling Leo's gorgeous cock filling me, ramming and jamming again and again.

For a fifty-one-year-old man he was a very active and long-lasting lover. He seemed to be refusing to come; just kept fucking me. When I got exhausted he slipped out of me and replaced Marika's two fingers inside her vagina with his still-powerful prick. While he fucked her I crawled between his legs and sucked on his balls. And then I somehow managed to maneuver my head between Marika's cunt and Leo's cock—talk about acrobatics! At this point, Leo was on his knees, and while I had to pull onto Marika's ass, this made it possible for me to go down on her clitoris and play with it while he was screwing her. This way I was in no danger of getting my head slammed by Leo's supercharged, thrusting body, and at the same time we were combining to give Marika a doubly-pleasurable orgasm.

And indeed, when she came, it was just wild. I was still sucking her clitoris, and Leo was still piledriving his incredible cock, when she suddenly burst into spasms of joy, writhing beneath our attentions, her breath coming in quick, hot gasps and her body flexing in the grasp of a total orgasm.

Having brought his wife to fulfillment, with a little help from me, Leo pulled his cock out of her satisfied cunt (he still hadn't come) and slipped it—glistening wet, rosy, and ever-rigid—into my again-hungry pussy, but this time from behind—doggie-style. He was still in tip-top shape, and for some reason I found myself feeling very masochistic as he banged me from the back. He was so strong, so masculine, and so animalistic that I was dying for him to hurt me and spank me. I begged him as he fucked me, hissing, "Spank me, Leo, hit me. Go ahead, hurt me." I'd barely said it when he began slapping my buttocks. His fucking became more fierce, and his spankings began to sting, and the combination nearly drove me wild. The burning hot feeling of his cock within me and his smarting strokes on my bottom were just too much, and I quickly reached my second superb climax.

We carried on and on like this until eventually we were terribly tired, and ended up together in a very warm *carezza,* as Leo called it—just lying in each other's arms, very quietly, almost motionless, just enjoying the vibes. *Carezza* is Italian and means to stroke gently, to hold, to fondle, or as the sound suggests, to caress; it doesn't particularly imply fucking.

This *carezza* with Leo was the most enjoyable moment in the whole swing. It was fun to get spanked, and exciting to get fucked so beautifully, and great to participate in the ménage-a-trois, but this, the tender, emotional moment of the lovemaking, was the very best. It was then, as we lay together softly, that Leo—though he'd been active for almost an hour—finally reached his orgasm—with me. It was very gentle. We were just hugging each other, holding our bodies completely still except for the almost imperceptible movement of his rock-hard cock inside my spent vagina, and with a soft and a satisfied groan his hips arched and he flooded me again and again and again with his precious hot jism.

And even then, when the very last spurts of his well-earned climax were completed and his prick began to lose its erection, we still lay together, his exhausted cock resting in my warm cunt.

Marika had been watching us all this while, and I could see that though she'd enjoyed it on one level, and in fact had brought herself to another climax, there was a certain understandable envy in her eyes. I think she knew intuitively that there was more than just another swing going on. Perhaps she sensed that Leo and I were embarking on a longer-lasting relationship, that something special was happening between us.

I didn't want to hurt her feelings, so I gently got out of bed, almost embarrassed about those final, tender moments with Leo and our subdued mutual orgasm. I washed up a bit, put on my summer dress, and whispered an affectionate good morning, thanking them for the lovely evening and for bringing me to Paris as their guest.

I LOVE PARIS IN THE SPRINGTIME

The next morning brought another beautiful, sunny day, and just knowing that I was in Paris made me feel bright and optimistic. After my morning *toilette,* I took my *petite déjeuner*—breakfast, or literally "little lunch"—in the hotel lounge.

My all-time favorite beverage, orange juice, isn't as commonplace a breakfast drink in Europe as it is in North America, but I ordered some and happily it soon arrived, freshly squeezed and delicious, along with hot-from-the-oven croissants and preserves. My willpower told me not to have that lovely croissant, full of butter, but my willpower isn't at its best first thing in the morning, and I just couldn't resist a taste. And if you're a food fan, you know how that first good taste leads to another and another!

After that wonderful night, I felt very close to Leo and Marika, but knowing that we mustn't consume all of one another's time, we stayed apart during the day. With so much beauty in Paris, it's hard to feel bored or lonely, so I didn't really miss them, and spent a full day being a grateful tourist.

Near my hotel in the Saint Germain des Près area were delightful surprises at every turn. The house in which Voltaire once lived, the Abby of Saint Germain des Près (which was founded in the sixth century), the cozy restaurants and cafes frequented by the Parisian arts-and-letters set and film stars, the Drug Store American-style . . . all were part of the wonderful collage that makes Paris the dynamic city it is.

Trying not to look like a typical, gaping tourist, though at the same time checking my little guide book every now and then, I poked around the Latin Quarter, which is right

next to the Saint Germain quarter, and dates way back to
the time when students there actually conversed in Latin.
The Sorbonne is there, and the famous boulevard Saint-
Michel. But I'm a woman, not a scholar, and I couldn't
resist the avant-garde fashion boutiques, the antique
shops, and the cafes along the Boulevard Saint Germain.

A short walk away was the beautiful eighteenth-century
mansion named Hôtel Biron, but better known as the
Rodin Museum—it was the home of the great sculptor
Auguste Rodin. It's located within sight of Napoleon's
Tomb, and the Eiffel Tower, and it was magical for me
that day in Paris to stand in the garden, surrounded by
Rodin's magnificent sculptures and the sturdy old trees,
knowing that for miles and miles around me there was history and beauty and life and love.

If you don't recognize Rodin by name, you know him
by reputation. You're surely familiar with his works, *The
Thinker* and the once controversial *The Kiss*. They're two
of the world's most famous sculptures. I remember being
very stimulated when I read the novel based on Rodin's
life, *Naked Came I,* and here I was this springtime day so
close to his wonderful work.

This incredible man had the ability to take a chisel to
marble and transform it into the most powerful beauty you
can imagine. It was almost overpowering with its loveliness,
but I spent an intense hour or so among it all, so far away
from the physical passion of the previous night—yet in its
own way a true orgy of sculptured beauty reflecting human
passion and desire.

Only later—damn!—did I learn that if one applies
for a special "educational" pass from the proper ministry,
one gets to see Rodin's truly erotic works, which aren't
otherwise available to public scrutiny. Oh well, win one,
lose one—I was moved, even turned on, if you will, by
what I did see, so perhaps it was best that I saved something for the evening.

Across the Seine, over the Pont d'Iena, lay the Trocadero
Gardens, and I decided there that this was as good a time
as any to explore *Le Métro*. I wanted to travel the way
Parisians do, so I checked the map at the entrance to the
station, and with my route all planned in my mind, went
underground and waited for a train. My first surprise was

when the train arrived. The doors didn't open automatically —passengers getting off or on had to open them. I nearly missed the first train, but luckily a friendly young guy saw my dilemma and opened the door for me from inside the train.

The Metro also has interesting laws about who can sit down during the rush hour—pregnant ladies and men injured in the war, among others, have priority. The signs didn't mention retired hookers, so I thought I'd better not press my luck, and I stayed on my feet.

The trains are clean and swift and silent (Paris was the first city to install rubber tires on subway wheels and Montreal and Mexico City have followed suit), nothing like those terrible underground dumptrucks that New Yorkers put up with. Anyway, with only one *correspondence,* or connection, and no goofs, I ended up at Place d'Etoile ("Place of the Star," literally, because it's like a star with streets radiating from it like rays), or as it's now called, Place Charles de Gaulle. Parisians must prefer their old traditions because many of the new Place Charles de Gaulle signs have been defaced, with Place d'Etoile written over them.

You may not recognize it by either name, but it's famous for at least two things: it's where the Arc de Triomphe is, and it's one end of the Champs Elysées. The arch is really huge and very beautiful. Napoleon had it built as a gateway to the city so that his victorious soldiers could triumphantly march through it. And, of course, the Champs Elysées is that grand avenue where the beautiful people are. It's lined with sidewalk restaurants, imaginative car showrooms, cinemas, hotels, and the most elegant office buildings.

By now I was weary from all my walking, so I stopped and relaxed at a sidewalk cafe. Sipping lemonade, I just sat back and watched the world go by—the lovely girls of Paris in their marvelous fashions, and that special breed of Frenchman that looks like Jean-Paul Belmondo.

I began to fantasize that one of them, a passerby impeccably dressed in spotless white, would come over to me, fling a few francs on the table to pay for my drink, then wordlessly take me by the hand and stroll down the Champs Elysées, perhaps to the nearby Hotel Georges V. Still without a word, we'd glide into the lobby and receive polite nods of respect and recognition from the staff. We'd get into the elevator, and then walk down a white corridor and into a white room.

There, perhaps to the music of Mozart, we'd make slow, superb, sensational love, moving our bodies together with all the grace of a slow-motion film. We'd finally—just as neither of us could stand it for a moment longer—burst into a mind-blowing orgasm, and the room would melt into a mellow yellow and the music would almost swallow us, softly changing into the theme from *Elvira Madigan*.

Later, still wordlessly, my lover would take my hand and lead me out into the warm sunlight and back up the Champs Elysées to my lemonade. And without even a word, let alone a goodbye glance, our hands would unclasp and he'd drift away up the street and out of my life.

A silly fantasy, I suppose, but it must have been in the air and just floated into my mind. I could hardly believe my eyes a few moments later when a gorgeous-looking man in a white suit approached my table. I was about to jump up and fling myself into his arms when he walked right past me and sat down at the next table. I waited for his special glance, but he didn't seem to notice me.

A few minutes went by and I was bursting with anticipation. Here was my fantasy lover, ready to make glorious love to me as soon as some unseen director gave him the cue.

Suddenly another beautiful man swept by me and joined the first. With a little telltale clutch of hands and that particular tone of voice that has *gay* written all over it, my fantasy burst like a pregnant soap bubble.

Here was Xaviera, all primed for the man of her dreams to sweep her off her feet, and he turned out to be a gentleman of the homosexual persuasion!

Oh well, I guess it takes things like that to make sure our fantasies remain fantasies. Besides, with all the good sex to be found in Paris, I'd be selfish to try to corner the market, wouldn't I?

Fantasy time over, for now, at least, I decided to indulge one of my genuine passions—beautiful clothes. With the help of my handy guide book and some friendly directions from passersby I found the famous Rue du Faubourg Saint-Honoré—home of France's political and fashion leaders.

The presidential palace is there, as are headquarters for Lanvin, Hermes, St. Laurent, and Courrèges. Nearby are Dior, Chanel, and Cardin—all legendary names in the world of fashion.

It's the street where you'll find Jacqueline Onassis at Alexandre, her hairdresser. Or any number of world celebrities, perhaps dropping into Roger & Gallet for a trinket, or into one of the art galleries to pick up "a divine little sketch."

Surrounded by temptation, I must have forgotten my usual thriftiness because in no time I'd spent several hundred dollars on a pair of suede pants and a matching suede coat.

Then I meandered over to the lovely arcades of the rue de Rivoli, another elegant shopping street near the Louvre, though not as expensive as Rue du Faubourg Saint-Honoré. I purchased some more irresistible clothes there, and decided to quit while I still had a few travelers checks left in my purse. By now I'd realized that prices in both Holland and France were easily as high as those in America; Paris, after all, *is* the fashion capital of the world, and the workmanship is excellent.

Exhausted from my walking and shopping and fantasies, I took a taxi back to the hotel and by a happy coincidence arrived there just as Leo and Marika pulled up in a taxi. Even out of bed we were coming together! We arranged to meet in the lobby at eight-thirty, giving ourselves plenty of time for a nap and bath.

TABLE FOR TWELVE, PLEASE

Preparing for dinner, I relaxed in a tingly-hot fragrant bath, and just grooved on what a great day I'd been having so far. Then, relaxed and refreshed, I dressed for dinner with Leo and Marika. I wore my green minidress with a completely bare back, and just two strings around my neck supporting a scanty front which slightly revealed my breasts. I applied a little matching eye shadow and because the night would grow chilly, I wore my white mink coat.

I must have seemed a strange sight as I met Leo and Marika in the lobby: here I was in sandaled feet, a summer dress, and a fur coat! But Leo complimented my appearance and Marika echoed his sentiment. She told me that we'd be joined by an attractive Egyptian-Jewish boy named Ahmed, and one of his many girlfriends.

Ahmed, I recalled, was a boy whom Marika had told me about once before. She'd confessed that they had spent two months together in St. Tropez, as lovers, when she'd been vacationing there on her own while Leo took care of business in Holland. He knew of the affair, though, and tolerated it, telling her, "As long as you have fun, you can even live with someone else when I'm not around, but just don't neglect me. In fact, when you're on vacation, go ahead and have fun and fuck whomever you want, whether I'm there or not." Certainly a broadminded contrast to my Larry's attitude.

Ahmed was indeed a good-looking boy, as I immediately observed when he joined us. He had dark hair and complexion, a matinee idol's smile, and a well-built but compact body, with a perfect ass. His girlfriend, Suzette, was a slim redhead with short hair, wearing black hotpants and kinky white stockings. She was a natural beauty, and her lovely, long eyelashes were particularly striking. I really dug her at first sight.

We strolled to a nearby restaurant, and by the time we were all seated around the table, I felt wonderfully warm and comfy. The restaurant was filled with attractive and charming people, all around my own age, and they were all so obviously enjoying life. It was contagious, and I sat there just glowing with happiness because I was surrounded by nice people who treated me kindly—such a contrast from my recent experiences in America.

I was in a very loving mood, and Suzette was so cute that I felt like hugging her close to me, right there in the restaurant. But my inherited North American hang-ups about not showing one's emotions inhibited me.

Suzette intuitively realized this, and made the first move. She lifted her long legs and rested them right on my lap, slowly pushing up my miniskirt until my tiger bikini underpants were showing. Then she came close to me and hugged me affectionately. Meanwhile, Leo and Marika were sitting across from us, and I began playing with his knees, then moving on to a game of footsie with him beneath the table. The fooling around continued on a very light level, with all of us feeling nice 'n close to each other, sitting there wordlessly smiling and nodding and getting stoned on the good vibes.

At the same time, we realized that we hardly knew each other, so Ahmed began to tell me about life in Paris, including the prostitution scene and the lesbian bars. Indeed, Suzette was working a few nights each week in one of these bars, as a cocktail waitress, to earn extra money. She was gay, but sometimes enjoyed doing a number with a guy, and had been known to give very creditable performances in a swing.

Aha! So Suzette and Ahmed were just good friends, as the saying goes. Well, he'd mentioned that he knew plenty of callgirls, and when I asked him how he made his living he just smiled coyly and murmured, "Guess!"

I immediately figured that he was being kept by some of the professionals, and he confirmed this. Here was a man who wasn't a real pimp and who was so charming that the girls just fell in love with him and made sure that he was well taken care of—both financially and sexually. But they all knew the score—there would be no serious involvement with him.

"There are two big madams in Paris at the moment," Ahmed told me, turning the subject away from himself for a moment.

I'd heard of one of them, a very old lady, in her seventies, with a worldwide reputation as the leading lady of them all.

"She's really the best," Ahmed confirmed. "Flies girls from Rome to London, or from Persia to Paris, you name it. It's big business, and some of her customers pay thousands and thousands of dollars."

He told me that she was rarely seen anymore, even though prostitution was more or less tolerated in Paris, and that she no longer had a house such as I'd had in New York. She had been vaguely associated with a murder case, which involved a bizarre combination of prostitution, homosexuality, and blackmail with a famous French film actor. The actor's bodyguard was shot dead right in front of her place, and since then she had moved several times, changed her telephone listing, and in the process lost many of her clients.

Now that she was getting on in life, she was taking things easy, though still providing girls for some of the wealthiest and most powerful men in the world.

Suzette mentioned the names of some of France's leading cinema actresses—names which I daren't repeat here—and said that they'd begun their careers as callgirls for this madam. She also told me that the wife of one of France's highest and most distinguished political figures was a regular client of the madam, who would arrange both young boys and young girls for this lady's pleasure.

I must say I was rather shocked when Suzette mentioned the lady's name, but Ahmed knowingly allowed that it was quite true, and not exactly a well-kept secret.

Well, why not? Just because you're a major statesman's wife, it doesn't mean you can't swing, does it? If it makes you feel good, do it—no matter who you are. But it is difficult to imagine some politicians at an orgy—like Richard Nixon and Golda Meir, or Queen Elizabeth and

Britain's former Prime Minister Ted Heath. It's like trying to imagine Jacqueline Onassis farting up a storm. You know they must do it sometimes, but it just doesn't seem probable!

Dinner was a sheer delight, and afterward we crossed the Seine and drove northwest through the night lights of Paris, past the Bois de Boulogne, to the outskirts. I was with a carload of swingers, so I knew we weren't on our way to a church social. Which was just fine, because I didn't happen to be wearing a hat!

Ahmed told me that we were on our way to one of the oldest swinging clubs, one which was frequented by famous personalities from the world over. Like other such clubs, he told me, they preferred couples, but a single man would be admitted here at six times the regular price.

Leo reminded me to relax and let whatever would happen, happen. "Que sera, sera," as Doris Day used to sing —though I don't think she had swinging in mind.

Soon we approached a lovely old French *maison* on the main road. We drove through the large gates, parked, and at the door Ahmed mentioned a name. A well-built, well-stacked young man in deliciously revealing tight bell-bottoms smiled and welcomed us into the bar. At first sight it didn't seem particularly exciting. There were perhaps ten couples in the bar, all dressed, and having a relaxed, quiet time.

I sat down on one of the bar stools and discovered, to my delight, that there was a little hole in the middle, just where my crotch touched the stool. And, looking around, I realized that some of the fellows chatting away were simultaneously fingering their ladies from underneath the seats. Hmmmm! Well, this was a good start, wasn't it?

Ahmed then took me around the entire house, which had all kinds of sexy little side rooms, and two large bathrooms. There was no difference in the bathrooms—I guess they were the first unisex johns I'd been in—and each was furnished with toilet, bidet, sink, and stacks of clean, fluffy towels. I also noticed a few used towels on the floor, in the corner.

We looked into some of the small rooms, and most appeared to be the same. There were attractive Moroccan benches, with tight little pillows, lining the walls, under a soft light, and a large oval table in the middle of each room. Although some people were smoking and drinking, the tables were completely clean, with nothing on them.

We returned to the bar, which adjoined an inviting, intimate dance floor, and the music sounded great. So Leo and I went out to trip some light fantastics, and—have you guessed it!—this was where I was gloriously fucked by my phantom friend from behind. It was such a good story that I couldn't resist telling you about it right at the beginning of my book! In fact, every time I think of it, or tell my friends about it, I can't help but burst out laughing when I remember how, after it was all over, I leaned over to Leo and asked him if my fancy fucker was at least good-looking! Now *that's* what I call a blind date, Charlie!

So there I was, still holding on to Leo and completely naked, fresh from a beef injection by a guy I hadn't even seen. His ejaculation was dribbling down my thighs, and while I didn't really want to leave the dance floor, I did want to clean up a little.

At the same time, I noticed I was getting some pretty amused looks from people, who had obviously gotten their rocks off watching me and my fancy rear-end dance partner. Some of the men voyeurs had pulled out their cocks and jerked off while it was happening, while some of the women had apparently performed a similar function for themselves or their partners. I'll bet there wasn't a dry pair of underpants in the house.

Even Marika, who'd been dancing with Ahmed when I last saw her, was now in the middle of the dance floor, quite naked, playfully pulling one man's penis while just beginning to release another's from his pants.

A young man who said he'd admired my tits from afar escorted me into one of the small rooms, which was already occupied by two or three men sitting on the benches. They actually stood up and stared at me as I came in, although one of them did have the courtesy to hand me a towel, and so I simply plopped myself on the table in the middle of the room and dried myself off. The boy who'd brought me into the room had his hands on his belt, and I could see the bulge of a huge hard-on just begging to get out from underneath his pants.

I dropped the towel to the floor, and thought that I'd be a bit of a cockteaser, so I lay back on the table in what I thought might be a mildly provocative pose.

In a flash—pun fun intended, optimistically—the young man who'd escorted me there had his belt undone, practically ripped open his fly, and pulled his pants and shorts down to his knees, and without bothering to undress any further he jumped on top of me and started fucking away as if there were no tomorrow. His movements were hard and strong, but sure—like a young bull. My legs were around his broad back, and my own back was flat against the surface of the table. I felt like I was being raped because he was fucking so forcefully that it hurt, plus the fact that he was almost fully dressed. His pants were still down around his knees and he had on a sweater, so all that could be seen of his body was his sexy little ass bobbing up and down as he slipped his furious cock in and out, in and out, again and again, drawing it almost completely out, then plunging it back into the depths of my by-now-squishy cunt. He was driving me right out of my mind, and I think I was doing the same for him. We were both panting and heaving, moaning and groaning, and the combined sight and sound of this incredibly aggressive fuck was bringing in another audience. Within no time there were twenty or more men crowded around the table, some already nude, some tearing off their clothes, all with prominent boners, as we used to say in kindergarten! The sight of almost two dozen stiff pricks got me even more excited, if you can imagine that, and I started arching my pelvis in rhythm to my fantastic French lover's thrusts. Knowing that he had such an audience must have turned him on even more, too, because the fuck just got better and better. Soon the bystanders started getting into the act, and I had pricks pushing against my ears, my hair, my neck, my armpits, everywhere. My body seemed to be covered with cocks, dongs, schlongs, dicks, pricks, peckers—you name 'em, I had 'em. I didn't know which one belonged to whom, or even what they were doing, because the most important one was the one in my cunt, which had just begun to make me ecstatic. Lights started flashing behind my eyes. My mind turned twenty different colors, my body pumped boiling steam, and I thought, this time I'll never stop coming. I'll just come and come and come until I die.

And as my vagina contracted in its spasms of joy, the superstick within it started gushing jism, and my wild lover groaned a long, satisfied groan, and we lay there together for another few minutes, completely spent.

Then he reached my mouth with his, and we exchanged our first—and only—kiss. He got off the table and stood up, looking so ridiculous standing there with his sweater all damp and twisted and his slacks around his ankles, so I asked him for a little favor—I asked him to take off his clothes so that I could admire his body. And he *did*. He had a lovely, firm chest with not a hair on it, and good shoulders and strong arms. But no wonder he was in good shape—he probably got more exercise fucking me than the average man in Milwaukee gets in a month.

But I didn't have much time to think about the value of sex as an exercise or conditioner. There were still twenty horny men in the room, and they didn't care what my just-finished friend looked like. They were interested in an inside tour of my cunt. Within the next forty-five minutes I must have been fucked by ten men, easily. Every way, too: doggie-style; kneeling on the table; from the back bending over the table; from the front while sitting on the edge of the table; and just for variety every now and then, the good old missionary position; I got fucked six ways from Sunday, believe me, and I enjoyed every drop of it. These guys did everything but suspend me from a chandelier. And if the place had had a chandelier, I think they would have tried that, too!

I was ready to call it a night when Ahmed came in, with a huge grin on his face and a tiny smile on the tip of his cock. Exhausted as I was, I couldn't help thinking how marvelously "humpy" he looked without his clothes. And so poor Xaviera, unable to refuse a pretty body, fucked one more for the road, making it a dirty dozen. I dug Ahmed and wished he hadn't been number twelve—oh! I'd like to have made love with him when I was a little fresher, but I gave it all I had and, if I say so myself, it was pretty good.

He was a gentle but thoroughly exciting lover, and knew how to use his cock for maximum penetration and pleasure.

When we finally finished he walked with me to the bathroom and when I'd used the bidet, he presented me with my underpants—the ones I'd lost so many fucks ago on the dance floor!

I must say, by then I was really pooped. I'd certainly worked out all my fantasies about being raped by a gang of studs. My body was black and blue the next day from all the pinching and pushing and squeezing.

On the way back to the hotel, we compared notes. I'd had twelves fucks, but Marika had had only one, while lovely little Suzette hadn't fucked any men at all, though she did manage to make love with a few ladies. Leo had screwed two women and Ahmed had made it three times. So I'd fucked more than the other four put together!

Leo said that I'd certainly turned in a virtuoso performance, and that I'd doubtless be a welcome visitor to the club for the rest of my life. (But unfortunately the owner of the club, which I'm calling Chateau Roger, was recently fatally injured and now the club is closed.) I was still mystified, as we drove back to the hotel, that I'd fucked so many men, while Marika had screwed only one.

"Didn't I tell you?" laughed Ahmed, and the others seemed to suppress a collective giggle. "It's a house rule that any time a girl lies down on one of those tables in the middle of a room, it means she's willing to take all comers! She has to fuck anyone who wants her!"

They all broke up at this, and the car was filled with hysterical laughter! I couldn't help but join in, of course, because it was pretty hilarious.

Marika had known about the rule all along, but hadn't told me—paying me back, I guess, for having given Leo such a super fuck the night before.

But I have to say that the joke backfired on them all. Oh sure, I may have been a little sore and weak in the knees. But, oh, did they ever miss out on a dozen dynamite screws!

GAIETÉ PARISIENNE

Well, when I woke up the next morning I wasn't at all horny. But I *was* hungry. So I resolved to pay a visit to a fabulous hotel I'd heard about from friends, and have my breakfast there. It was called, simply enough, l'Hotel, and it was reputed to be one of the city's more interesting hostelries and an absolute must for those who can spare at least a hundred dollars for an evening's accommodation. It's located on the Rue des Beaux Arts in the Saint Germain des Près area, and at the turn of the century was known as L'hotel d'Alsace. Oscar Wilde died there in 1900. I wondered to myself if this was the scene for a delightful story, allegedly about Wilde, that I fondly remembered.

The great writer and professional bon vivant had come to Paris after being imprisoned, for sodomy, in his native England. He had been a flagrant homosexual, and had now decided to turn over a new leaf. He would live out his life in France, but be a lot more discreet.

A friend met him upon arrival, took him to a hotel, and while Oscar was shown to his room by the page boy, his friend made arrangements for the luggage. This took some while and it was fifteen minutes later when the friend entered the room, only to find Oscar in a very uncompromising position on the bed with the boy.

"Oscar," the disappointed friend cried, "I thought you'd promised to turn over a new leaf!"

"Oh, I will," replied Oscar, " . . . I will. As soon as I get to the bottom of this page!"

These days you're likely to meet not the descendants of Oscar Wilde—but rather the likes of Marcello Mastroianni and Catherine Deneuve at l'Hotel, and perhaps stay in the same room where Brigitte Bardot gave birth to her son by Roger Vadim.

A French actor, Guy Louis Duboucheron, and a Texas architect named Robin Westbrook combined to transform the old hotel into a gay, modern masterpiece. Each room is distinctively decorated in art deco or genuine antique, and the ground floor is a cross between a lobby, a pet shop, and the hanging gardens of Babylon. Throughout the entrance hall and dining room are massive vines and greenery, colorful live pheasants, peacocks and parrots, and even a couple of monkeys. Several English hunting hounds wander about peacefully, with an occasional outburst of howls at the tempting birds.

Among the hotel's attractive little extras is the custom of welcoming newly arrived guests with a fresh rose on the pillow and a bottle of chilled champagne. There are just twenty-five rooms, and guests are accepted only by strict personal recommendation. For breakfast, however, I was accepted without a recommendation—or a reservation.

After breakfast I made myself known to the manager and was given a brief personal tour of the hotel. Then I decided to pay a visit to another very "in" place, the Cafe La Coupole on Boulevard de Montparnasse, where at any time, I'd been told, one may expect to see the outrageous.

Drag queens and transvestites battle for attention here with Europe's top fashion models, like Verouschka. New York's "trendies," such as Andy Warhol and Viva, drop in during their Paris trips, and you are likely to see Yves St. Laurent, or any number of famous Parisian designers. For that matter, you're also likely to be rubbing elbows with any number of famous men with their gay lovers. It's a scene, all right.

By interesting contrast, the waiters are incredibly ancient. I noticed more than one of them looking like a flamingo, standing on just one leg, rubbing it with the other—probably trying to restore long-lost circulation.

Numerous artists come in to La Coupole to try to sell their work, and with a surprising degree of success because the cafe always seems to be filled as much with interesting tourists as with local Parisians. You might also get hustled by an old man trying to peddle Moroccan carpets. I was, and I might have been interested if they'd been *magic* carpets. He promised me they were, but he couldn't produce a twelve-month, twelve-thousand-mile warranty, so I took a pass on it.

That night Leo and Marika and I went with Ahmed to the Alcazar Cabaret on Rue Mazarine. Ahmed led us upstairs, away from the tourists, to the private areas where the artists get together and relax between performances. It was right out of the Liza Minelli film *Cabaret*. There were the lesbian "stage door Johnnies" waiting for their girls to finish work, and there were plenty of lovely gay boys, flirting with the male dancers and some of the customers.

Because it was so crowded, many people were standing on little chairs, straining to see the stage. We finally managed to find a comfortable spot in the balcony, from where all the action could be seen, and a good thing, too—the show ran from nine in the eevning till four in the morning, and "anything goes" was the password. Burlesque, transvestites, slapstick comedy, new singers making their debut: it was everything you'd expect from an old European music hall.

Best of all was a hilarious scene with Vera DeKova. She must have been at least sixty-five or seventy, still very well put together, with thick wigs, layers of makeup, and many a face lift. She appeared seven nights a week in the wildest of costumes—feathers, lace, multicolored gowns—and accompanied by five very gay boys. One was a muscular black, and the other four were typical, French, slim-hipped, cutie-pie faggots. She sang in a low, put-on voice and danced on her wiggly high heels with a little dribble-drabble step to the left, then to the right. You had to be there, I suppose, because while it may sound grotesque it was actually thoroughly amusing.

Ahmed told me that Vera had been married at least five times to five different millionaires, each of whom had left her a bundle when they'd died or divorced her. At one time she'd been a singer and dancer, but was never very successful. Now that she was old and wealthy, she was into her own ego trip. Performing was her kick. She wasn't paid for her nightly appearances . . . in fact, she paid the management for allowing her to perform! And of course, she paid her five dancers, for their costumes, and for the musicians.

As I looked at her I wondered what I'd be like at her age, and decided that if I had the panache and *chutzpah* that she did, I'd be a happy old broad. She was doing her own thing and digging it and, best of all, she was somehow carrying it off with style. Vive Vera!

Some of the other acts included a whorehouse skit—an old-fashioned French brothel with various kinds of customers arriving. The madam was played by the club manager, in drag, and his performance was delightful. There was a scene with an innocent young sailor coming to have his cherry popped; a freak who liked to stick needles into girls' bottoms; a masochist who wanted a crazy thrashing; a professor who wanted to dress up as a cooking teacher; and other kinky kooks! At least it didn't make me nostalgic....

Another act involved girls wrestling each other and falling off the raised stage into the arms of five or six dancers. They really seemed to be wrestling, or at least put on a convincing performance. It made me think of the old line, "She may not be much of a wrestler, but you ought to see her box!"

Just before we left, a gorgeous knockout of a girl came on, doing Marlene Dietrich and Marilyn Monroe impressions. She turned out to be a transsexual—not a transvestite—who had already undergone the operation to develop breasts and was soon expecting the final surgery which would turn him into a complete woman.

The show was nowhere near as slick as the Las Vegas spectaculars that I've seen, and there was plenty of obvious improvisation, but it was great fun and grand entertainment.

THE FRENCH CONNECTIONS

Until my "dirty dozen" experience on the table at Chateau Roger, I'd never been involved in such a big or busy gangbang. I'd had sex with perhaps five or six couples, all together, but certainly never with twelve different penises. But that was greasy kid stuff compared to what was coming. (Oh, *dear*....)

The big performance—opening night, I guess you might call it—was at the home of a multimillionaire industrialist, whom I'll call Claude Sevigny. Together with Ahmed, Leo, and Marika, I went out to his villa, hidden at the top of a hill on the outskirts of Paris and carefully guarded by two men who turned out to be actual Paris *gendarmes*, hired especially for the occasion. Some pretty famous people could often be found at Sevigny's *partouzes* (swings), and there'd been trouble once with reporters who'd barged in during an orgy. They were paid off, and the story was never published, but Sevigny now hired guards to keep them out in the first place.

Since group sex in France is not illegal, as long as minors aren't involved and there's no blackmail, Sevigny was able to get official police protection, too.

Arriving visitors were met by the guards, who used a walkie-talkie to announce all guests. The villa itself was surrounded by trees, and was very dimly lit. As we got closer I realized that the only glow from the house came from flickering candlelight within. We parked the car and just as we were about to ring the door chime, the door opened and we were welcomed by Sevigny's wife, Camille. Wearing nothing but a smart string of shells around her neck, she embraced Leo and Marika, shook my hand, and kissed Ahmed on the mouth, doing all this roughly at the same time. Then she invited us inside.

The house was huge, yet at the same time it felt quite intimate because of the soft candlelight and comfortable-looking furnishings. Just off the entrance hall was a grand bar, where people could help themselves to drinks. There was also an enormous buffet, loaded with cold cuts, an astonishing assortment of cheeses from around the world, fresh French bread, a variety of salads, pate, and desserts.

The large living room was furnished with contemporary beige leather couches and chairs, with thick carpets underfoot. It was thoroughly inviting. Through a big studio window, a large bottom-lit heated swimming pool could be seen. There were two lovely naked girls frolicking in the pool, caressing each other, stroking each other's breasts, and kissing and fondling in a very tender manner.

For that mater, *wherever* I looked about the house there were attractive naked bodies. Most of the people there were between twenty-five and forty-five, and in better than average shape. I don't mean that they were all perfect specimens, but they were mostly trim and attractive. Because almost everyone was naked, you didn't say to yourself, "Oh, look at that guy in the green sweater."

It was more like, "Oh, look at that guy with the moustache and the thin pecker!"

We soon found our way to a dressing room, where the four of us slipped out of our clothes and then continued exploring the house. For one thing, I couldn't begin to count the people there—probably well over two hundred.

Back in the living room, I noticed that the pool action was getting better. The two girls were still playing with each other, but five or six men had gathered on the sidelines. They looked like an honor guard because they were standing in a row, each with a prick standing at attention.

One of the men started stroking his prick slowly, holding it the way you'd hold a lightbulb, and ended up jerking off, spraying his jism into the pool, much to the delight of the girls and his fellow onlookers. At that point the girls became even more playful and invited the men into the water. In no time the pool was full and well on its way to supporting a moist ménage.

There was quite a crowd gathering at the window by now, watching the floating free-for-all. It was an interesting view because the pool was lit from beneath, so all the bodies seemed to be floating softly in the blue water. One of the guys had lost his hard-on in the water, but the others were well maintained and were soon being utilized.

By now I was pretty turned on, so I found my way outside and immediately started working on the guy who'd lost his erection. He was floating on his back in a shallow section of the pool, so I spread his legs and stood between them, then began a little mouth-to-cock resuscitation. Next, I'd float on my back for a few minutes, and we'd float apart, then come together and kiss and caress. It must have made a pretty sight, all those bodies floating in the water; I imagine that we might have looked like a big flower with its petals spreading open, then closing again.

My pool pal had cultivated a waterproof prick by now but rather than attempting anything in the pool, he invited me to go downstairs with him.

We'd been quite intimate, but hadn't introduced ourselves. His name was Martin. He was about five feet nine —not terribly tall—and had a broad-shouldered, narrow-waisted body. His longish hair was more red than brown, and he was one of those men with not just a hairy chest, but light curly hair on his shoulders and back, also. His wonderfully formed cock, neatly circumcised, had hung pendulously when it was soft, and now it stood up long, thick, and rigid. His body was well tanned and he had a magnificent, snug ass and nice flat belly. His soft blue eyes sparkled, and a light smile on his lips suggested a friendly personality and warm sense of humor.

We were still wet from the pool, so he showed me to a large bathroom, where we each took a fluffy beach towel and dried each other. As we did this, other couples came in to use the toilets or bidets, and we watched one couple enter, hand in hand, looking sweaty and exhausted. I told Martin that they had obviously just finished a great fuck, and he agreed. The girl squatted over a bidet, and her lover helped clean her, adjusting the flow of the spray. In fact, for a moment I thought she was going to have another orgasm right on the bidet, she seemed to so enjoy splashing the water on her clitoris.

Then her partner stooped over the bidet while his girl splashed water on his limp penis and lovingly helped clean him.

They then took towels and dried each other off, turning each other on all over again in the process. Her nipples grew hard, and so did his penis, and they exchanged a kiss which went on for so long I thought they'd probably both come before it was over. Finally, however, they broke the clinch and with a sheepish smile toward Martin and me, they left, again hand in hand.

My friend and I were dry by now, externally, but speaking for myself, at least, becoming rather moist internally.

This was Martin's first time at an orgy, he told me, and I guess that's why he'd had the soft-on earlier, in the pool. The situation took some getting used to if you were a new swinger. However, he was less embarrassed now, and obviously ready for action. As we headed for the basement of the house, where most of the action seemed to be taking place, the sound of sweet music reached my ears—the unmistakable moaning and groaning of dozens of copulating couples.

The basement was almost cavelike, the walls and ceiling irregular, and the room itself wandered on and on, rather crazily.

The huge room was furnished with big plastic couches and Moroccan benches, smaller leather sofas, and comfy, velvet-plush chairs. Parts of the floor were marble tiled, while other areas had thick rugs and animal furs. The walls were white, with some mosaic designs here and there, and hung with magnificent originals by Dali and Picasso. There were antique candelabra along it at regular intervals, and the flickering candles cast strange shadows on the many bodies in the room.

I suddenly realized the reason for the plastic couches, which, at first, I'd felt were rather out of place. The plastic made everything nice and juicy; the human perspiration made them warm and slippery so that it became like making love on an oiled waterbed.

What a scene! Hundreds of humping bodies were in the room. In one corner were three girls in a daisy chain, eating and caressing one another. As I watched, the two girls from the swimming pool came and joined them, so then they were five, all playing together. Two dildos were brought into action, and the girls began to take turns, expertly fucking each other with the artificial cocks, slowly and smoothly drawing them out, then plunging them deep into the waiting vaginas with all the skill of an experienced cocksmith. Two guys watching this do-it-yourself dong-along got so stimulated by it that they began sucking each other's cock and fondling each other's balls, and this attracted the girls' attention. Since they outnumbered the two guys, they took them over and forced them—there wasn't any resistance, to be truthful—to fuck and suck as many females as possible. So there was an enormous five-girl, two-man daisy chain happening, and there was so much going on within it that I don't think I saw everything!

But this was no time to be watching and not participating. Martin's penis looked like it was primed to fire and I was terribly excited, so, almost as if we'd rehearsed it, he put his arms around me, lifted me into the air, and gently let my more-than-ready recreation spot slide over his rampant ramrod. Deep, deep, deep it slipped within me, and I put my arms around his hairy shoulders and my legs around his waist. We started riding each other slowly, each thrusting away from each other, then against each other, and just going wild with sensation. We built up speed gradually until we were fucking like a well-oiled locomotive, and when the pleasure was beginning to get unbearable, Martin sucked in his breath and with a little croaking noise in his throat, starting shooting load after load of jism into me, and my vagina gripped his cock with every spasm so that together we milked the orgasm to a fabulous finish.

We were exhausted from this little exercise, so we squeezed ourselves into one of the plastic couches and relaxed together. We were surrounded by fuckers and fuckees, and all manner of sexual excitement. On one side a girl was spanking an older man and he was wailing with delight and pain as she flogged him and cried that she'd beat him harder and harder if he didn't stop wailing. He didn't, of course, so she began to threaten him with an enema if he didn't shut up immediately. This, of course, practically freaked him out there and then, and he made even more noise, screaming for mercy and forgiveness while obviously hoping that she'd beat him silly and then give him the enema of a lifetime. The last thing I noticed was the girl sternly leading the man toward the stairs, no doubt to find the appropriate equipment for their freaky little scene.

Martin and I were grooving on all the action, quietly cuddling each other, and his limp cock gradually began to show signs of life again. It was sort of flopped against my tummy, so as it began to get semihard I started breathing deeply, making my stomach rub against it. In two shakes of a lamb's tail, Martin's wonderful whang was rigid and ready for action again. I obligingly sat on his lap, with my back to him, and we started working on our encore. He caressed my ass with his hands as I bounced up and down on him, and I was able to reach between our legs and play with his balls, and even managed to wriggle my finger along the sensitive ridge between his scrotum and anus, much to his delight.

We both seemed to have a little more control this time, and we were able to keep it up for a good long time, slowing down the pace, then speeding it up almost to climax level, then stopping short, and pacing ourselves into an easygoing we've-got-all-the-time-in-the-world rainy-day fuck. My vagina was well lubricated from our first encounter, and his good thick cock made an amusing and sexy squishy noise as it plunged in and out of me. This, together with the feel of his hairy chest and hard nipples against my back and the sound of all the other couples, was just fabulously erotic. I closed my eyes and tried to freeze the moment in my mind so that this great feeling would never stop, when I felt the unmistable touch of a cock against my open mouth.

Martin was a great lover, but he sure wasn't this versatile! I opened my eyes and found myself staring at a one-eyed wonder, about eight inches tall, and attached at one end to a great big man. Like Martin, this newcomer appeared to be in his early thirties. But there the resemblance ended. He was about six feet four and had lovely blond hair, which he had styled just below his ears. His chest was perfectly hairless, and while his cock was long, it was very lean and very flexible. And still perched on my lips.

Martin didn't seem to mind, and I endorsed the idea, so while he and I continued fucking, I took the newcomer's cock into my mouth. He leaned down and whispered his name to me. Gunther. I would have introduced myself but had been brought up not to talk with my mouth full.

As I went down on Gunther's cock, taking as much of it into my mouth as I could, then slowly drawing it almost completely out again, he put his fingers on either side of its base and gently massaged it. This really seemed to turn on Martin, whose thrusts got more and more aggressive until finally he reached out his arms and threw them around Gunther's ass. This served to push Gunther's entire crotch against my face. The surprise and excitement of this got to Gunther and within a few seconds he had made a deposit in my oral sperm bank. So what could I do? With one cock shooting into my snatch and another into my mouth, I shuddered into a deliciously thrilling climax, and the three of us collapsed among one another's sweaty limbs.

Ahmed, it turned out, had been watching these proceedings with glee, and was more than ready to participate. Although we two had had a pretty good fuck the other night, he had been number twelve, so this time he'd obviously decided to come early.

He joined me in the pile-up on the floor and, without giving me a chance to clean myself for him, firmly shoved his pecker into me. After a few tentative strokes, he pulled out, his dark-hued cock glistening with the sperm of his predecessor. I thought for a moment that this had turned him off, but *au contraire!* He crawled down a little and started enthusiastically slurping away at my pussy, giving it the cleaning it so richly deserved.

He had a fantastically talented tongue, I soon discovered, and while blowing warm air into me, he made all sorts of silly noises, and fooled around with his fingers, first in my cunt, and then, his fingers nicely lubricated, with my rectal rosebud.

He also redoubled his efforts with his tongue and lapped and sucked away, all the while fingering my behind. It was lovely! Ahmed's tongue, fingers, hands, and whole body were moving with a rhythm all their own, ready to move in an instant from cunnilingus to coitus.

Gunther decided it was encore time, too, so for the second time he slipped his slender member into my mouth, squatting over me. So I went down on him again, licking and sucking while again exploring his anus with my lubricated finger.

However, this time Gunther was eager to fuck me, and felt it would be a waste to come in my mouth. Similarly, Ahmed was enjoying the *bouffe-baba* he was giving me, but was doing it really to set me up for a fuck. So the two of them agreed to fuck me simultaneously. First they both wanted to go in the same hole together, but I vetoed that on the grounds of one's company, but two's a crowd. So Gunther arrived at a compromise. He told Ahmed to lie on his back. Then I would sit on top of Ahmed, my legs spread to either side of his body. However, I would lean forward a little on my knees, thus pushing my ass upward. Ahmed would fill my cunt with his generously thick prick, while Gunther would slide his suitably slim slammer into my ass.

Even though Ahmed had been fingering my anus, and Gunther's prick was nicely lubricated, it still hurt a little being bum-fucked like this. But with the excitement of the situation, and the good feel of Ahmed's cock fucking me up front, I got tremendously turned on.

Not to be outdone now, Martin, my randy redhead, got back into the act and stood facing me so that I could suck him off. Here I was, double-fucking and sucking at the same time. The rhythm was fantastic; first a counterbeat with Ahmed pushing in as Gunter pulled out and I tongued my way down Martin's shaft. Then we all managed to get it together, in a uniform rhythm, and it was superb! My whole body rocked back and forth with their bodies, and as we did, I felt the incredible sensation of three distinctly different cocks moving in and out of me.

I'm usually not too enthusiastic about anal intercourse, particularly with a man who's well endowed. A thick rod can hurt tremendously, but this particular scene was super-satisfactory, and I was loosened up—in every sense of the word.

We continued this way for almost twenty minutes, much

to the amusement and delight of many onlookers, but my legs were getting tired and beginning to ache from holding the same position.

We managed to change positions, with me sort of on my side, and Ahmed still in front with Gunther in back, and Martin in my mouth. It was a little crowded and a little tricky, but it sure was fun and we made it work.

Gunther came first, I guess because my tushy is so much tighter than my cuntie. Although Ahmed had no complaints about the latter. It was juicy but tight enough to keep a firm grip around his prick. I, in the meantime, had reached orgasm about three times, just finishing the third as Gunther climaxed into my backside. Within another minute Martin shot his load into my mouth, leaving Ahmed and me undistracted to work toward a great big exploding volcanic comequake. Which we did!

Thoroughly spent, the four of us hugged each other affectionately, and after a few moments' rest we stumbled upstairs to the washrooms.

We met Leo and Marika on the way upstairs, and they were having just as great a time as I was. They were with Claude, the owner of the house, and he told us that he was giving the party to celebrate his birthday. We hadn't known this, of course, and we weren't prepared, but I did have a copy of *The Happy Hooker* in my purse, so I excused myself and got it from the cloakroom.

We presented it to him, after I'd autographed it, wishing him *bonne fête* and many happy returns of the day. Although he spoke English he didn't understand the title because, of course, it's an American slang expression. When we translated it for him, he seemed quite delighted, and mentioned that there were two prostitutes at the party who loved to combine business with pleasure.

I never got to find out who they were, and I must say I was curious to know whether they were giving out free samples at the party—as advertising for future business—or if they were charging for their charms. If they were charging, how? Cash on the line? I wondered, or did they perhaps send discreet invoices later?

One curious character I noticed there was a fellow in his early forties, walking around with a permanent hard-on. If he wasn't walking around, he was screwing somebody—

but either way, he must have had a constant erection all night long. His name, I discovered, was Sasha, and he was a famous swinger in Paris. Anytime a *partouze* was happening, he'd always turn up, ready for all the sex he could get.

His mind was completely consumed by sex, I was told, and it had ruined both his marriage and his business. He'd driven his wife to distraction by wanting sex almost every hour, and had actually raped most of the girls in his office. Even now, after several fuck-filled hours, he still wasn't satisfied, and prowled the party like a panther, looking for his next lay.

I felt rather sorry for Sasha because obviously he wasn't getting any real satisfaction from all his sexploits. I'm sure the only satisfaction he derived was from counting the number of cunts he'd visited.

Another unusual guest was a tall, lovely brunette with firm, small titties and long legs. I'd seen her in action with several guys, and at one point she was screwing right next to me, having the fuck of the century, judging by her undulations and gyrations, but she was one of those silent screws who never utter as much as a little moan. I assumed that this was probably a condition that she'd cultivated as a result of sharing a thin-walled apartment with others or maybe from trying to get laid at home without disturbing her parents.

But later I noticed her talking to a friend—probably the man she'd arrived with—yet she still wasn't making a sound. The girl was obviously, I realized now, a deaf-mute, and she was talking a sign language!

I was surprised, of course, that a deaf-mute would be at a swing like this, and then I understood that I was only reacting to my own prejudices. Why should a deaf girl, or a blind man, or any handicapped person, let his or her physical disability interfere with sex? It's just society's awful narrow thinking that suggests that disabled people are a different breed and should be confined to simple, unpleasurable activities.

This attractive, deaf-mute girl could enjoy a swing as much as anyone else. She liked sex, she was clearly good at it, and all she was missing out on was the sound of everyone else moaning and groaning. Sure, that's a turn-on, but I'll bet she made up for it by having developed more heightened sensitivity in other areas.

And I was glad to see that so many people at the party had accepted her without making fun of her, or passing rude remarks, or otherwise taking advantage of her infirmity. She was having a good time, and giving others a good time, and that's what really counts, right?

I also noticed a fairly elderly lady at the party—probably in her late fifties, or even her well-preserved early sixties. You could see that she must have exercised a great deal in order to keep her figure moderately trim. Her hair was dyed superblond, and she wore long white leather boots and all kinds of chains around her neck, partially distracting attention from her somewhat droopy boobs.

She was desperately searching for young men with whom she could run off to the sheets, but I don't think she had much luck, poor thing. While there were plenty of older men making it with young girls, it seemed that nobody was interested in a vice versa situation. So even at an enormous orgy like this, it's not always a case of "everything goes." Underneath all this swinging lay some pretty deep-rooted middle-class values.

For instance, while there was plenty of lesbian activity, there was virtually no male homosexuality that I could see. Before that large, mixed daisy-chain there had been the brief bit of cocksucking, but even that was only with those two really liberated guys, who were probably bisexual anyway.

About the only buggery going on was my scene when Gunther had given me a Hershey Bar special. Or "a fast freight up the brown route," as I'd once heard it called! I certainly didn't see any male-to-male bum-fucking.

I was having a ball, in many more ways than one, and was quite satisfied with the variety of sex I'd been getting. But suddenly I spotted a familiar face coming into the room—it was Suzette, Ahmed's lovely redheaded lesbian friend. She stood there naked except for a shy smile on her lips and a gold chain about her waist.

"Ooh la la!" she called as she spotted me, and burst into a broad, happy smile. "Hello, Xaviera," she whispered, and gave me a little hug. "You look as beautiful as I guessed you might."

I realized that we hadn't seen each other in the nude yet, and thanked her for the compliment.

"Oh, and you're lovely yourself, Suzette," I told her truthfully. "You're so petite, and your hair—it's so short and boyish and red. Red's my very favorite color for girls."

She stood there, with an innocent smile on her face, looking more like a fourteen-year-old than the twenty-one she was. She put down her wine glass and put her arms around my neck. Taking her head between my hands, I dropped a little kiss on her forehead, then pressed my lips against hers. Her mouth opened slightly and her tongue began to explore my lips—it was warm, hard, and soft all at the same time.

"Pardonnez-moi, Suzette, un moment," I whispered to her. "Forgive me for a moment, I just want to go and wash up. Don't go away."

"I won't, Xaviera. I'll be right here," she said, and planted another soft kiss on my lips.

There was a hand-shower in the bathroom, so I cleansed myself thoroughly and used the bidet. I'd fucked and sucked so much that I wanted to be clean and fresh for lovely Suzette, who was making me feel hornier than anyone else had so far that night. When I was clean and fresh again, I rejoined her. As promised, she was waiting patiently for me.

"Did you come by yourself tonight?" I asked her.

"Well, not really. Ahmed had asked me to come along earlier, and at the time I had an engagement for tonight. But it ended early, and I was able to get a lift here with some other friends. I'm glad I did," she said with a special smile, and gave my breasts a little kiss of their own. "Have you been busy?" she added.

"Well, to be honest, busy is an understatement. I've had my share of fucking for tonight. But I haven't really made love—if you know what I mean," I replied.

As we looked around the room, all the beds and couches and chairs and rugs were filled and covered with copulating couples. Or thrill-making threesomes. And even some fornicating foursomes! I didn't know where to take my little lover until I noticed an empty Moroccan bench, which looked perfect for her.

"Come over here, *ma cherie*, it's perfect. Here, sit back

—the leather's warm. That's it. Here's a spot for you. Comfortable?"

"Oh, Xaviera, you're great. Yes, of course it's comfortable. Now you make yourself comfortable." And with that she opened her legs to me. I dropped to the floor and buried my face in her lovely honeypot, with its soft red pubic hair.

I pulled her closer to me so that her pussy was just above my face. Then, on one knee, I kissed her and caressed the pouting outer lips of her vagina.

"Oh, Suzette," I whispered between kisses. "You're so beautiful, and so young. So undeveloped yet, like a lovely sixteen-year-old. You're so fragile. You're my Lolita!"

Then I was silent as my tongue busied itself within her tight little lips, licking inside her cunt, then searching for her tiny clit.

I must have found it before I realized, because she softly moaned, "Oh yes, Xaviera, yes—oh, yes, yes," sounding like a character out of James Joyce.

My petite French Molly Bloom had a lovely, small clitoris that slowly began to blossom under my tongue. As I sucked on it, it grew and grew, almost the way a man's penis would swell in a woman's mouth. It grew to the size of a pea, and responded nicely to my tonguing.

Until now she'd been passive, but suddenly she held my head in a scissor-grip with her thighs and crossed her ankles behind my back. And with her hands she gently pushed me closer so that not just my tongue, but my mouth and nose and entire face were buried in her lovely quiff.

Ahmed wandered over while Suzette and I were making love, and without hesitation he put his cock into her mouth while I was eating her. Although she was lesbian, she wasn't averse to a little cocksucking and eagerly gave Ahmed a beautiful blow-job.

The sounds and sight of Suzette giving head to Ahmed, plus my own licking of her, got me even more excited than before. Just then someone got behind me, and since I was on my knees eating her, he got on his knees and entered me from behind. My vagina was good and moist, as you can imagine, and his cock was good and stiff. I wasn't going to have a "blind date" like I'd had the other night on the dance floor, so I turned around for a moment to see who the newcomer was. I might have guessed! It was Leo, who thought he'd have some fun and be my second phantom fucker. As my tongue went back to work on Suzette, Leo slipped into me and made a good scene even better.

After the men had had their jollies, Suzette and I stayed together for a while, caressing each other and generally sharing some pretty good vibes. Then, because this was a swing and we were committed to the swingers' principle of not pairing off (much as we may have wanted to), we parted with a gentle kiss and went our own ways, knowing that we would see more of each other before the night was through.

By two o'clock in the morning I think I'd fucked another eight men, and two more girls, and it seemed to me that anything more would be just plain gluttony! It didn't take long to track down Leo and Marika—they'd done pretty well, too, incidentally; Marika had taken at least five men—and Ahmed and Suzette. We were all pretty pooped, and quite ready to leave. Although we were satisfied sexually, there was still so much adrenalin pumping through our veins that none of us was ready to sleep. So we decided to go out for some fresh air and perhaps try to find a late-night discotheque.

And so we got dressed and said farewell to the two hundred or so playmates who were probably more used to a big scene like this, and for all I know planned to fuck and suck till dawn's early light.

It was just then, as we were leaving the cloakroom, that I met Michel.

He was a tall, very well-dressed, very virile-looking man with a thick dark moustache, black curly hair, and piercing brown eyes which twinkled as he smiled. He was a perfect blend of the best of Burt Reynolds and Marlon Brando. We looked at each other and we could see little alarm bells going off behind our eyes!

He introduced himself, and since he, too, was on his way out, he invited all of us to a discotheque just off the Champs Elysées. Like a teenage girl with a mad crush, I suddenly forgot how exhausted I was and how much sex I'd had. Just being next to Michel made me feel fresh and free all over again. And I was glad that I hadn't met him during the orgy because I had a sudden craving to make passionate but private love to him. Alone, just the two of us, without a few hundred onlookers.

CHEZ MICHEL

Michel took us to a chic disco just off the Avenue des Champs Elysées on the Right Bank. It was an intimate club, and quite crowded for three o'clock in the morning. Much of the music was French and hot, but there was also a fair amount of English-language hit-parade stuff. I recognized an Aretha Franklin tune, "Day Dreaming," and a good boogie record by the American Dennis Coffey group. That was also the big summer for Roberta Flack's "First Time Ever" and Cat Stevens's "Morning Has Broken."

Michel and I danced to them all, getting closer and closer as the hour grew late. Somehow I was able to forget all the men I'd had that night and concentrate on him. This particular man, fully clad, attracted me much more than all the nude bodies I'd seen. Imagination and anticipation can often be much more of a turn-on than bare nudity offered on a platter.

He was about two heads taller than I, and I had to stand on my tiptoes to put my arms around his broad shoulders. He spoke very good English, with an American accent, and I was curious about this.

"I worked in New York for about six years once," he told me in his soft, low voice. "Let's just dance now, and I'll tell you all about myself later. At my place."

As we danced to the music I reached my hands inside his jacket and lifted his shirt out of his slacks. I softly scratched his back with my long nails, higher and higher, then unbuttoned his shirt halfway down and saw his hairy, appealing chest.

A Françoise Hardy record was playing, and we continued dancing even though we were both getting progressively more aroused. Michel was fondling my buttocks and I was lovingly nibbling his left nipple, feeling his erection against me.

We were both getting weak with excitement, and I knew that if we didn't pass out we'd have to fuck right there and then, or else go out of our minds. So we said a quick *adieu* to my friends—Leo giving me a broad wink—and left.

We crossed the Seine to the Left Bank, where he lived on a lovely street just off Boulevard Saint Germain. As we got out of his car he put a finger to his lips.

"Sshh," he whispered. "My eight-year-old-son is with me. Pierre. He'll be sound asleep."

But despite our best tiptoe efforts, the boy woke up as soon as we got to Michel's apartment, on the first floor. He hid his sleepy little head under his sheets and cried, "Why did you wake me, papa? Why did you wake me up?"

I gently pulled back the sheet so that I could see his face in the darkened bedroom.

"Hello, Pierre," I said. "Please don't be angry, we didn't want to wake you up."

"Oh, all right. Thank you, madame."

"Pierre, you're such a beautiful young man," I couldn't help telling him. He had long, dark hair, big, bright eyes, and certainly had inherited his father's good looks.

Michel bent over and hugged the boy in a nice fatherly way.

"Don't worry, my son, just go back to sleep."

But once awakened, Pierre started paying attention to me. "I like this lady better than Elsa last week," he announced, to my delight. Nor did Michel try to suppress a little chuckle.

I thought it was a pretty quick judgment for such a young man in the middle of the night, but received it with pleasure and a smile of thanks. And as I gazed at the shape of his gorgeous little body under the sheets, and his lovely face, I felt very warm—in more than a motherly way, I must confess.

Michel brought a bowl of cherries and a pitcher of juice from the kitchen, then led me by the hand to his spacious living room/bedroom. It was a big white studio, with wall-to-wall white broadloom and a big white bed on a raised pedestal.

All the furniture was white, too, including his stereo speakers. The two of us provided the only real color in the room. Suddenly my mind flashed to my afternoon fantasy at the sidewalk cafe of the white stranger leading me to love, and I wondered if it hadn't been a premonition of some kind. If Michel had offered to play a Mozart concerto, I think I would have fainted. But he didn't. He lit a candle, turned off the lights, and began to undress. I dismissed the afternoon fantasy from my mind, but couldn't help marveling at the coincidence.

I slipped out of my light summer dress and joined him in bed. We were both still at a fever pitch of excitement from the discotheque, but we still managed not to attack each other. We ate the cherries and sipped the juice and got to know each other better. I was full of questions about him.

"Once upon a time," he playfully responded, "I married a very pretty girl. She was one of the top fashion models in Paris. Lovely, elegant, charming. I was struggling to make a dollar, in and out of many different businesses, hustling to stay alive. She fell in love with me. We married, we struggled, she gave birth to Pierre. My wife got a job in New York, so the three of us moved there."

Michel slipped out of bed and searched in a white cabinet until he found an envelope of photographs. He lit another candle, poured more juice for me, and showed me the pictures.

"She's very beautiful," I said truthfully. She was brunette, tall, and slim. "This must be Pierre with her, but who's the other boy? Is he your son, too?"

"Yes, he's Pierre's younger brother, also a very attractive child. The pictures had been taken about two years earlier, when Pierre was six and the other boy four."

"Where's the other boy now?" I wondered.

"With my wife. When we divorced, I got custody of Pierre, and she took the younger."

There was an edge of bitterness in his voice, so I asked him more questions so that he could get the full story out of his system.

"When I was in New York," he explained, "I finally landed a terrific job, working for a rich old man who needed someone like me to sell twin-engine planes for him. As I became more and more successful, my wife gradually gave up modeling and gained a bit of weight. And our marriage began to deteriorate. My wife, Elaine, couldn't really cope with my newfound success coupled with her decreased work."

"Were you still in love with her?" I wanted to know.

"Of course. I never cheated on her during six years of marriage. I loved her totally. But she began having affairs with other men. Just to reassert her independence, I think. Unfortunately, at that time I had to fly some planes to Morocco in a sales pitch."

"It's always the way, isn't it?" I observed. "Just when the relationship is at the straining point, business pressures make things worse."

"You don't know how worse," he replied. "When I landed the plane in Morocco—with a copilot I didn't know much about—the Tangier police searched the aircraft and seized a package behind my seat. They told me it contained marijuana mixed with tobacco. I was thrown in jail at once, and got really rough treatment.

"I was treated like an animal for five days, until finally I was able to contact my wife. She flew to Morocco and was able to visit me in prison. It was then that I realized how insensitive and naive she was, asking infuriating silly questions. The police had put a bail of fifty thousand dollars on my head, so I gave my wife a list of people—my lawyer, accountant, banker—and asked her to have them get to work on it.

"You know what the stupid bitch did, Xaviera? As soon as she left the jail she threw away the notes I'd made. Then she left Morocco, and shacked up in New York with some guy she'd met in Rome. She didn't give a damn about me!"

Michel was raising his voice a little now, and I could feel the fury and frustration filling him. He went on to explain that after five months in jail he eventually found a trustworthy lawyer in Tangier, who contacted his friends and lawyer in New York. They raised the money and he was freed.

"I felt like throttling the bitch when I got back to New York," he hissed through his teeth. "She'd changed the locks on our apartment, and told the kids they'd never see me again. I nearly killed her. We had a tremendous fight when I caught up with her. She sued me for divorce, and it became final three months ago. And because of the Moroccan business—in jail and all—I was asked to leave the United States."

Well, I certainly knew all about that, so we did have something in common. He concluded, telling me that a friend—our host at the villa, actually—had helped him get back on his feet in France.

He leaned back and sighed. He'd purged himself of his sad experiences and I was glad that I'd been a good listener for him.

"That's my story, Xaviera. It's crazy, but it's true. And it's all behind me now, so let's forget all about it. Look, it's almost five in the morning. Let's just make love."

With those words he took me in his arms and hugged me tenderly but with vast reserves of strength. We'd hardly touched each other in the past hour, as he'd talked, but now his cock began to grow. It wasn't particularly long but it was thick and strong, and it throbbed against me. I caressed his nipples while he kissed mine with his warm mouth.

Soon we were lost in a sea of love—not too quick, not too slow, it was a calm sea—and we floated together, gently bobbing up and down.

Our lovemaking was straight and simple and very, very good. All our pent-up emotional energy came to the surface in a wonderful way. This wasn't fucking or screwing or humping, or anything like that. It was making love. And it was great.

It was almost sunrise, but this morning our brightest hour had been just before the dawn. And we slept, huddled together like innocent children.

At nine o'clock, little Pierre came running into the bedroom and threw open the curtains, letting in the brightest sun imaginable. My fantasy again! The room turned from white to yellow as it filled with sunshine.

Pierre looked adorable. He was dressed in suede pants

and a bone-colored turtleneck. He came over to me and kissed my nose.

"Good morning, how are you?" he asked in his best-mannered voice. "My name is Pierre, in case papa hasn't told you yet. Who are you?"

"Xaviera."

"But that's a French name. And you're not French, I can tell by the way you talk."

I told him that my father had wanted a boy, but my mother had borne a girl. My father had already chosen the name François-Xavier before I was born.

"But what happened?" he asked. "You became a girl, didn't you? And what about your name?"

"Yes, I was a girl, all right. So I had something less than a boy had, didn't I? And my father decided that since I didn't supply him with everything he'd expected in his child, he wouldn't give me the full name he'd chosen. So he took off the François and added on *a*. And I became Xaviera. Can you figure that out, little Pierre?"

"Yea-a-ah," he answered in a long gasp, but he was paying less attention to my conversation and more to my right breast, which had slipped out from under the bedclothes.

His father told him to go prepare for breakfast, and the three of us spent a family-style day together.

That afternoon Michel and I made love again, and this time Pierre hovered around us and even participated—playing with my breasts while his father filled me with a beautiful fuck. What an example to give a young boy! I can't recommend this open an attitude for father and son, even for those who have the sensitivity and instincts to handle it carefully. I'm sure it can be an unsettling experience.

Michel proudly told Pierre and me that when the boy was twelve or so, and ready to fuck, he would call me in, and I could receive his virginity. I said I would think about it.

The day went by so quickly and soon it was night and Michel and I joined Leo and Marika for dinner. They liked him as much as I did, and the four of us spent a wonderful night together, in a final swing before we were to leave *la cité des lumières*.

Too soon, I had to bid *au revoir* to Michel as I returned to Amsterdam with Leo and Marika. Fortunately, Europe is snug, and wherever I went, Paris wouldn't be far away by jet, and I was sure that Michel's and my paths were meant to cross again.

HOLLAND, HOME, HEARTBREAK

Arriving at Amsterdam's Schiphol Airport from Paris with Leo and Marika, after a fabulous time spent in the French capital, presented me with a scene quite different from what I'd faced in April. Coming into Holland from the United States, I was miserably depressed, and that morning had been cold and rainy.

I had left New York under the pressure of an ultimatum from the American government: leave voluntarily within ten days or be deported. I chose to go quietly.

And six hours later, standing in Schiphol Airport just after dawn, I could see my mother waiting. She looked hypernervous and suddenly I could see why. A gaggle of newspaper reporters had gathered at the arrival gate, eager to flash photos of me with my beagle pup and trunk after trunk of luggage. Six years earlier I'd left Holland as an unknown secretary; I now was a world-famous ex-madam and best-selling author.

The reporters were from the major wire services and Dutch papers. In America I'd become used to the press, and even got to rather like them for pushing my book. But in Holland they were out to crumple my image. Maybe they were jealous; after all, every writer dreams of having a best-seller, and I'd *done* it, without first spending umpteen years as a low-paid reporter.

The Dutch authorities also barraged me with questions, but about Bagel, my four-month-old beagle: "Where did you get that dog? How old is it? Male or female? Color? Pattern? Breed? What is *beagle* in Dutch? Is it a hush-puppy? What shots has he had? Which company manufactured the injections? Doctor's name?"

Then, after making me fill out their small mountain

of forms, they took Bagel off to be quarantined for two weeks. As they dragged him off to his cage, he howled and cried and screamed all through the airport. It struck me as ironic that Xaviera Hollander had traveled to her freedom in Holland, whereas her little puppy arrived to be imprisoned.

My mother was happy that her lost child had returned, and yet was somewhat uneasy with my presence, for she'd been shocked by the details of my past life. My father had written a few books shortly before the war, and she hoped I might share his talent. When I was a teenager, she'd once told me, "Xaviera, I know you like to write and like being chief editor of your school paper. Then why don't you do some serious writing?"

I hadn't much thought about it in those days. And I'm sure she hadn't expected me to write a famous sex book!

"Xaviera," she said a few days after I'd returned, "why don't you write a book about butterflies or something next time, instead of always writing about sex?"

"But mother," I replied, "basically I *am* writing about birds and bees!"

However, it was difficult to be frivolous now that I was back home because I had to face the reality of my chronically ill father. He had suffered a stroke in 1965, and through the years had become more and more paralyzed, kept alive only by my mother's around-the-clock care.

Friends couldn't believe that this man was alive after so many years of suffering. In a hospital, he would have died within weeks, the victim of indifferent care. Just to give you an example, once, because of a careless nurse, my father fell from his bed.

I was twenty-one when, after his first stroke, he was carried to the nearest hospital. That first day, as he lay paralyzed and incoherent, we feared he'd die.

A couple of months later, though, he was home again. He had been taught how to walk and, with the help of crutches and my mother and I on either side of him, he could move about clumsily. It was depressing to witness this once-vital and vivacious man, the center of our attention, reduced to a crippled existence. The doctor said my father had a thrombosis cerebrae on the right side of his brain, causing paralysis to the left side of his body. At least then he could speak, though his sparkle was gone and he seemed to have aged ten years. And he could still leaf through a newspaper and comprehend some of what he read.

Actually, however, despite his robust appearance he had never completely overcome the damage to his health suffered as a result of the torture he'd endured at the hands of the Japanese during World War II. I'd often seen him taking injections to relieve the residual pain he experienced as a consequence of those concentration camp years. But that condition was nothing compared to the state of his health when I left Holland in 1966. He had lost a great deal of weight and by then was almost completely paralyzed. It may have been cowardly of me, but it was his constant deterioration which partly prompted me to leave Holland. I just couldn't stand to see this man, whom mother nicknamed the Lion (I used to call him Pipadoxi), becoming little more than the shell of a human being whose only pleasure was that he could still recognize his loved ones and greet them with his eyes and a little smile.

Now I was back, after six years of absence, and girding my courage to see my father again. As we were driving home, my mother warned me to prepare for a shock, but no warning she could offer could really prepare me for the sight of my father for the first time in six years.

Immediately after I'd put away my suitcases, my mother opened the door to his bedroom for me and no matter how bad I had imagined it would be, seeing him was like a hard smack in the face. Tears flowed from my eyes. He was no more than a skeleton. If I hadn't moved close enough to hear his breathing, I'd have thought he was dead.

His cheekbones protruded from his face. He still had his thick, graying-black hair, neatly combed, but there was no color to his skin. His nose seemed twice as large as I'd remembered because the rest of his face was pinched and sunken. His mouth was like a bird's beak, and most of his teeth were missing.

As I walked over, he didn't see me. His large, brown, velvety eyes were apathetically gazing at the ceiling. I finally attracted his attention and for about a minute his eyes fixed on me as I stood in front of him. He tried to lift his hand from under the cover, and though his eyes turned away, I knew he had recognized me.

He was covered by blankets, with his pajama top loosely draped over his shoulders. I gently pulled back the covers. My mother wanted to prevent me from doing that, but realized that I would eventually see his poor body.

I had braced myself against the shock. His body looked like those I'd seen in pictures of people starving in India. It was fleshless, just bones covered by a thin veil of skin. My mother had to get up three times each night to turn him around, changing his position so that the pressure of his bones wouldn't break the skin.

His left hand, lying on top of the cover, had grown into a clawlike shape; two nails had turned blue already and, in order to stop the fingers from digging into his own hand, my mother had put a rolled-up handkerchief into his fist.

Looking at this immobile frame, I began recalling how when we'd been in Italy on vacation my father would sometimes parade up front, or walk behind my mother and me. Meanwhile the young *paparazzi,* those charming, horny Italians, were chasing us two women, yelling, *Gli belle blonde sorelle! Ah, que' belle gambe!"* ("The beautiful blond sisters! Ah, what beautiful legs!") My father would smile, knowing that he still was boss, unafraid of the competition.

Now this same man—once so vital in word and deed —was lying powerless before me. All that seemed alive were his eyes, and even they had become almost expressionless. If, like my mother, I had had to take care of him for eight years, I'd have gone berserk. I preferred to remember him when he was vivacious and strong.

I can't stand the sight of others suffering. And I know this: my father would have preferred a quick death.

One afternoon, two weeks after he'd entered the suburban Amsterdam hospital as a result of his first stroke, my mother and I drove out to visit him. As I then had a regular job and she had a number of things to attend to, we could only travel that distance every other day.

I entered the hospital while my mother parked the car.

Walking along the hallway toward his room, I saw mostly older people sitting about in wheelchairs, chatting.

As I approached his door I saw a woman of about forty, nearly seventy percent paralyzed, calling feebly for help. She had to go to the bathroom, but the nurses were eating lunch, and so she had to wait.

When my mother joined me after parking I told her, "Look, ma, this woman has to go to the bathroom. Maybe you can help her, since you were daddy's assistant. Why don't you help her, or try to find a nurse, while I go in to daddy?"

My mother, whose concern always extended to others, wheeled the woman to the nearest toilet. Later I learned from her that this woman had suffered a stroke shortly after the birth of her first child, when she was thirty-five. She was now thirty-eight and almost completely paralyzed.

Meanwhile, I walked into my father's room and immediately sensed that something was wrong. I had never seen him covered so highly with the sheets; they almost covered his chin. He looked at me like a beaten dog, with a very guilty look in his eyes. I'd never seen that expression on him before.

When I moved closer to the bed I noticed that the alarm clock I'd brought him for the hospital was gone from the small sidetable. Looking at where it had been, I said to him, "You did something bad, didn't you?" He looked at me more guiltily.

At that moment I pulled down the sheets and noticed heavy scratches on his neck. I pulled them down some more and saw bloody scratches at the wrist of his left arm—the paralyzed one. Lifting his pajama jacket, I saw more scratches near his heart.

I then understood why the clock had disappeared. It was under the pillow. My father must have grabbed it with his still-healthy right hand, tried to break the glass against the bedframe, and then attempted suicide.

He must have known exactly how long and painful his suffering would be, not only to himself but to his wife and child as well. He no longer wanted to be a burden to anyone, and had acted in despair.

I remember my mother telling me how many times he

had begged her to give him a fatal injection. But like so many who argued against euthenasia, she always hoped that a cure might be found, and could not bring herself to be the instrument of his death. And so he was still alive —which in his case was quite a cruel fate.

MEMORIES: PIA[1]

Being around my father, I was reminded of a close friend I once had named Pia. From the time I was fifteen, we virtually grew up together. We went to the same high school, and rode our bikes together to and from school.

Pia wasn't particularly pretty. Her claim to fame was beautiful, blond, kinky hair in the Afro style, which wasn't fashionable in those days. "You sure you don't have Negro blood?" we'd ask her jokingly. She used to try to straighten her hair, but we always told her to leave it natural.

She came from a large Dutch reform family of ten children. Though not well-off, her parents always dressed her nicely but simply.

One summer's day, when she was sixteen, while we were out riding our bikes, I noticed that despite her good suntan she looked very pale and tired. Her nose and cheeks were particularly whiter than usual.

"Take it easy," I told her. "Let's get off our bikes and get some ice cream."

When we'd finished the ice cream we walked our bikes to school because she still seemed exhausted. I asked her whether she'd gone to bed late the night before.

"No," she said. "I've been going to bed early every night lately. I've been feeling awfully tired the past few months. I don't know what it is!"

She was studying hard; we had another two years of high school ahead of us. Pia was an average pupil who usually couldn't tolerate excessive strain. Our teachers would be nice to her and ease off, even if she'd done something wrong.

She and I balanced perfectly. Pia was quiet; I was an

extrovert. She was sweet and never nasty; I was a naughty, wild kid, always cracking jokes, distracting the class, clowning around, doodling all over the place.

Despite our different personalities, we were very good friends, and now I was becoming quite concerned for her. One day, on the way to school, she fainted. Then it happened again.

"Pia," I almost scolded her, "you've got to tell your parents."

"No," she insisted. "I don't want to tell my parents. I don't want to scare them."

"Pia, look, my father is a doctor," I said. "I want you to go see him. I want him to give you a checkup."

I finally won out. After my father, who was then healthy and had a flourishing practice, had given her a complete checkup, he was very depressed. She'd been to dinner at our house a few times and he knew she was one of my best friends. But he told me the truth: that she didn't have long to live. And he made me swear not to tell anyone.

"What do you mean?" I asked him.

"I don't give her more than a year," he replied. "She has to come back once more for an examination before I'm completely sure of my diagnosis. I think it's leukemia. I'll have to tell her parents."

He sent her to a hospital where she could be treated by a specialist.

From then on, I remember watching Pia go downhill physically. She became thinner and thinner, and more and more listless. Every month she missed about a week of school because she was too feeble.

Then she had to be given a lot of drugs and they caused her to partially lose her beautiful, kinky, bushy hair that she'd become proud of. It started falling out in big patches.

It got worse: her neck, thighs, and arms started swelling while the rest of her body remained slim. She said it was a result of the injections.

One day she finally told us—the kids in her class and her favorite geography teacher—that it was no use keeping the secret anymore . . . she knew she was dying of leukemia. We were shocked and didn't know where to look; we realized it might have been true, but refused to accept it.

"Are you crazy, Pia?" we told her. "You don't have leukemia. It's just some kind of bleeder's disease. You just need to eat more steak and eegs, and let the doctors give you more shots. Don't you see you've gained weight already?" We tried to cheer her up.

"Yes, but what about my hair? And the weight is only in certain places and makes me look very ugly. I've got a big bull-neck now."

It was true: she looked very bad. Her eyes looked fishy and small above her puffed cheeks. When she smiled, they looked even more squinty.

"I know I won't live longer than my seventeenth year," she said. "I don't give myself more time than that. I think I better tell the doctors so that they won't lie to me anymore. I wish they'd tell me straight how long I've got to live. I've been reading in books about my symptoms. I'm sure it's leukemia."

We couldn't say anything anymore. After this, she became more and more religious, and started reading the Bible almost night and day.

A month before she died, she developed heavy lumps in her breasts and stomach. Besides leukemia, other forms of cancer were destroying her young body. More lumps appeared under her arms and on her neck. She lay in the hospital, awaiting her death.

She used to compare death to the big black thunder clouds so common in the sky over Holland. In those clouds she saw death coming to her rapidly, chasing one another to be the first to grab her. Yet they'd never touch her, but slip by. She was intrigued by those clouds, and often during my visits to her in the hospital I'd catch her off guard, staring out the window at the overcast sky.

Shortly before she checked into the hospital for the last time, while she still could walk, the doctors suggested that her parents take her on a vacation. She had never been beyond the outskirts of Amsterdam. They urged her parents to take her to a sunny country.

Money was a problem, but the school, the parents of some of her friends, her classmates, and acquaintances all collected enough for a trip to Rome. It was the city her parents had chosen upon the advice of a local travel agent.

Pia didn't particularly want to go to Rome. She preferred beaches and woods where she could sit and watch the waves and leaves, the clouds and sunlight. She wanted to go to Spain or the Riviera, but her parents thought that the two weeks in Rome would be more educational for her. When she returned, she was even more depressed.

"I didn't know how tragic it could be," she told me. "Rome is beautiful, but it's a dead city, full of dead bits of stone. My parents took me to a huge cemetery, thinking they were doing me a favor by showing me ruins and tombs. How naive can they be! Don't they realize that in a month or two I'll be lying in a cemetery! Why didn't they show me flowers and woods and beaches and lakes and boats? Why didn't they take me fishing or on a ship?"

The day before she died, her seventeenth birthday, she asked the nurses, upon her death, to recite certain psalms that she'd chosen from the Bible. She told her mother that she wanted to be buried in her yellow babydoll pajamas with her hair combed neatly. By now she was halfway bald and she wanted the lumps on her body covered carefully. She even chose the makeup she wanted to wear. Listening to her daughter prepare so calmly for her death, her mother almost had a breakdown.

When I went with my mother to pay my condolences, I saw that Pia's instructions had been followed exactly. And around her neck was a thin gold chain with a heart on it, my gift to her when she turned sixteen.

Looking at her lying in the coffin, I suddenly burst into hysterical laughter. Her parents, confused, didn't know how to react. If my mother hadn't explained my hysteria —that I laugh, as a nervous reaction, when I'm experiencing great sorrow—and apologized, I doubt that they would ever have forgiven me.

For Pia's funeral I had been chosen with three other girls to carry the dark purple cloth that is placed over the coffin once it's closed. I was under control, calm and serious. When the organist began playing the hymns Pia had chosen, I began to break down, sobbing deeply.

Reaching into my pocket for a handkerchief, I momentarily let go of the coffin cloth. I recovered it and looked around me, slightly embarrassed, but realized that dozens of other boys and girls and adults at the funeral were also weeping and wiping their tears with handkerchiefs. The grief was overwhelming.

This was one of the most emotional days of my life. It was the first time I had buried someone very dear to me. Whenever I see a funeral procession, that sense of loss returns to me and my heart aches not for the person who's died, for he or she has found peace, but for those who must now continue living without someone they love.

MEMORIES: BIBBY

Yes, being back in Amsterdam flooded me with memories, both good and bad. The famous line by T. S. Eliot, "April is the cruelest month . . . mixing memory and desire," came to mind more than once, and even though April quickly became May, I was still going through heavy changes.

Sights and sounds from my younger years would continually materialize, and I spent much of my days in revery, relating the times that had been, those years ago, with the times that were to be, searching in my past for the shape of my future.

One day, strolling along the Leidsestraat, lost in another world—wondering what I would do with myself, worrying about my poor father—I glimpsed a familiar figure on the other side. He didn't see me.

But I'm sure it was Bibby.

Oh, what a flood of memories that released. I recalled that first morning back in 1965 when I walked into the offices of a small Amsterdam coffee company as their new girl friday, and was immediately struck by the looks of a slender young man. The contrast of his dark, heavy eyebrows, long black eyelashes and black slightly wavy hair with his big blue eyes fascinated me. His eyes weren't a watery blue, but the shade that suggests a very emotional, sensitive personality. His mouth was small and sensitive, and when he smiled he bared a lovely white set of teeth. His nose was nice and straight. His name was Bruno; I immediately gave him the nickname Bibby.

It was a hot summer day, and I was wearing a slightly low-cut, simple black dress with pink and red flowers. Just a tempting bit of my breasts was exposed by the dress, decent yet sexy enough for my first day on the job. I've always hated to wear stockings or closed shoes in the summertime, so I was wearing open slippers and soon got known as "the girl with the slippers."

Bibby, who had been working there for about a year, was assigned to give me a tour of the place, which suited me fine. There were only about ten employees, their small offices separated by glass windows. Apart from the coffee maid, I was the only woman working there, and as she was older, I expected quite a jolly time there.

All the other men were about ten years older than Bibby and I, and seemed easygoing. In this relaxed atmosphere, the work seemed easy and the pressure slight.

From the start, things clicked between Bibby and me. I liked the fact that he wasn't pushy at all. In fact, he was rather innocent, almost shy, and we spent quiet lunch hours together, just talking.

Eventually Bibby began to ask me out for dates. I couldn't accept because I was already involved with another boy, Felix, but I never explained this to Bibby . . . I simply refused vaguely. Finally, he was begging to know why I wouldn't go out with him.

"Look, Bibby, I've had this love affair with a guy for about a year," I said. "He's very jealous and possessive, and he sees me almost every night and usually during the weekend as well. Honestly, I'd like to go out with you. But first I'll have to break off with Felix in a gentle, tactful way, so that none of us gets hurt. After all, he's very hotheaded and stubborn, and might do something crazy."

Bibby was patient, willing to wait for as long as I wanted him to. So far we'd gone no further than holding hands at the back of the office during lunch hour, plus an occasional kiss. And sometimes, as we walked along the canals hand in hand, inhaling the gorgeous summer air, his body pressed against mine, but still in an innocent way.

I was so happy to have found a man who didn't come on superstrong that I purposely acted naive. I certainly didn't want to let on that Felix and I were balling about every other day.

It was a strange yen I had for Bibby. Somehow I wanted to be innocent again, a virgin. And if I had talked to Bibby about all the things I'd done with Felix, he would have been appalled. Besides, it didn't even seem appropriate to talk about sex with Bibby. We talked about so many other subjects, and I enjoyed the feeling of mental communication; but I also wanted his body.

One day I went to Felix's apartment and said, "Felix, I think we're finished."

"What?" he exclaimed.

"We're finished," I repeated. "I've met someone I love more than I love you and it's time to change. We have mutual interests—he loves art, theater, music—and he's very good-looking."

Felix said abruptly, "Have you gone to bed with him?"

"No," I admitted, "I haven't. For all I know, he might be a failure or he might be great. Right now that doesn't matter."

"How do you know you love him if you've never slept with him?" Felix asked.

"You don't have to go to bed first to know that you love someone," I told him.

"I wish you all the luck in the world, baby," he said, "but he can never love you as much as I do—you know that. You'll be back with me as soon as he's let you down."

It sounded cynical and sarcastic. Then Felix forced me to make love to him, and I knew for certain that I no longer felt for him as I had a year ago. My heart was empty, longing for Bibby.

When Felix reached his climax, he suddenly pushed his face into the pillow next to my head and wept for ten minutes, hugging me painfully. He then got up abruptly, his face turned from me, but the pillowcase was damp from his tears.

Felix was an emotional kid, and must have sensed that this was actually our final fuck. He had never been in love before, nor had he ever had a steady affair with a girl before me. When we'd met, we were young and green and crazy, though sexually we were a perfect match. But mentally I outgrew Felix. I needed a man who could develop an interest in the cultural as well as the physical aspects of life. I loved reading and regularly played the piano. I'd also accumulated a large collection of classical records. But Felix had absolutely no interest in any of that.

That final scene with him was painful, but Bibby had told me at the office that if he was to start a relationship with me, he wanted to be sure I was through with Felix. He said that he'd be heartbroken if he knew I was cheating or playing both sides of the fence. Being a Gemini, it was naturally difficult for me to choose just one partner, but I truly yearned for Bibby.

Bibby lived in Bussum, about an hour's drive from Amsterdam. He commuted by train; our office was only a five-minute walk from the main station.

In the beginning of our relationship, there was no sex. We'd go out for dinner or to a movie or spend the evening with my parents and about the only action was a secret kiss in the doorway, almost like teenagers.

We finally agreed that I'd spend a weekend in Bussum, and my parents didn't object, thinking we'd be properly chaperoned.

Bussum was a very pleasant town, set amid woods and pasture land, with its houses surrounded by trees and lawns. Its streets were lined with pretty houses, fine boutiques, art shops, and galleries.

Bibby, as I'd recognized the first time we met, was a very emotional person behind his large, melancholic blue eyes. He also seemed very vulnerable, easily hurt, quite unlike Felix, with his broad grin and small brown eyes hemmed with wrinkles from laughter.

Not surprisingly, therefore, Bibby spent most of his non-working hours at home. He had an excellent collection of classical records and a grand piano in his room. I knew about this but it was a great pleasure to discover that he played beautifully. I had twelve years of classical music lessons behind me, yet music played a far larger role in his life than in mine.

That first weekend I spent at Bussum, I arrived by train early one Saturday morning. Bibby met me at the station and took me to his house, where I met his mother. (His father had died of cancer when Bibby was sixteen.) She was a woman in her mid-sixties, dressed simply, without makeup, a typical sweet old mother from a middle-class background. I was also introduced to his two brothers, both of whom seemed quite bright.

Bibby showed me around the house and finally took

me to his room. It was on the second floor, spacious, with a large window overlooking trees. It contained a large, square wooden table with four chairs, an open fireplace, the piano, two easychairs, and, against the wall, a small bed. It was a warm, pleasant chamber.

Above the bed I noticed a large Persian rug next to which he had mounted five different swords. I felt a bit scared.

"Aren't you afraid they might fall off?" I asked him.

"No. I collect big krises and swords. They're ancient historical krises. This one is from a Chinese war and you can still see the blood and some hair of one of the enemies on its tip."

Maybe so, but I didn't care to check.

I was pleased by the contrast between Bibby's sunny, well-kept quarters and the messy room where Felix and I had been fooling around. Felix's lack of neatness had turned me off; I can't stand dirty things lying around a room. I breathed a sigh of relief, for I liked the house, his brothers, his mother, and most of all I liked Bibby and his room.

That afternoon we were alone in the house, and we were finally ready to make love. It had been so long and the anticipation was great. But did we hop right into the sack? Well, no. . . .

First he played some Chopin etudes on the piano for me and I felt utterly romantic, and thought I'd melt. However much I liked his piano, though, I really wanted to see his organ!

Finally he came over and embraced me. I felt so innocent . . . I wished I were a virgin. He was very, very nervous.

He stared at my suntanned legs, then at my bare toes with their pink nailpolish, then at my hands. His hands were tightly clasped around mine, squeezing my fingers yet gently caressing my palms.

"You have such lovely fingers," he whispered, inching closer.

I started playing with his tie. He removed it, so then I ran my fingers up and down his spine. He shivered. His blue eyes gazed at me questioningly. Bibby was just too bashful to make the first move.

"Do you have any good music we could dance to?" I asked him.

He put a Sergio Mendes and an Astrud Gilberto album on his turntable and we danced closely for about half an hour. I felt something beautiful rising in his pants, his body pressed closely against mine, his breath in my ears, in my hair, on my neck.

Bibby was taller than me, so I had to look up to meet his eyes. He then kissed my eyes, my nose, my forehead, at the same time his delicate fingers touching every part of my face. I restrained myself, content just to blow kisses on his neck and ears.

Then, when it got too intense for me, I pulled his head lower and kissed his mouth fiercely, more passionately than I had ever kissed him in the office or at the door. My tongue slipped into his warm, eager mouth, exploring his teeth and lips. His tongue then probed mine.

Entwined by kiss and dance, I guided him toward the bed. We sat down and I suggested that he relax and stretch out. The music still playing, I slowly worked my fingers through the hair on his chest and head. His hands remained immobile; he was uncertain of what to do.

I bent forward and took off his shoes and socks. As he lay there, I noticed the bulge in his pants. He blushed when he saw me looking at it, pulled up his legs and tried to cover it with one hand.

"No, Bibby, leave it, leave it!" I urged. "I want to look at you."

I covered his face with kisses. I'd become so horny that I could have come just by tightly squeezing my legs together. But I waited patiently, for though I had cared for my previous boyfriends, this was really different. What I felt for Bibby had to be true love.

Usually the man is more aggressive, but Bibby's innocence aroused me. Then suddenly I guessed its cause: he was a virgin. But I wouldn't ask him until after we had made love.

I unbuckled his belt. Then I unzipped his fly. Under his cotton underpants, his erection formed an exciting, snowclad mountain. But he got embarrassed and moved to close up his pants.

"Come on," I begged. "We've waited weeks for this moment. Let me do it!"

"But what about the curtains . . . the neighbors?" he asked nervously.

I wanted to say, "Screw them!" but instead I replied, "Okay. One minute. But, meanwhile, won't you take off your pants?"

After drawing the curtains I walked across the darkened room and saw him lying in the half light, clad only in his white briefs. His erection was sturdy and he seemed less nervous.

There were no pillows on the bed because it was made up like a couch. I said, "Let's take off the bedspread and open up the bed. Tell me where the pillows are."

Bibby pointed to the closet. I walked over while he carefully removed and folded the bedspread. I removed my shoes, and then stepped out of my dress.

Bibby looked at me admiringly. He had never seen me in my sexy French panties and bra. Perhaps he'd never seen a girl so undressed; indeed, judging from his pale complexion, I doubted that he'd ever gone to the beach.

As he looked at me he reached out, touched and kissed me as if I were unreal. Gradually he became more aggressive. He kissed my belly and then tried to take off my bra. Inexperienced as he was, it took him what seemed like half an hour to unhook it.

When the bra dropped he eagerly took hold of my firm breasts and lovingly caressed them. My nipples were like bullets. I pushed my body against his. Bibby again seemed shy, so I decided I'd better take the lead again.

I stepped out of my purple bikini panties and dropped them nonchalantly beside the bed. Taking one of his hands that had been delicately fondling my breast, I put it on the bushy brown triangle at my thighs. At that age I didn't know about trimming pubic hair, so I had quite a luscious jungle. Though I'm a natural, silky-soft blond, my eyebrows and pubic hair have always been dark.

After Bibby naively stirred my pussy, ignorant of exactly where to find my clitoris, I gently guided his index finger to the precise location. I was already very damp, very ready for him. Meanwhile, with my other hand I pulled off his briefs. I was delighted to see the fine thick cock with a pair of superb balls shielded by long black curly hair.

While he was playing with the "man in my boat"—my clitoris—I stroked his rigid "man in my hand." Bibby was uncircumcised, but he was very clean. His foreskin easily slid over the head of his penis. I began pulling it back and forth, and could feel how sensitive he was there. And because it was all so new to him, he was ready to explode.

I climbed out of his arms and moved down his body. I lay between his legs and without hesitation went down on him, caressing his balls lightly with my fingers and cupping them in my hands. Then I kissed his lovely cock.

Bibby got very excited and begged me to make love to him whichever way I wanted to, meaning I was to take the lead. Since I was between his legs, lying on my belly, I decided to wriggle higher and tease his erection with my cunt. My vulva was warm, juicy, readily awaiting his pulsating cock. I yearned to have him fill me.

At last Bibby was inside me—with a little help from his friend—but he was ready to come any instant. So I had to give him two crash courses in self-control, keeping perfectly still while we were entangled.

When I was reasonably sure that Bibby could hold off awhile, I resumed fucking.

Pressing tightly against his heated body, I slowly moved back and forward, my legs around his and my body over his, and it wasn't long before I exploded. To be fair I just had time enough to try to give Bibby, who was trying so hard to hold back, advance notice.

"Come, Bibby, give it to me, please, deeper! Give it to me! All the way!" I groaned at him in ecstasy.

At that point we simultaneously peaked. It was a long, gulping, wonderful feeling, and I felt his semen gush into me. It had been worth waiting for, I instantly told myself.

We lay there that afternoon, exhausted, happy, utterly content. Those aftermoments were as precious as the climax. We whispered sweet things to each other and caressed each other, eyes closed, feeling, touching faces, breasts, arms, hands.

Perhaps we were almost embarrassed by our act of love, like young, innocent kids. I felt as if I had never slept with anyone before.

I then asked Bibby the question that was to be asked. It was about an hour after we had made love, and he was again getting a hard-on.

"Bibby, was this the first time you ever made love to a girl?"

He nodded shyly. "Yes. You're my first girl."

It was exciting for me to know that here was this man, a few years older than me, who had been a virgin when I had met him and who was going to have me as his first lover and steady girlfriend. Because we mutually hoped this would be a long-lasting, happy relationship, I determined to be the best tutor he could dream of. Day by day, I expected our sex life to improve. I knew I had a lot of teaching to do, but Bibby was an eager pupil. If he could play my instrument as well as he played the piano, there'd be no worries.

A few weeks later, while performing 69, something I'd introduced him to, an awful accident happened. I had taught him to eat me, caressing and stimulating my clit with his fingers as well as with his tongue. While making love this way, we both got very excited and wild, but while Bibby was careful not to bite or hurt me, I became so passionate that I bit his cock so badly that it started to bleed.

That same day he went to his family doctor, who laughingly told him that I'd almost circumcised him. The doctor bandaged the organ and applied medication and cold compresses. Fortunately, no real damage had been caused.

When Bibby had recuperated, we very carefully started making love again. But there was more to us than the fucking and sucking such as I'd had with Felix and could have had with Bibby or any other man. There was a deeper emotion... love.

Bibby and I became inseparable... our days at the office, our nights at concerts, cafes, theaters, parks, our weekends together in his room.

Sometimes we would even manage to get together and make love one night during the week, but most of the time our lovemaking was restricted to weekends. So you can imagine how explosive our sex sessions were, as together we'd release the pent-up love and lust of a sexless week.

At one point we had been going to the theater a lot and the concept and excitement of performing intrigued me. Luckily I was able to join an American cabaret group which was performing in Amsterdam for the summer. I worked a few nights a week as their girl friday, and as an usherette, dressed in the national Dutch Volendam costume (including wooden clogs!). At the time I really felt like I was part of the troupe, and it was so exciting that I soon joined another theater company. There I was involved in all kinds of little theater work, including makeup, which I quite enjoyed, and eventually I was writing comedy sketches for the show.

Bibby would proudly sit in the audience during performances, or sometimes just meet me at the stage door, always lovingly encouraging me.

We'd been going steady for a year, and Bibby was getting more and more serious about our relationship, which somehow frightened me. If nothing else, I knew I wasn't ready to make a lifetime commitment.

It was also about this time that my father was hospitalized after his first stroke. Bibby suffered almost as much as I did from the loss of my father's companionship. My father had become very much his own, and day after day, month after month, Bibby would go out to visit my father and push him around in the wheelchair. Heat or cold, rain or snow, Bibby was so true to him that I sometimes felt, however irrationally, that I was being neglected.

Still, those were beautiful, carefree, happy moments when I was young and in love with Bibby. Whenever I listen to the music of Tchaikovsky or Bach or Brahms or Chopin, those lovely hours return to my mind and I could weep remembering how kind, devoted, and faithful Bibby was to me, how much he loved me.

But it was too good to be true. Bibby was just terribly sensitive and got hurt too easily. In the long run that made me edgy. I almost started feeling the way I'd finally felt with Felix. But where Felix had been too boyish, Bibby was too serious for me.

Bibby always played the gentleman. I doubt that he ever owned a pair of blue jeans. Even on weekends he wore a shirt, tie, and jacket, or else a suit with a vest. I appreciated his courtliness, but I sometimes felt like shaking him up and telling him to act young and nonchalant for a change.

So while he continued to be a shipshape gentleman, precise in his choice of clothes, neat in his room, cleanbodied, kind toward his mother, attentive to his brothers, and loving toward me, I felt more and more repressed. In his world, I could never do anything wrong. He had stuck me up on a pedestal, and I was finding it stifling up there. He wouldn't let me relax. I had to promise to marry him, and I just wasn't ready to settle down yet.

Though I didn't want to be destructive, I soon realized the relationship was fading. And one day I impulsively announced, "I think I'm going to America, Bibby. I've decided that as of now, we're through."

He said nothing. He turned pale. Then he took his Vespa and drove home.

At two o'clock that morning his elder brother phoned me.

"Bibby's had an almost fatal accident." Somewhere along a dark road he'd rammed his scooter into a tree. He would have to spend weeks recuperating in the hospital.

I felt terrible about the incident. I knew he hadn't deserved such a blunt goodbye from me. Then, to make matters worse, while Bibby was in the hospital, I became infatuated with a strong, dominant man named Pieter. Pieter had his own room downtown, and before long we were fucking regularly. I quit the coffee company, too.

Bibby recovered and took me back as his girlfriend. Though I was turning on to Pieter more and more, I pretended that I still loved Bibby, which in a way I did. But I'd already destroyed any hopes he had of marrying me. I simply wasn't the type of girl to live quietly with him in a nice suburb, bored stiff listening to the neighbors gossip about the weather. Apart from the art and music we mutually liked, there was no excitement, joy, youthfulness in our days together.

After our reconciliation, Bibby again got more attached to me, while I unconsciously began hurting him again. Pieter and I were fucking and sucking each other dry as nuns on weeknights, while Bibby was in Bussum with his mother and brothers.

I still hadn't told Bibby about Pieter. One day Pieter and I were strolling, warmly entangled, along one of the canal banks. I'd forgotten that it was lunchtime and that Bibby, whose office was near Pieter's room, might be out for a walk as well. When I saw him coming, it was already too late. He had spotted us and his face changed color. I couldn't help but introduce my lovers to each other.

Pieter shook Bibby's hand and looked at me questioningly. Bibby shrunk from the vicelike grip, apologized for having to leave quickly, and then, looking at me with tears in his eyes, asked me to call him later that afternoon. I did, and we arranged to meet that evening. It was supposed to be our final scene together.

We met in his uncle's house in Amsterdam because I didn't want to go out to Bussum. We had the use of a quiet room on the sixth floor. It was a warm, clear summer night, and the window overlooking the street was open.

Bibby stood near the window. He cried softly as I told him our affair had really ended. Suddenly he rushed toward the window. I grabbed his coat, but he shook my hand off. He had one foot on the sill and was leaning out over the building's steep facade.

"Please, Bibby," I literally begged him, "don't do anything foolish."

"There's no reason to live anymore," he whined. "I've lost you. You're my ideal woman. I love you. I want you to be my wife and the mother of my children. But you've turned me down. What have I now got to live for?"

"Bibby," I said, "I'm not worth it, I'm not worth your death!" Now we were both weeping.

I asked him to forgive me for the pain I'd caused him. "It's not in me to hurt people because I hate to get hurt myself," I explained. "But just once in a while I wish you had handled me like a strong, powerful man."

Bibby looked at me with tears in his wide blue eyes. He looked like a beaten dog. He finally realized it was over.

I had a restless night after he dropped me off at home. Scary nightmares kept waking me.

My intuition told me that something was wrong in Bussum. Bibby was doing something dreadful. In a dream I'd felt a sharp pain in my wrists, the sensation of a sharp blade. Then I remember blood spilling everywhere and I awoke terrified.

When I didn't hear from Bibby the next day, I told Pieter I was worried. "Don't call him." Pieter said. "Let him work it out himself."

Two days later, when I still hadn't heard from him, I called his office.

"No, Bibby isn't in," I was told. "He's sick. We don't know what he's got, but he'll be away for quite some time."

I was worried. Finally I called his house. His mother answered, and her voice was gloomy.

She told me I couldn't speak to Bibby. I begged her to tell me what had happened.

"You've certainly made a wreck out of our Bibby," she complained.

"What do you mean?" I asked her.

"You remember what happened the night you first broke up with him, the night he had that scooter accident? Our Bibby didn't want to live anymore. The scooter accident wasn't an accident. He did it purposely. . . . Now this time you broke up with him, the other night, he—"

"Don't tell me!" I exclaimed. "The swords?"

"How did you know?"

"I had a nightmare. I knew he was doing something awful and I wanted to call him that night to stop him from doing it."

"Xaviera," she sighed. "It's hard to grow up. When I was young I didn't suffer like you people do. I married when I was seventeen, and he was my only man. But you young kids, you jump from one lap to another. Xaviera, do you know how badly my Bibby wanted to marry you? He was a good kid, and we love you here. You were his first girlfriend and he was so happy with you. Why did you have to make him suffer?"

When she'd finished I begged her forgiveness. "I didn't want to hurt him but I had to end the relationship. I didn't love him enough to marry him. Things weren't working out between us as they should have."

"I left you free all weekend long," she said. "You could sleep over at our house. I never told you to stay away. I never forbade Bibby anything. You locked yourselves up in his room for hours and hours on weekends. Sometimes it was embarrassing! But I must say you were good to us, like a happy sparkle in the house. Why did you have to leave my Bibby? But *ach*, Xaviera, you know best how to live your life."

"Tell me," I pleaded, "what did happen to Bibby?"

"His brothers took him to the hospital when they found him. He had cut his wrists and was bleeding, bleeding heavily. It's good he didn't fulfill his wish to die. He's badly cut up . . . he'll always have big scars on his wrists to remind him. He lies in darkness most of the time now."

I felt very guilty, like I'd dragged him through genuine horror.

"Please, Xaviera," his mother urged, "it's better if you stay out of his life. Just let him recuperate. Let him find himself again. . . . Xaviera, go out on your own, but don't destroy anybody else. Don't let anyone fall in love with you unless you love them as strongly, or you'll only hurt him."

For quite some time after that I never heard from Bibby. Eventually mutual friends told me that he had recuperated, but that he wasn't dating any girls, and kept strictly to himself. Music was his only interest besides work.

I occasionally wrote Bibby from wherever I went . . . South Africa and then the United States . . . but I hardly ever got a response. If I did, it was simply a polite acknowledgment of my greeting. His words were cool and aloof, and carefully neutral. Once or twice a sentimental thought would find its way between the lines, but the ultimate message was either that he no longer had anything to say to me, or else the pain was still strong and he didn't want to admit it. I hope for his sake it wasn't the latter.

He still spoke to my mother, though, and visited my father faithfully.

My mother reports that he's advancing comfortably in business, and that lately he's settled down with a mistress fifteen years his senior.

Poor, dear Bibby . . . we each had so much to give each other . . . but it wasn't the right chemistry.

A few years later I fell in love with Carl, my American fiancé, and was left deeply hurt by him when we broke up. . . . It was only then, when I suffered deeply, that I understood what I'd done to Bibby.

If I'd known then what I know now, I thought at the time . . . but even so, I still would have done what I did. Bibby's ideals were unreal, I'm afraid, and had we married, we would have been doomed. Somewhere along the line the hurt would have happened, and I think it was best to get it over with early rather than go through the charade of an impossible marriage.

It's such an incredibly thin line between love and hate, between good feelings and bad, between heartening and hurting. I'll always regret that the love between Bibby and me ultimately produced only hurt.

NO DUTCH TREAT

Being back in Holland again, after having been away for so long, was really putting me through changes, as the saying goes.

My father's illness, memories of friends like Pia and Bibby, and the gloomy weather all combined to make me feel rather depressed. Amsterdam was such an abrupt change from New York City, too, so my social life became very different. I spent a lot of time at home, of course, and my mother just coddled and spoiled me, so happy to have her daughter back under her wing.

Most of my old friends, I'd found, were happily settled, and we no longer really had much in common. But Marie, a girl I'd gone to high school with, was still single and she called one night to suggest we go out on the town together. I was anxious to get out of the house for an evening, so I eagerly accepted. We made a date for the next day.

My mother offered me the use of her car, so I took advantage of the opportunity to drive around my home town. I had heard of many changes in the city but now I'd get to see them firsthand. I picked up Marie and let her reacquaint me with the city while I drove.

If you recall your American history, New York was originally called New Amsterdam. Amsterdam itself has been called the Venice of the North. Others even compare it to Boston because of its twisting streets and baroque architecture. But Amsterdam is only one thing: Amsterdam.

The Venice analogy, of course, is based on the main feature of the city, which is the network of numerous canals running through it. For the tourist, the best way to explore them is in the glass-topped sightseeing boats, where a multilingual guide will point out the various spots of historical and architectural interest.

At one point, before the city fathers erected foot-high guardrails along the canals, a popular attraction was hauling cars out of the water . . . especially after Friday-night binges.

The canals were first dug about four hundred years ago, and I sometimes wonder if the water in them doesn't date that far back, too. The politest thing I can say is that the water is the color of coffee. And it's said that even an atheist can walk on it!

The canals seemed familiar to me, but I'd forgotten about the noisy, unorganized traffic. With the Amsterdamers' perverse sense of rights, it's much safer to walk around the city than to drive a car—or even worse, a bike. So I parked the car and we walked around.

When we came to the Rembrandtsplein, one of the primary squares in the city and one of my very favorite spots in Amsterdam, I just didn't recognize the place. Everywhere I looked were hippie kids of all nationalities, young men and women both, thick as pigeons—no wonder I'd heard that Amsterdam had become the hippie capital of the world. As we walked around the Rembrandtsplein I saw that a lot of these kids were really quite attractive under all that hair, and they certainly seemed carefree and good-natured. And I also realized that some of them were no older than sixteen or seventeen, which shocked me a little at first—being far away from home at such a young age, but then I remembered my own youth and my need to get away, and I was partially able to admire their gumption and facility for getting around on little money.

"How do the good city fathers feel about all these kids flocking here?" I asked Marie.

"Oh, it was not greeted with *huzzahs* at first, but everyone soon got used to it, and I suspect that some of them are even a little proud that all these kids chose Amsterdam as their mecca. . . . These days, anything goes in this town."

I could certainly see that—because Amsterdam, in addition to attracting hippies like swallows en route to Capistrano, was also rapidly becoming the gay capital of the world. Planeload after planeload of gay boys and girls arrive every week, Marie told me, seeking the freedom the country offers to those of their persuasion. And the evidence of their presence was everywhere: there were scores of gay bars, clubs, and hotels all over town, and no one seems to get hung-up at the sight of all these gay blades and non-Dutch dykes. To the standard adjectives applied to the Dutch—dependable, honest, stoic, clean, industrious—I guess you'd now have to add tolerant.

The drug scene is also booming, Marie told me, with the influx of hippies—again drawn by Holland's tolerant attitudes. And, Marie said with some wonder, the radio even gives stock market quotations on dope prices each day!

Okay, already, I felt we'd had enough counterculture inspiration for one day. Amsterdam is also a great shopping city and since it was still early evening, I suggested to Marie that we do some window shopping—and maybe even buy something!—on several of my favorite shopping boulevards anywhere, Kalverstraat and Rokin Leidsestraat. So we headed that way and spent a pleasant hour or so strolling through this area. We looked at the diamonds—which can be a real bargain in Amsterdam if you know what you're doing—in the glittering window of the house of Bonebakker, diamond merchants for six generations, and we admired the beautiful Delft china in the windows of Focke & Melzer, especially the unusual items—not the traditional blue Delftware, but the one-of-a-kind items, the red and gold Pijnacker, the multihued Polychroom and the lovely green Delvert. Prices for some of these pieces run as high as four hundred dollars, but you do have to remember that each piece of Delftware is hand-painted under the glaze.

By now Marie and I were feeling the need for some refreshment after all our walking, so we went back to the car and drove over to the Leidseplein, Amsterdam's main square. Then we headed for the cafe in the American Hotel. This used to be *the* place for many groovy young models, writers, painters, journalists, stewardesses, and secretaries. But the crowd had changed, I soon realized.

A tough-looking older man stood at the door checking out the arrivals and the once-bohemian atmosphere had been shattered by the requirement that men wear ties and jackets.

But despite their required clothing, the young men there were mostly loud and arrogant and lacked any sense of class. For the most part they were clumsily engaged in either just staring at passersby or exchanging loud comments.

"Hello, how are you, Madame X?" they addressed me. "Back in Holland again? Don't you think you're pushing your luck?"

I smiled disdainfully at them.

Marie, who though she's pleasant company isn't one of the brightest girls I know, started flirting vaguely with one of the better-looking loudmouths. Then, only a few moments later, two of the loudmouths—without invitation—came over and sat down at our table.

One of them, with long, greasy hair, a dirty shirt collar and coffee stains on his tie, leaned across the table to stare into my face. When the waiter returned with our drinks, my stunned admirer was able to stir himself enough to noisily order a scotch for himself and a screwdriver for his buddy.

Yet another fellow came over and claimed he knew me from high school. I couldn't remember his name, but his face appeared vaguely familiar. He, too, sat down, and Marie and I soon found ourselves surrounded by a group of men, mostly aged between twenty-five and thirty-five, and none of them the least bit shy or polite.

A few of them had read my book or newspaper stories about me, and they had trapped me into a stupid conversation. "Great fans we are of you, great fans! You must be a millionairess by now, eh, honey? Fabulous book, but bet you can't make a dime here in your old profession!"

"You guys couldn't afford my prices," I laughed in response. "That's why I rely on writing sexy books. But

I really don't need or want your comments," I added. "Why don't you leave me alone?"

By now the table was crowded with even more drinks and various snacks the men had ordered. Marie seemed to be having a good time, but I definitely wanted to be rid of these clods. So if they weren't going, I *was*.

Well, the moment I suggested to Marie that we take care of our share of the bill and go elsewhere, the guy with the long greasy hair sprang up and said, "Oh, one second. I've got to make a phone call, but I'll be back in a minute, all right?"

"Hey, I've got to take a pee and then I want to buy a newspaper," said a second, and he left behind the first. They were going off like a string of firecrackers.

The third was blunt. "I'll see you later. Thanks for the drinks and snacks." And he led a major exodus from our table.

By this time I was becoming quite upset. "What *is* this?" I exclaimed. "What the hell is happening here?"

The waiter came over and laughed. "They've really taken you for a ride, haven't they!"

"What do you mean?"

"That's their way, how they act. We can't keep them out because they dress up like the regulations require, even if their clothes are sometimes filthy. But they're a bunch of leeches taking advantage of girls. . . . Hey, now I recognize you! You're Xaviera who just got here from America! Right?"

I nodded assent.

"They must think you're a millionaire by now," he said in a gentle voice. "In any case, they've stuck you with the bill."

I was feeling kindly disposed toward this nice old man who at least was treating me with some courtesy and understanding, but then he, too, disappointed me. "Excuse me, Miss Hollander," he said, with a sort of two-faced grin, "since I was pretty sure you'd end up paying for them, I've already put everything on one bill."

I seized the check from his hand and glared at it—it amounted to seventy guilders, or about twenty-five dollars —and fortunately I had enough money in my purse to cover the bill. But it was an expensive lesson to be learned about these male Dutch parasites. At least in the old days they would go Dutch treat. So I had every right to feel pissed off at these cheap, chintzy con men. And at Marie and myself for walking right into the con job.

We left at once, and I suggested to Marie that we try The Paradiso, which once upon a time was a popular bohemian spot. But she said that times had changed it, and that it had degenerated into a crowded hippie scene. We ended up at the Sherry Bodega, a wine-tasting place with three floors, a rather "in" crowd, and open from four to seven P.M. Then, later on, Marie took me to the Fietsotheque in the Hilton Hotel. *Fiets* means bike, and that's the theme: even the entrance is a bicycle ramp. It's a good bar and a good disco, attracting an equally good crowd. We danced with some of the single men out looking for action, but I have to admit that most of them turned me off. I also recognized several guys from my teenage days who I knew were married—or at least had been married—and now they were out on the prowl. We left the Fietsotheque soon and went to another discotheque, the Voom-Voom.

Although the clubs are open late in Amsterdam, we really weren't having a fantastic time, so we called it an early night, and I dropped Marie off at her apartment.

When I got home that night I was quite depressed—depressed by the way people had treated me when I hadn't done them any harm, and by the sleazy uncouth, unattractive types I'd seen in the bars and in the streets. Dutchmen still seemed so basically immature and clumsy in their relations with women, and I wondered if they would ever grow up.

I spent the next few days at home, catching up on my writing and reading. I enjoyed the quiet at home, but at the same time missed the many friends and telephone calls and social evenings I'd become accustomed to in New York.

Then on Friday I went downtown again and met Ned, whose number a friend in New York had given me. And Ned led to Leo.

The rest you know. Leo and his wife and I quickly

became great friends, and soon we were off to Paris together.

We had now been back in Amsterdam for almost a month, seeing each other constantly. But I was still living at home, which was, I'm afraid, very depressing. As May turned into June, I again needed a getaway. And Leo and Marika again obliged.

RIVIERA XAVIERA

St. Tropez on the French Riviera!

Whoever the good Saint Tropez was, I doubt that he ever realized that his holy name would one day grace one of Europe's leading fleshpots.

He was, I've learned, a Christian centurion in the first century A.D. He was beheaded, for his faith, by Emperor Nero, then his body was cast adrift in a boat with a dog and a cock—a rooster, that is. The idea was that the bird and the beast would devour the Christian's remains ... but they didn't; he remained as intact as he could under the circumstances, and the boat, body, bird, and brute washed ashore on the French Riviera. Tropez was immediately sainted for his martyrdom and successful passage, and the spot where the boat washed ashore was named St. Tropez.

Leo and Marika took me with them from Amsterdam to the South of France early in June, and we spent the entire month there, at the home of their friends, a well-known swinging French couple named Marcel and Brigitte. They have a fabulous villa in Ramatuelle, just twenty minutes away from St. Tropez itself.

The French Riviera, as you know, is the country's southern coast on the Mediterranean sea. Tiny Monaco and the Italian border are within a hundred miles, and the islands of Corsica and Sardinia lie south in the sea.

The climate on the Côte d'Azur—the azure coast, reflecting the beautiful Mediterranean—is subtropical, and popular the year round. Hard to believe that it's on the same latitude as Chicago or Toronto! The big difference is the sirocco, a hot wind that blows across the Mediterranean from North Africa, serving as a year-round hot-air supply.

We arrived in St. Tropez before the "high season" began,

so it wasn't as jam-packed then as it got during the summer. The town is small, and it's *the* spot for wealthy sophisticates, yacht-owning swingers, and beautiful bodies of every persuasion. Anything and everything goes in St. Tropez; the most outrageous behavior barely raises an eyebrow.

Our hosts, Marcel and Brigitte, were gracious and friendly. Marcel is a quiet businessman in his late forties, and his wife is a vivacious thirty-eight. Although they've been married for many years, their children are recent arrivals—a boy of five, and a two-year-old.

During the week, Marcel and Brigitte live a fairly square life with their kids in Nice, the fashionable capital of the Riviera. On weekends they go to their Ramatuelle house, just outside St. Tropez, because that's where all the action is.

There, they have open house all weekend long, with lavish lunches and dinners for their friends. Sometimes it turns into an open-air *partouze* out on the terrace and around the swimming pool, where their Moroccan gardener pretends not to notice what's going on! In fact, nobody seems to care much about exactly what's happening. Everyone walks around in the nude, and the atmosphere is very casual and relaxed.

Marcel and Brigitte were able to stay only long enough to make sure that we were comfortable in their home, then had to return to Nice. So unfortunately I was unable to get to know them very well.

Our first night there, Leo and Marika took me to dinner at l'Escale, a very popular St. Tropez restaurant right on the waterfront. They'd even arranged a surprise for me—Gunther was joining us.

I was delighted to see him again. We'd had a ball together (in five or six different ways, come to think of it) at that massive orgy in Paris. Because of the anonymity of that occasion, he'd been only another cock in the crowd, but I'd admitted later to Marika that he was a gentle and attractive man, and that I wouldn't be opposed to getting to know him a lot better. She mentioned that she'd often seen him in St. Tropez, and suggested that we'd probably bump into him.

Obviously Marika not only had a good memory, but was enough of a matchmaker that she'd contacted Gunther and had set up this dinner date in St. Tropez.

He's a good-looking, tall, slim German with a beautiful face. He's in his mid-thirties, and fluent in at least five languages; his reputation as an internationally known furniture designer is well established.

As the four of us chatted at the bar of l'Escale, a stunning blond walked over to our table. She was wearing a light denim suit and clearly had on not a stitch underneath. She paused behind Gunther and started vamping him, just like a scene from an old movie. She ran her fingers through his hair, put her arms around his shoulders, the whole number! She was in heavy heat for him but Gunther seemed rather indifferent to her. Leo and Marika and I certainly weren't indifferent to her beauty, though, and couldn't resist inviting her to join us at dinner.

Freda was her name. She was in her early thirties, born in Hamburg and rather Slavic-looking; Freda speaks perfect French, German, and English with a cute cosmopolitan accent. A professor of biology at the University of Heidelberg for approximately two-thirds of the year, the rest of the time she is able to travel around Europe—particularly southern France, Italy, and Spain.

As the evening progressed we discovered that while she was trying to be friendly, she remained somewhat uptight and cool. Like most Germans (if I can indulge a generalization) she had no sense of humor. Leo, a natural Dutch-Jewish comic, teased her all night long and she took much of what he said literally. However, she was certainly attractive and managed to intrigue all of us except Gunther, who seemed to already know her rather intimately.

Then things got awkward: Freda had drunk too much Bordeaux and became loud, and so we decided to call it an evening. But because we wanted to know her better, Marika invited her to join us for lunch the next day at Ramatuelle. She recognized our address, and it turned out that she knew our hosts well. This was a good introduction for us because any friend of Marcel and Brigitte's would be gladly accepted into our crowd. As they say in French, *les amis de mes amis sont mes amis*—the friends of my friends are my friends.

We parted after dinner—Leo and Marika to the house, Freda to hers, and because we hadn't been able to talk together during dinner, Gunther and I walked home to his apartment.

That night we stayed in his cozy flat and made love for hours and hours, till the sun rose next morning. However, the problem with Gunther (although I don't think it bothers *him*) is that he's basically impersonal. In bed he's tender and emotional but the next day he's just not interested in you anymore and, indeed, is out looking for a new woman. Worse yet, he's one of those men who doesn't have to bother looking very hard for a new girl because they flock to him like pigeons after popcorn. Still, no matter what he's like the morning after, he certainly knows how to treat a lady in bed.

I still remember a fantastic fuck we shared that night. I was on my knees and elbows, and slowly let my arms and legs slide straight until I lay flat on my belly, my face pushed into a pillow. Gunther had been standing behind me while my ass was elevated, then he moved over me and slowly lowered himself to his knees, slipping into me from behind. I stayed quite still for a few moments when he entered me, but then, with long slow strokes rocking back and forth, he started fucking, his cock going almost all the way out with each deep stroke. Each cycle grew deliciously slower and slower on the out stroke, then faster and more exciting on the inward stroke. And did I respond! At the peak of an in stroke, he must have felt my vagina contracting at the onset of orgasm, so he drew his cock out of me with an incredibly protracted slow stroke, magnificently elongating the delicious preliminary shudders of my orgasm. Then he drove into me all the way!

My hips twisted frantically, out of phase with the muscular jerks that twitched my back and legs. Hmmmmmmm! I can feel it now, that moment when I came. Gunther remained quite still, his cock deep within me, his balls squashed against me. He filled me with his warmth and I tingled something silly with every drop of it. We remained in that position and gradually his cock went soft within me.

Gunther fell asleep beside me, and I savored his slumber, too. I cradled his blond head and enjoyed the rich sensation of lying close to him, the drying warmth inside my thighs, the waning contentment in my nipples, my breasts, the curve of my cheek, the fullness of my eyelids—and most of all, being enveloped in all the soft, rich odors of love. I drifted away, too, and we slept for an hour or so.

We awoke lying together spoon-fashion, his back nesting

in my belly. I put my arm around him and found his nipples, stroking them awake and arousing a swelling in his crotch. He wriggled his ass into my pubes, starting the sensations all over again.

I moved around and down so that I could kiss his cock. My tongue started at the base, then along the shaft, licking and kissing and teasing. I slipped my mouth over its bulging head, sucking more and more, taking into me as much as I could of its eight inches. I gorged on it, stuffing it into my mouth with greedy gobbles. Gunther tensed his hips and thigh muscles and lay rigidly still. He was close, I knew.

I frantically sucked him, plunging my nose into his pubic bush, twisting my head as my mouth slithered up and down him, and with a sudden lurch of his hips, Gunther ejaculated again and again, and still I sucked, swallowing it all until he was totally spent. I reluctantly kissed *au revoir* to his penis, catching a final, pearly drop on my tongue. And we slept again.

At eight o'clock our room was filled with the Mediterranean sun. Although we'd put in an energetic night with not much sleep, I was relaxed and gladly stirred awake. Gunther, cool and beautiful, was still sleeping. I wanted to hug and kiss him all over from top to toe, and I did, cuddling him awake. Then we kissed and kissed, gobbling each other's tongues as if they were cocks. Guther was slim but I could feel his strength as we kissed, and somehow I felt in the mood for a good, violent, farewell fuck.

I hadn't really had a good, burly bang since Paris, so I looked at him teasingly and said, in my best Mae West manner, "Come on, big boy, sock it to me."

Gunther was not amused. Perhaps his Germanic pride was offended by my aggressiveness. But he was aroused, all right.

"Okay, lady, you want it bad, you're going to get it bad," he said, and jumped on top of me.

My legs were spread wide, and I barely had time to flip a pillow under my bottom before he jammed his long cock into me.

"You want a real fuck, sweetheart, you're really going to get yourself fucked," he said with determination. And then he reared up, holding down my upper arms with his hands, his arms fully outstretched, his pelvis still against mine, skewering me with his prick.

"Oh God, Gunther, you'll hurt me," I protested, but his fingers dug into the flesh of my arms and his pubic bone ground against mine as he continued thrusting.

"Come on, you bitch, get with it," he roared, and I moved my hips to match his beat.

"What do you want me to do to you?" he demanded. "Tell me, Xaviera!"

"Fuck me, I want you to fuck me!"

"Tell me again!"

"Fuck me, Gunther!"

"I want you, you bitch," he growled, and pounded his body against me, driving his cock in hard, again and again, smashing the breath out of my body. He was so tough that all other sensation, all my thoughts and fantasies, were completely overpowered by the one incredible sensation. My body became a total fuck—nothing else.

I could barely catch my breath as his belly smashed against mine, faster and faster, and only by submitting myself to his mounting rhythm could I get a few gulps of air.

His cock seemed to be made out of steel, and it repeatedly violated not just my vagina but my entire mind and body. The bed rocked like a shingle in a hurricane and our bodies slammed together with unbelievable speed and fury.

"Don't, Gunther, you'll kill me," I heard myself blurt as his energy somehow increased. I was afraid that every bone in my body would crumble under his onslaught.

But he didn't answer or acknowledge me, he was so intent on his jackhammer action. My eyes closed under the relentless pounding and my lower body buckled, entirely detached from my upper torso, and a warm flood filled me. My own spasms brought a final fling against me and Gunther tensed, about to come.

As the spasms continued, tears streamed down my face and I started begging.

"More, Gunther. Don't stop now!"

He held the tension, then abruptly pulled out and savagely dragged me around to the edge of the bed. This time he stood on the floor and with me on my stomach, held me down with one hand on my hip while with the other he guided his sopping cock into my cunt from behind.

His rampant hard-on was a deep purple-red, and must surely have been tender from all the violence. As he shoved it into me in this, one of my favorite positions, it felt bigger than ever.

My insides were like thick soup or warm whipped cream, and I was stirred into slow waves by each new movement of his cock. He slowly brought me up to the edge of orgasm and held me there until my tension built up enormous wells of energy. Then he began a furious pumping motion, his thighs thumping against my buttocks, starting a chainlike cycle of orgasms where every stroke of his prick set off a new spasm.

I was thrashing like a fish, impaled by his spear of a cock. My hands gripped the sheets and tried to dig into the mattress. My back arched like a bow and snapped with thrill after thrill. I wanted punishment suddenly.

"Hurt me, Gunther," I gasped, but my head was in the blanket and he didn't hear me at first.

"Gunther! Spank me. Hurt me. Please, Gunther!"

And he did, beating his hand and body and cock against me, and I filled the bed with my muffled groans until finally the pain was so intense that I screamed with each new stroke.

He brought me along with him, higher and higher, and finally flung himself against me, his body flat on top of mine, and his cock gushed and spurted and flooded me.

We collapsed on the bed, exhausted. But in a few moments the mood was abruptly over. Quietly we washed, dressed, and said goodbye.

We never got together again. What a pity. He was such a fantastic lover, physically . . . but it ended there. He walked off to his office and I found a taxi to take me home, and I'm not sure that he even gave me a second thought.

FREDA THE COOL ONE

Leo and Marika were still asleep when I returned to the villa at Ramatuelle. I took a hot bath to relax and unwind, then, because it was such a beautiful morning, I went outdoors and let the sun dry me. Then I oiled my body and stretched out on a mattress next to the pool.

I should have been quite satisfied, yet in a strange way I still felt horny and ready for action—not with Gunther, though, and in fact not even with a man. Freda was due to arrive later on for lunch, and I couldn't stop thinking about her, about her beautiful body and seemingly complex personality.

Gunther had told me the night before that he and Freda were from the same home town, that she was indeed very complicated, and that he just didn't dig her. She had sexual problems, he said, and when she had been together with four people once at a swing—at least she was willing to try —no one had been able to bring her to orgasm.

So, thinking about how I could seduce lovely Freda, and with lusty memories of my night with Gunther, I dozed off under the Mediterranean sun.

The crackling of tires on the gravel driveway woke me. It was Freda's Volkswagen. She walked around to the pool and, with a smile, sat down next to me. She was wearing pink, lightweight tight pants and a pink shirt, buttoned down the front.

While we chatted—mostly about St. Tropez—Leo and Marika joined us. After more small talk, Marika and I went into the kitchen and prepared lunch—a light salad with lots of juicy European tomatoes and plenty of spicy pâté. We returned with the food and wine, and juice for me, and it was a relaxed, most enjoyable lunch.

After lunch I began to talk about the work that still had to be done on my second book, and the need to select all the letters for the third book as well. Freda seemed very interested in the work I was doing and asked if she could see the manuscript.

There was only one copy, and it was in my room, so Freda and I excused ourselves and headed for the house. Leo and Marika gave me a quizzical look and Marika said, in Dutch, "So you're going to try and seduce our German friend, are you?"

I shook my head at her. I did *not* plan it that way. Freda was a very complicated girl, and she would need time. She wasn't the type whose clothes you could rip off without first winning her trust and affection.

As Freda leafed through my manuscript, she relaxed on my bed, stretching herself out quite alluringly. And as she read my manuscript, I sat on the edge of the bed and dictated into my tape recorder answers to letters I'd received from readers.

Some of the letters obviously intrigued her—they were from people in need, people with sexual problems and fantasies, the lonely, the desperate, the frustrated, as well as from happy people sending me their approval or congratulations or just a horny hello. As I continued dictating, Freda snuggled a little closer to me. She put her head against my shoulders, and just then the bottom button of her shirt popped open.

I knew she had a beautiful body, but when her shirt opened I notice that she had some light pigmentation spots on her belly. I was curious and asked her to show me them. She smiled at me, childlike.

"Don't be worried," I said. "Just let me see your tummy."

And I gently unbuttoned her blouse, revealing a pair of beautiful titties—strong, not too large, with an intriguing light area surrounding her big nipples.

She'd been to Tahiti Beach in St. Tropez, and her body was nicely tanned. But she had these same light pigmentation spots on her breasts, too—which was strange-looking, but at the same time rather sexy. She told me they covered her all the way down, and I asked her to show me more. She unzipped her pants and pulled them down to her hips, revealing a beautiful brown belly with white spots around her pubic area.

I purposely didn't want to pay too much attention to this part of her body, but I simply couldn't resist touching her belly.

She gave a soft sigh, and with the slight clumsiness of innocence, took off her blouse completely, showing off her lovely breasts and shoulders. Encouraged by this, I grew more daring and pulled down her pants. She wasn't wearing panties, but her hips and bottom showed the outline of a bikini, where she was less tanned. She had slim hips and small buttocks, and the childlike, translucent, untanned skin made her pose and the boyishness of her loins all the more exciting.

The house was quiet. I suspected, in fact, that Leo and Marika were in their own room, enjoying a nooner, while they thought I was seducing Freda. But, if anything, she was seducing me!

I felt I needn't wait any longer, and before she knew what was happening, I covered her body with kisses, from under her long, straight blond hair down to her pubes.

Freda didn't know what to do with herself, and covered her groin with her hands as she questioningly smiled at me. I told her to just relax, lie back, and let it be.

So far, I had always succeeded in making any woman come quicker than any man could. But I would proceed slowly with Freda—to be sure. I nuzzled my face into her crotch, ever so gently, and my tongue searched for her clitoris. When I finally located it, hidden away, she didn't become as responsive as I'd hoped for, so I continued licking and sucking and caressing. Then, slowly, tantalizingly, I insinuated my finger into her vagina, but to my amazement she wasn't getting at all juicy. She seemed to be enjoying what I was doing, but her body wasn't really reacting—although there was a warm glow on her face and she occasionally giggled like a teenager.

To put it bluntly, I was working my ass off, yet she wasn't getting turned on, and I finally realized that this girl was indeed frigid.

She kept telling me that she loved every bit of what I

was doing, but that she could simply not have an orgasm. She'd never had one in her life—and she was thirty-one.

I felt sorry for her, and began to understand some of the things she'd mentioned to me. Sex to her was something which she could enjoy only with someone who could offer her a long-lasting relationship. But Freda knew she wouldn't find such people in St. Tropez. It's constant butterflying, from flower to flower, in a vacation area such as the Riviera. So much so that men like Gunther are famous for their successions of one-night stands.

Gunther, in fact, was the only man with whom Freda had truly enjoyed sex, but even though fucking Gunther had been great, even he—great as he was in the sack—had been unable to make her come. It was my opinion that her frigidity must have been very deep-rooted, psychologically, and that she had a very long way to go before it would all be sorted out. She was obviously well-educated, but—on an emotional level—just a child.

However, this was neither the time nor the place to get into a heavy discussion about her problems. I thought at least I could make her afternoon pleasurable. Even though she wouldn't reach an orgasm, I knew that I could make her feel wonderful—because there are stages of enjoyment in sex. If you don't go all the way to the final destination, you can still enjoy the trip. Before you can get off you've got to start by getting it on!

Poor Freda, she so badly wanted to get fucked. When I had her warmed up I put one finger into her cunt, then a second, and then she tried to get my whole hand in. She really pushed, working my fingers in and out, as if I were a man hand-fucking her.

At that moment, I must confess, I found her so adorable that I felt a strong case of penis envy. How I wished I could have sprouted a cock, then and there—a thick, hard cock that I could have used to trigger her to orgasm. But as often as I'm attacked by penis envy, I have to remind myself that I'm a woman, and I have to satisfy my sisters with my mouth.

All this was quite new to Freda, which pleased me, because the girls I like best for lovemaking are fairly innocent and virgins to lesbianism. I don't expect them to go down

on me, and as you probably know, I prefer that they don't—
I like to remain the aggressor, the butch.

Freda was again trying to have me fist-fuck her, and I got the message: she wanted a man. I excused myself for a moment and tiptoed down the hall to Leo and Marika's room. I knocked, then pushed open their door. The room was dark and they were both asleep, but Leo woke up at once and quickly stood up next to his bed—virile as ever. For a fifty-one-year-old man, he's amazing. He can fuck and fuck for hours with tremendous self-control, and only climax when he feels he wants to. He can spring a lovely hard-on at any time of day or night—a talent many young boys in their so-called sexual prime might envy.

Marika woke up, too, and realized why I'd called on her husband. "Go right ahead," she smiled through sleepy eyes, "and enjoy it. If it's all right with you, I'll just continue with my nap." So, with his wife's blessing, Leo accompanied me back to my room.

I was to be there strictly as a voyeur, now. Leo started eating her and caressing her breasts with his hands. Then he wriggled a finger up her ass and put another finger into her cunt, and if she wasn't getting horny, I sure was. Anyhow, I couldn't stand just watching, so I put my lips to his firm cock. We almost formed a daisy chain except that Freda had nothing to occupy her mouth or hands. She just lay there and enjoyed, and as she warmed to the activities, Leo slipped his organ out of my mouth and swept it into her pussy.

Justice must be served: Leo tried, and *tried*. He fucked her six ways from Sunday—her hands holding onto his shoulders and her legs wrapped around his neck, or with a pillow underneath her and her legs around his waistline—or any number of positions that help heighten sensation. Yet the only emotion Freda displayed was occasional hysterical laughter, which unfortunately only served to turn Leo off. The poor girl—she should have been one of the most fantastic lovers in St. Tropez, but instead was a frustrated, hung-up lady.

After more than a half hour of steady fucking, Leo finally gave up and climbed off her to make love to me. Of course, I had no problem reaching a climax, and all the while I could see Freda watching us curiously, amazed at my flexibility in bed as Leo and I tried various positions and made certain that we didn't neglect any part of each other's bodies.

It was clear from her eyes that she was interested in Leo, and would like to know him better. No magic had happened this time for her, and we left it at that. Leo returned to his room while Freda and I showered, then went out by the pool and enjoyed the afternoon sun.

Later Leo told me that he thought she needed more simple sexual experiences, with no emotions involved. He felt that a few good fun-fucks would possibly straighten out many of her problems. I agreed, and added that she would also have to face reality and give up some of her illusions about men and True Love.

A DAY IN THE LIFE . . .

I had been in St. Tropez for two weeks, and still managed to find something fresh every day that surprised me with its beauty.

I was having a marvelous time because I was actively hunting for excitement—excitement of any kind. An interesting mind, a lovely view, satisfying sex, a good meal—whatever. I wanted to live it up as much as I could, to enjoy the total freedom that I'd never really known during my years in the United States. It's also true that I was reacting to the depressing times of the past few months. Americans have their fun spots, sure, such as Miami and Las Vegas and parts of California, but none of them can touch the giddy good life of the French Riviera, where they really let it all hang out!

One day I'd be turned on by a far-out fashion in one of the boutiques, and another day I'd get my kicks from chatting to a couple of young tourists. The dress shops have clothing that you'll never see anywhere else in the world, the kind of clothing women dream about—supersexy silks and satins. I couldn't help myself! I'd see a lovely handmade gown or pantsuit, and I'd have to have it! Just like that day in Paris—my traveler's checks were disappearing like tickets at a lumberjack's gangbang.

Another time, I was near the yacht basin when an attractive young couple asked me for directions. She was a gray-eyed, five-foot version of Barbra Streisand (but prettier), and he was a pixie-faced six footer with twinkling blue eyes. They asked me—in careful French, of course, with all the correct guide-book phrases and pronunciations—but I could recognize their North American accent underneath it. Teasingly I answered them in Italian, but they'd just come from a week in Florence, so they tossed a few Italian phrases at me. I tried my Dutch on them, and they bounced back with a bit of German! Finally, as I could see they were getting bewildered, I spoke to them in English and it was great fun to see the relief in their eyes when I did. They'd just arrived in St. Tropez that morning in a rented car that they introduced to me as Melmoth. (They had a zany sense of humor! That was the name Oscar Wilde chose when he moved to France.) The little car was loaded to the bulging point with tents and sleeping bags and knapsacks, and they were wondering if I could direct them to a campsite for the night.

As it happened, I'd just passed by one the day before on my motorbike, a lovely camping ground high on a hill overlooking not only St. Tropez, but the entire Riviera, right down to Nice. It was a lovely view, and must have been breathtaking at night, when the coast is a string of lights as far as the eye can see.

I began to give them directions, but it became rather confusing, so with a shift of all their baggage, they made room for me in the car, and I was able to escort them directly to the camping grounds. They checked in—it cost just a few francs to rent tent space—and then drove me back into town. They were anxious to go swimming, so the three of us went to Pamplona Beach— it's the more touristy one, but I wasn't sure how they'd react to the jet-set ones such as *Plage Tahiti*. It possibly wasn't the best introduction to the swinging Riviera for them, because there were big-bellied businessmen with tired, shapeless bodies, and their dumpy, defeated-looking women. But there were also plenty of groovy-looking singles and couples. Ken and Valentina didn't have bathing suits with them, but he was wearing bikini underpants and her panties easily passed as a bikini bottom. Although Pamplona wasn't an entirely topless beach, neither she nor I wore tops (nor did he, for that matter!) and she couldn't stop giggling about the sauciness of it all. Ken was fairly turned on, not just by seeing his wife's and my bare breasts, but there were plenty of other good-looking topless girls around, and it seemed to me that his bikini got a little tighter at the sight of all that lovely flesh.

One sad note was the globs of oil that had washed onto the beach from passing ships. As we ran toward the water,

Ken lightly stepped over what he'd thought was a rock. It turned out to be a huge wad of thick oil. Fortunately, most of the St. Tropez beaches are operated as private clubs, so they're well maintained, and oil slicks such as this are soon cleared up.

On the beach was a gorgeous brunette who was fully dressed, but extremely sexy. She was wearing tight, hiphugger pants, which didn't reach much above her pubic hair, plus a small top and an open jacket, topped off by a big hat and an extravagant pair of sunglasses. She was surrounded by topless girls with good bodies, yet she looked sexier!

The great scene was when she slowly peeled off her clothes. First her jacket, then her hat, top, and glasses. And the way she stepped out of her pants was enough to make me suffer a wet crotch. Yet once she was down to her bikini and bare boobs, she looked like every other topless girl, and the thrill was gone.

Ken, Valentina, and I spent an hour or so swimming and chatting on the beach. Although Valentina had been born in Europe, this was the first visit for both of them as adults, and they were tremendously excited and overwhelmed by it all. They told me about all the spots they'd seen so far, and I filled them in on some of the cities they'd be getting to later. It was also their first day in the summer sun and their skin was quite pale, so they didn't risk a first-day sunburn. They also wanted to pitch their tent and do some shopping, so we said goodbye and that was it.

We never saw each other again, but the time we spent together was pleasant and easy—the kind of up-front openness that's so characteristic of Europe and so often foreign in America. Why be shy and afraid when it's so easy to turn strangers into friends?

BEACH BALL

Every beach in St. Tropez has its own special atmosphere and its own distinctive clientele.

At all but one *plage,* it's perfectly commonplace to see topless girls—in fact topless is more the rule than the exception. Both men and women wear skimpy bikini bottoms, which cover the essentials but do little to conceal a good crotch or a nifty ass. The one exception, Pamplona, is largely frequented by shy or uptight tourists whose sense of style is not as liberated, many of the women keeping their bikini tops on, or perhaps wearing a full one-piece suit, and the men (with that typical North American reluctance to display their goodies) wearing shapeless boxer trunks.

Full nudity is reserved for the one nudist beach, which is a twenty-minute walk from *Plage Tahiti.* Since I'd been to nudist camps in the United States, I was thinking of checking out the St. Tropez nude beach to make a small survey on behalf of the U.N., which hadn't yet given me a grant to make the survey, so I settled on going there with Norbert, a Canadian enjoying a European sabbatical. He, too, was curious to see the nudist beach, but too shy to go alone.

Norbert was tall and pleasant-looking, with an easygoing manner and friendly brown eyes. He hadn't spent much time in the sun, and his body was still fairly untanned, but his face was nicely freckled. As we walked from Tahiti to the nude beach, he told me how he'd invested in the art market in Canada, and had made enough to take off a year or so in Europe.

We arrived at the nudist beach and slipped off our swimsuits. I noted with approval that he was circumcised and, with delight, that he had a funny little mole on his chubby right buttock.

This record album is rated X

...as in

Xaviera!

By The Author Of "The Happy Hooker"

Send check or money order to: Milidomo, Inc., Dept. XWBI, 527 Madison Avenue, New York, N.Y. 10022

Please send me _____ copies of Xaviera! I prefer ☐ records ☐ 8-track ☐ cassette. I have enclosed $_____ ($6.73 for each record, and $7.73 for each 8-track and cassette which includes 75¢ each for postage and handling).

I certify I am over 21 years of age _____
(signature)

Name_____
Address_____
City_____
State_____ Zip Code_____

NYC residents please add 7% sales tax.

Milidomo, Inc., Dept. XWBI,
527 Madison Avenue, New York, N.Y. 10022

Xaviera.

The Happy Hooker has gone on record with her latest contribution to the sexual revolution. Xaviera Hollander, world-renowned speaker of the house, has earned her X this time, with a vivid narration of the freedoms of life and the joys of love and sex. Listen to her honeyed Holland voice pouring sugar into your ears, rolling each phrase for its erotic sound, searing you, the listener, with the hottest audio experience ever.

It's a no-holds-barred discussion of her views on sex, her experiences as a pay-for-playgirl... coupled with explicit passages of her personal encounters.

The segments include: "My attitude towards sex: The threesome and six other *uncensored* cuts that give you a scorching taste of devine Dutch decadence."

Xaviera! is definitely a no-no for children, moralizers and tenants with thin walls. It's a must for you, the loves in your life and free people of every stripe and persuasion. Just $5.98 for records and $6.98 for 8-track and cassette, plus postage and handling. Mail your coupon today and swing along with Xaviera!

Milidomo, Inc., Dept. XWBI,
527 Madison Avenue, New York, N.Y. 10022

We spread our beach towels over the warm, soft sand, and sat down—not far from a super-looking beauty. She had a sweet, roundish face with long blond hair drifting down past her shoulders. She couldn't have been a day over nineteen. Her skin was lightly anointed with suntan oil, and as she lay back, her legs slightly apart, she looked like an athlete at rest. Her boobs were just glorious—soft, round mounds, perfectly proportioned, with charming, perky nipples. Where her thighs met we could see her delicious golden fuzz, trimmed short, blending into a slightly darker color as it curled toward her navel from its heavenly triangle.

Norbert couldn't keep his eyes off her, and I noticed that his little friend between his legs was stretching up to take a peek (or is it peak?) for itself.

Most people at the beach were pretty blasé because they were so accustomed to nudity and pretty bodies and they didn't seem to care much whether it was Sophia Loren or Twiggy lying next to them. But as Norbert and I admired this blond beauty, we were amused to see an elderly man (easily in his sixties) with a flabby belly and a limp, dangling cock. At first he looked like a lost soul, but as soon as he spotted Blondette, he shuffled as close to her as politeness would allow (about twenty feet, I suppose), flopped down on the sand, and lay down on his stomach, suddenly taking in the sun.

He was wearing big dark sunglasses, and Norbert and I agreed that he had to be a voyeur because he had that special kind of excited expression on his face and now and then he would lift up his glasses to get a better glimpse. He didn't seem to notice us watching him, and after a few minutes he shuffled about five feet closer to the girl. Then he waited awhile, looked around to see if anyone was watching him, and shuffled progressively closer. Before long he was right next to her, though she remained completely oblivious to him.

Then she stretched herself very languidly and picked up a spray bottle of suntan lotion. She spread apart her golden legs and slowly sprayed up and down one leg, then the other.

This was too much for our tubby peeping Tom—and I must admit it was a turn-on for Norbert and me, too.

The girl was still paying no attention to her audience of three, but obviously was aware of our presence. She put on a great erotic performance, anointing herself from her toes to her knees to her thighs, then slowly and lovingly rubbing it around her pussy. At the sight of this the old man actually shivered and Norbert himself had sprung a tremendous red-hot rod-on. I was pretty turned on myself. This girl was giving a fabulous cocktease performance.

She kept rubbing herself with oil, massaging it into her beautiful breasts, making her nipples stand even more erect. Finally she lay back on her mattress, spreading her legs wider apart than before. Norbert and I and the old man had our eyes glued to her crotch, where the combination of oil and perspiration under the hot sun made it look like the treat of the century.

With a sigh I reached over and pulled Norbert's head onto my lap and let my cheek rest on his thigh so that I could feel a warm body close to me as I gazed into the girl's inviting honeypot. I started daydreaming that it was *her* thigh that I was leaning against, and that it was *her* head in my lap.

And then I was stroking her body with my right hand, very lightly, until it rested on her golden fleece. With my left hand I caressed my own body until I was fondling my own triangle. Both hands pointing downward, I gently rippled my fingertips over my labia and hers, and then with my ring and index finger I slowly opened the outer lips so that my middle finger could start the soft circuit of massage.

With the middle finger of each hand, I was nuzzling both her clitoris and mine. The slightest caress there can provide easy stimulation for a great orgasm; as I began this gentle massage my mouth fell open for breath and with closed eyes I abandoned myself to the mounting sensations. My fingers moved faster and faster as I finger-fucked her and played soppy solitaire with myself.

From my very first touch, I knew that she'd been waiting for me. She didn't shrink away from me, she didn't make a sound. Instead she slowly rotated her hips, steadily picking up the pace until she and I were both moving with the same rhythm, and we worked so well together that we soon reached our orgasms together, in great violent spasms.

Norbert, meanwhile, had been watching all this with a throbbing erection, and at the sight of us climaxing he had begun stimulating his balls with one hand while milking his cock with the other.

He was nicely hung and his cock, for one foolish moment, reminded me of a big snake rising out of a basket. Its blind phallic eye was staring right at me, and as he moved his hand up and down on it the veins stood out and the head grew dark, almost black. As he jerked off faster and faster, his cock grew even bigger and harder, and when I saw his eyes begin to glaze over, I begged him to slow down and hold back. But it was too late. Just as I bent over him, the pearly white fountain shot up into my face, and I opened my mouth to catch his hot jism in my throat. He must have been saving up for this one . . . to paraphrase the radio slogan, the come just kept on hitting!

Norbert was completely exhausted from his five-finger exercise and lay back quietly, almost semi-conscious. So I moved back to the blond and buried my head between her inviting legs. I blew softly and warmly into her vaginal lips and tongued her clitoris. She moaned with pleasure, and although I was so involved that I'd completely forgotten him, I could hear Tubby Tom echoing her groan. I stretched my arms up her torso to fondle her breasts, and took her hard nipples between my thumb and forefinger while my tongue rapidly flicked on her clitoris, darting in and out of her.

When I felt she was about to come, and her clitoris grew in my lips, I stopped teasing her and smiled at her with sadistic triumph.

"Oh please, please," she gasped in French, "give me more . . . please!"

So I climbed on top of her and squeezed my leg in between her spread legs; my breasts were touching hers, our erect nipples pressing into each other's. I drew back her head and kissed her shoulders and neck, and nibbled her earlobes. I put my hand under her shoulder and the other under her bottom so that her short pubic hairs would rub against mine. I was now wild with passion, pressing kisses into her perspiring face, kissing her eyelashes, eyelids, her nose and forehead, her sweet cheeks. I worked my way toward her mouth, eager and moist with excitement. She began to moan and I rocked against her, up and down, up and down, higher and higher, and her body was warm and slippery. Wow! We pumped together like rutting stoats, moaning and whimpering and grunting.

Norbert had come around again (all right, Norbert had revived himself!) and grown another lovely boner. So as I knelt in front of Blondette, my ass in the air, he moved behind me. And as I went down on her, he stimulated my cunt with his fingers, found it to be hot and moist, and began rubbing his prick back and forth between my ass and pussy.

I sank forward, burying my face in the girl's crotch, and the old voyeur suddenly shouted, "Bravo!" We turned toward him just in time to see him bring himself off in his hand, with a super-satisfied smile on his face.

A good time was had by all—in my mind, at least. I'm afraid the hot sun had warmed me into fantasyland, and as I opened my eyes I realized that I hadn't moved and none of this had happened. My cheek was still on Norbert's thigh, his head on my lap, Blondette was still sunning herself and Tubby Tom was still grooving on her.

Then the girl noticed the time, got up, and walked away —unfucked and unsucked—and the old man shuffled off moments later, in her direction, his limp dick still dangling forlornly.

Even though Norbert and I were left alone, I thought we might at least be able to turn part of my fantasy into reality. So we found a shaded spot and got it together very nicely, thank you. Not quite as exciting as the fantasy (it's hard to beat a good imagination), but nevertheless a fine and fulfilling fuck. I missed the beautiful blond, since she had started it all, really, but she was certainly with us in spirit.

FREDA'S PLASTIC FANTASTIC LOVER

After an exciting day at the beaches, I returned home to Ramatuelle at about five o'clock. Leo and Marika greeted me, almost beside themselves with excitement.

"Xaviera!" they shouted as soon as they saw me.

"We did it!" Leo called, looking like a grinning gnome, Marika hugging him and bouncing on her toes.

"Wait a minute, wait a minute. You did what?"

"Oh, Xaviera, Freda made it! She had an orgasm!"

"Fantastic. What happened?"

"This afternoon, after lunch, Freda and Marika and I were feeling very pleasant," Leo told me, "and we went upstairs together for our siesta. One thing led to another, of course, and we were kissing and petting, with a little threesome going."

"Leo was screwing her for quite a while," Marika cut in, "and she was enjoying it, you know, but as usual nothing was happening. So I brought out my vibrator—the big one."

"Oh, wow. The ten-incher?" I'm not a great vibrator freak myself, but I'd seen this one, and it was a biggie.

"Yes, that's right," Leo said. They were both so anxious to tell me, they practically tripped over each other's tongues. "Well, Freda was on her back, and we'd been going at it hard and heavy. So when Marika gave me the vibrator, I pulled out and before she realized what I was doing—"

"He jammed it up her!" Marika interrupted gleefully.

"And she came! Her hips thrashed and her body shook all over and she moaned in the agony and ecstasy of it all." Leo was becoming poetic in his excitement.

"Oh, Xaviera, you should have been here. It was wonderful, she got all flushed and her body turned red. And she cried, and we laughed, and she laughed and we cried . . . and it was so fine."

"I'm so happy . . . the poor chick, she's waited thirty-one years for this! Where is she?"

They told me she was sleeping in her room—her first post-orgasmic nap! So I didn't disturb her. I just hoped it would be the first of many for her, and wondered at it all. She'd finally found a satisfactory lover—a plastic cone that trembled and jiggled to the erotic stimulus of a dollar's worth of batteries.

Well, you take it wherever and whenever you can find it, right?

That evening we had a celebration dinner for Freda in St. Tropez, at a quaint little restaurant atop a hill. It was one of those places that didn't look like much from outside, but once we were inside, the atmosphere was so welcoming. There was an open fire, crackling and friendly, and lots of happy people. While it's true that there were plenty of arrogant and phony people in St. Tropez, they were happily outnumbered by the crowds of decent people from all walks of life—not just the rich and famous—who were liberated, fun-loving, and easy-going.

We began our celebration meal with escargots (sounds so much better than snails!) in drawn butter and garlic. Marika, Leo, and Freda ordered a chilled white wine—Puligny-Montrachet, I think—and pronounced it excellent while nonalcoholic Xaviera joined the toast with apple cider. For the main course I had beautiful beef, grilled medium-rare over charcoal and smothered with Béarnaise sauce, accompanied by tender, buttered asparagus tips. Freda chose *poule sautée a l'estragon,* which was chicken breasts sauteed in white wine and cream, spiced with tarragon. Leo and Marika, together as ever, shared a platter of *rognon de veau flambé*—tender veal kidneys dramatically flambéed in cognac at our table. Since we were all having rather heavy meals, we had a light salad—just tomato vinaigrette. To accompany their main courses, the others ordered a bottle of Chateau Kirwan (a red Bordeaux), while I stayed with Chateau Hollander and sipped my trusty cider.

We took a pass on dessert, much to the waiter's disappointment, who was hoping he could do his crepes suzette act at our table.

It was a wonderful dinner and a wonderful night. Perhaps it was my imagination, but I'm certain that Freda had a little more glow to her face. We didn't talk too much about it during dinner—it was enough that she felt so good, we felt good for her, and she knew we did. We just had a good time and grooved on being together. Afterward, she came back to the villa with us, and since she'd had such a fulfilling day (we all had, for that matter!) we wordlessly agreed not to possibly mar it for her by attempting another sexual scene, which might leave her frustrated again. So instead we sat around the living room, softly lit with candles, and listened to music on the good stereo system.

I was delighted to find one of Leonard Cohen's records there, and during the course of the evening we covered the musical spectrum from Stan Getz to the Beatles to Herbie Mann to Beethoven, and ended the evening listening to a lovely piece by a composer I'd never heard of before. He was a contemporary of Bach, and I've since learned that he had some influence of Bach's music. His name was Johann Pachelbel, and the work was his "Canon in D Major." It's a lovely, flowing piece of music and since we couldn't think of anything as beautiful to play after it, we played it again, then decided to let it close the evening for us. We were rather dozy anyway, and so we trundled upstairs to our respective bedrooms and fell asleep—as the cliché goes, tired but happy.

FEUD FOR THOUGHT

After a few weeks of hectic activity in St. Tropez, Leo and Marika and I began to tire of the relentless pursuit of pleasure. Leo suggested we take a rest-and-relaxation visit to Ile du Levant.

It's a beautiful island about half an hour by boat from the Côte d'Azur. The ferry to the island leaves from Le Lavendou, which is an hour's drive from St. Tropez. The entire journey wasn't very long, but we decided to take it leisurely, and stopped on the way in the lovely little town of Mole, which is famous for one of its restaurants.

Freda was accompanying us, and it was she who had suggested that we stop at Mole. Soon we were seated in the shade of the trees, being served delicious homemade bread and five differents types of pâté, each one more exquisite than the one before it. I've never had such suberb pâté anywhere, at any price. We stuffed ourselves—we just couldn't resist one more mouthful, then another.

Fully booked (which is my polite euphemism for a stuffed belly), we drove to La Lavendou and eventually boarded the ferry. It was a large island and our first stop was Port Cros, an attractive harbor dotted with lovely white houses topped by orange brick roofs. High up the green hill stood an impressive castle.

A hydrofoil, operated by a wildly colorful character named Lou, then picked us up to take us to our final destination, which was a simple dock at Ile du Levant. A young man in an old truck met us there, ready to take us into town. It was unbearably hot, so we took time out first to get ice cream cones and cool drinks from a nearby cafe. Next door to it was a small shop selling "minimums": brief bits of cloth, with strings attached—just enough to cover the genitals. Ile du Levant is a nudist island, but the rule is that minimums are worn in town, and in shops and restaurants.

Leo had been coming to this island regularly for almost twenty years.

"I remember an old lady—in her fifties, I guess—who was elected mayor here one year," he told us. "But she didn't last very long. She didn't approve of topless dancing and even campaigned to have people wear more than just a minimum!"

What surprised me was how she'd been elected mayor in the first place with an attitude like that.

We each bought a minimum—the women's were crocheted and decorated with pearls, the men's were a little bigger for obvious reasons—and they seemed like nothing more than G-strings. We also each bought linen shoes to climb the island's steep rocky hills . . . we had arrived wearing leather sandals, which would be much too slippery.

Then back to the truck and a ten-minute drive on a narrow road which led straight up until we reached a small village at the top of a hill. It was called Heliopolis—Greek for "city of the sun."

Leo had made reservations at the Brise Marine, the most luxurious hotel on the island. All the rooms had running water and bidets (no other hotel on the island did!) and the entrance was flanked by two lovely patios with flowers, plants, and fountains.

Various hotel guests were nonchalantly walking about in the nude. One was a sweet old Englishman, a retired lawyer from Birkenhead. Another was a big fat Texas oil tycoon who'd come to the island for its quiet atmosphere. He was a loner, and never left the hotel because the climb down the steep hill was too much for him. The exercise might have done him a world of good, though. Then there was a sexy but fully dressed Italian couple who arrived when we did. I later saw him naked; he seemed not exactly masculine and was very strangely hung. Two other guests were a middle-aged surgeon from Paris and his overweight young mistress. Most of the guests were couples; there were a few single men, and Freda and I were the only single girls at the hotel.

Freda and I were sharing a room. We unpacked, freshened up, and dressed in our terrific new suits—mine in blue denim, hers in lavender. We joined Leo and Marika, whose room was downstairs from ours, and together walked over to The Minimum. That's the name not only of the G-string, but also of the only terrace restaurant in Heliopolis. We had a light dinner there to make up for all the pâté we'd wolfed down earlier in the day, and then decided to go over to La Payotte, the nearby discotheque.

Like so many men and women, I find one-night stands irresistibly exciting sometimes and began looking for an attractive man. I need the security of a steady relationship, the knowledge of that continuing care and affection, but at the same time I frequently find myself overcome by the crazy desire to bounce up and down on top of someone I've never seen before and will probably never see again. Those situations are completely free of pressure, obligation, and emotion—and sometimes I need that.

Leo and Marika could never understand this kind of relationship so we got into a discussion on it.

"Why is it that you can meet someone really nice, who wants to be your friend," Marika asked, "and all you want to do is spend one session in bed with him, then turn him out of your life? Aren't you missing out on a real relationship?"

Leo had a theory. "You're still reacting to the days when you were a prostitute in New York. You had to become accustomed there to short-term sexual relationships, completely devoid of any emotional involvement."

"That's right," Marika agreed. "And that also made you accustomed to having a large variety of men in your life."

They were partially right, of course. All these men coming into my life for a few hours, or a day at the most, and my relationship with them a combination of business and pleasure. Hell, yes, it's obviously had its effect.

In a way, I was also reacting to a lack of steady emotional warmth. It had been over two months since I'd left New York, and no matter what the quality of our romance had been, I did miss Larry. Even if we argued every day, it was at least involvement—you have to care for someone to be able to keep coming back for more arguments! It sometimes made me feel a bit jealous to see Leo and Marika so happy together.

And to make things worse, I wasn't contributing to their happiness. Our discussion about my flitting around led, as such discussions generally do, into much more basic feelings. And the fact was that they were disappointed in me as a friend. It was all coming out now.

Leo and Marika saw my one-night stands as an act of disloyalty toward them. They felt that if I found a man—or a woman, for that matter—I shouldn't keep it as a twosome. If I found someone I wanted to go to bed with, then I should share him with Leo and Marika.

Eventually, when I tried to point out that there's nothing abnormal about a simple twosome, and that I had no intention of supplying them with a continuing supply of orgy partners, they became quite defensive.

They both jumped up, and said almost together, "No, no, no! Don't say that. You don't have to bring anyone here for us to fuck. You don't have to swing."

But Marika added, "If you do have a lover, though, isn't it selfish of you to keep him to yourself? Shouldn't we all be able to enjoy his company in bed, as well as out of bed?"

To tell the truth, I was becoming a bit fed up with the swinging scene. Why did these two people so desperately want a constant parade of different bed partners? They were continually searching for new talent. And I suppose I was the perfect matchmaker, bringing home girls and boys both.

One thing we did agree on when it came to swinging: It's no fun to go to a party, take off your clothes, and hump away. There has to be something more than just the opportunity for sex—either interesting people, or an appealing atmosphere, or something exciting. Orgies may be great for working off one's sexual urges, but emotionally they can be numbing.

I thought the arguments were over, but no, there were more to come.

Leo, Marika, Freda and I were at the dinner table. Leo and Marika were reliving old times, talking about people I didn't know, and frankly I became a tiny bit bored. Freda somehow seemed to know who they were talking about, so she stayed with their conversation. It was a casual situation, and we were waiting for the entree to be served, so I had no qualms about taking the opportunity to write a few postcards to friends in Europe and America.

At the sight of this, Freda suddenly went into a big Gestapo number, telling me it was impolite to sit there and write postcards and that I should have sufficient manners to participate in the conversation.

"It's bad enough that you sit by yourself all the time, talking into your little tape recorder! But now we're about to have dinner and you're treating us like pieces of shit!"

I half expected her to snap her fingers and summon goose-stepping soldiers to come in and take me away. Unfortunately the combination of her cold, abrupt manner and guttural accent made her sound like a character from a wartime "B" movie. I refused to take her seriously, so, trying to let her words just roll over me, I didn't bother to retaliate. But then Leo and Marika chimed in, agreeing with her in raised voices. Every multilingual person in the restaurant was listening.

A Swiss man at the next table murmured that I should get an award for putting up with all their crap. A good thing they didn't hear him, or they would have dragged him into the target area, too.

It was probably not very polite for me to write postcards, but neither was it polite for the others to chatter away in a closed conversation, without even trying to include me.

The yelling and screaming just went on and on . . . it must have been twenty minutes, though it seemed like all night. It was really getting to me, and at least five times I ordered Freda to shut up, but of course to no avail. When she kept on haranguing me I excused myself to Leo—my host—and joined a sympathetic couple who'd heard the whole row and had invited me over to their table.

They were Austrian; she thirty-five and he forty-five, and most pleasant. While I was with them, Freda left—to go play with herself, unsuccessfully, I hoped bitchily—so my new friends—Leopoldine and Gustav—and I rejoined Leo and Marika. The five of us took seats on the terrace, and now that peace had been reestablished, we relaxed and talked.

Gustav, who said he was of royal blood and had the title of Count—which didn't count for much these days, he laughed—owned a winter resort in Austria, even though he hates snow and cold weather, and can't even ski. He enjoys his guests, though—a select group of well-to-do winter sports fans, the majority of them rich German industrialists.

Leopoldine was his public relations officer, as well as his mistress. She was a wild young thing with a great body. And she couldn't ski, either.

"And I suppose none of your staff skiis, either, Gustav?" I couldn't help asking.

"Well, as a matter of fact, Xaviera, I don't want them to. It's so hard to find competent personnel that I really can't afford to have any of my people going out skiing and possibly breaking a leg. It's happened before."

They were such pleasant people that we sat and talked for a good part of the evening, and the unhappy moments I'd experienced at dinner were forgotten. Our conversation was quite inconsequential, with nothing that especially bears repeating, but it was warm and friendly—and that's what we all needed that night.

Although the possibility of a swing—Leopoldine was definitely the type, I felt—was in the air, we all somehow seemed to sense that there wouldn't be one that particular night. Which is fine. Swinging simply for its own sake is pointless.

Before we parted company for the night, Gustav and Leopoldine made certain that we each had matchbooks advertising their lodge, and we gave them our telephone number in St. Tropez.

So far Ile du Levant had been a lot of sun, several arguments, and little else. I couldn't say I was having a particularly good time. So I decided to find some fun—create it, if need be. Perhaps find myself a new fun friend. . . .

What would be the name of my new fun friend? Well, would you believe Moustaffa?

MOROCCAN ON THE ROCKS

Moustaffa was a twenty-two-year-old Moroccan servant boy at our hotel on Ile du Levant. I had once been warned to stay away from Moroccans because they have a violent nature, but like most of the staff at the Brise Marine, Moustaffa was polite, bright, and spoke excellent French.

He was also very cute. He had a nice firm ass and had a short but rugged build. After seeing all the nude men walking around the hotel—the old Englishman with his dangling dinky dick, or the revolting fat American with his parts hidden away by flab and pubic hair, or the Italian who'd been shot in the back and had big scars on his ass, or the surgeon and his fat girlfriend—I'd been rather turned off to sex, and the only one who got to me was this cute young man, walking around in bathing shorts. He had a lovely, darkish face with pitch-black, fiery eyes. His mouth was sensual, his hair was bushy and black, and his hands were strong and large, as were his leather-sandaled feet.

Whenever he walked by me his hands were always ready to touch me—to stroke my hair, or gently run his finger over my back at exactly the sensitive region, or to softly squeeze my hips. From the moment I saw him on our first day, as he carried our suitcases, I lusted for him.

"Don't touch him, Xaviera," Leo had warned me, realizing that I had a fuck in mind.

"Why? D'you think he might have a dose?"

"Well, aside from VD, let me tell you something you might not be aware of. On this island, most of the hotel owners are gay, and the boys they employ are often kids they've picked up in Marrakech or Casablanca or Essaoria. They hand-choose these kids, not only to work in the hotel, but also to be their personal catamites. These are hired bumboys, Xaviera, brought over like willing slaves."

It seemed incredible that this was happening in the middle of the twentieth century.

"Listen, there's a French territory called Djibouti just east of Ethiopia in North Africa. Young boys there are sold as slaves to buyers from Europe. Not just house slaves, but sexual slaves. For about nine hundred pounds sterling, you can buy a kid there and he's your for life!"

"But, Leo," I asked, "are you suggesting to me that Moustaffa is a slave here?"

"All I'm suggesting, my dear, is that if his services here go beyond the regular hotel chores, his master may be very angry if the boy is seduced.

"And what's worse, Moroccans are very jealous lovers. If you make it with the boy, and he likes it, which he probably will, then sees you taking another man up to your room, the boy's liable to get so jealous that he'd stab the man in the back!"

"Oh really, Leo, you're in a fantasy world. These things only happen in the movies," I suggested.

"And on islands like this. Listen, three years ago, right here, a friend of Marika's had an affair with a Moroccan bartender here. Then, after a few days, she brought another lover to her room, and the bartender just freaked out. Caused an enormous fuss, and all of us nearly got thrown out of the hotel. So I'm warning you, the kid isn't worth the chances."

Well, it was a good story, and I believed it, but I somehow couldn't visualize Moustaffa making it with one of the hotel owners. All I could visualize was him and me together, doing the delightful deed of darkness.

One day friends invited Leo and Marika to dinner at their cottage. Freda, who was still sharing the hotel room with me, joined them, and I knew they'd be gone for several hours. So I arranged a rendezvous with Moustaffa. Just to be on the safe side, we made a date for just after the restaurant closed, when his boss would leave the hotel and spend the evening in his own house. Moustaffa didn't need any seducing—obviously our lustful feelings were mutual.

He arrived at my door fully dressed, no longer in his bathing shorts. He wore a brownish sweater and a pair of tight black slacks that did a super job of outlining his sexy ass. As soon as I opened the door, he came right in and hugged me close to him.

"Do you want to fuck?" he asked, clearly a young man who comes right to the point.

Does a bear shit in the woods? Is the Pope a Catholic?

Still, I couldn't help laughing at his blunt approach. At least his prick was still in his pants.

"First, Moustaffa, since we can be honest with each other, let me ask you—have you ever fucked your boss?"

"No, I haven't. Never." He seemed indignant at the suggestion.

"Is there any chance your boss is in love with you?"

"No, not a chance. Not with me. If there's anything happening, it's between him and the cook. They've been friends for eleven years, I believe."

"Then, yes—let's fuck! Here, let me undress you . . . oh, let me loosen your belt here, and get these pants down. Oh, look at it, it's beautiful, and so big, ohhhh . . . It's such a dark purplish color . . . and so nicely circumcised . . . and so thick . . . oh, look, it's getting bigger! It must like me! Oh, Moustaffa, I'm all juicy already, let me get undressed . . . here, thank you . . . oh, baby!"

We fucked deeply, quickly, and forcefully. He was dynamite. And such a super prick! Shaped so much bigger than average, and such a deep purple hue.

After he ejaculated, Moustaffa left my bed and went to the bidet to wash up, and Miss Hygiene was delighted to see that he had such sanitary habits. Clean as a whistle (and what a whistle to blow!) he flopped back on the bed, while I used the bidet myself.

Then we caressed and explored each other's bodies. He put body lotion on my back, which was still a little tender from a day on the beach, and just the feel of his strong hands on my skin got me all hot again. The feel of my body got him pretty randy, too, particularly as I moved my head toward his stomach, and with gentle circles my lips moved around the top surface of his belly, then made larger and larger circles until they brushed his curly public hair. Then

I brought the hard head of his prick between my lips, and crouched on the bed, going down deeper on his hard organ.

On hands and knees now, my head sunk low, my sun-burned ass sticking in the air, I moved my head up and down on his cock, savoring the flavor of its skin, my tongue feeling the differing textures of the glands, the circumcision scar tissue, and the hard-veined shaft.

When his cock was so big and hard that I couldn't wait anymore, I sat on top of him, legs spread on either side of his body, and I plunged up and down on his thick, meaty cock. He moved me up and down with his hands, faster and faster, and I could feel him filling me up. With screams of pleasure he began to jerk up into the air, just holding me on his cock. His strong hands closed tight against my waist, slamming me deeper into him and, as I quivered on top of him, my cunt closed around his entire member in one huge gulp, the wide-open lips settling around his balls.

He couldn't help but scream from satisfaction while I, at the peak of my orgasm, just collapsed on his chest.

Utterly satisfied, we rested for a while, then cleaned up, dressed, and went out, hand in hand. Moustaffa insisted we go to Le Couvent, a discotheque which was much more of a fun spot than La Payotte. Le Couvent's music was much better, the people seemed brighter and friendlier, and every now and then the music would stop and there'd be a short, amusing transvestite act—perhaps an Edith Piaf or Josephine Baker imitation. Nothing special, but enough to keep the audience and atmosphere cooking.

Happily for me, Moustaffa was as good on the dance floor as he was in the sack—he really knew how to use his body. Soon we were grinding against each other, my arms around his neck, his hands on my buttocks, firmly pressing his penis against me.

At the side of the dance floor were two young kids—eighteen at the most—dressed in the military uniform of the French Marines, which had a base on Ile du Levant. One of them, a boy with a cuddly baby face, was staring in wide-eyed fascination at Moustaffa and me, rubbing against each other, and Moustaffa was also occassionally fondling my nipples by simply reaching under my skimpy top. It was obviously driving the young marine to distraction.

When the record ended I asked Moustaffa if he'd mind my dancing with the kid. "Of course not," he said, and I walked over to the young boy, took his hand, and led him onto the dance floor. He was so young and skinny that it was like holding a kid brother in my arms. His baby face was birdlike, with a skinny long neck and a protruding Adam's apple. His short, straight hair was carefully plastered down with cream, his hands were shaky and nervous, and his big marine boots stomped on my toes with every fourth step.

As I pressed myself against his white pants, I could feel him gaining an erection. So I maneuvered my hands from his shoulders to his back, then to his spine, then his hips, then a bit more to the front. And finally I felt his cock standing smartly to attention. I squeezed its head with my fingertips and rubbed my vaginal mound against the spot where I estimated his balls were. As we danced—his head on the side of mine, his nose in my hair—he uttered a thousand words in French, none of which I could understand because he was speaking in dialect, and very rapidly.

He wanted to kiss me, but I gently avoided that. Poor kid, all I wanted to do was excite him. After all, I was with a jealous Moroccan and I didn't want to start a free-for-all. Besides that, even if I had wanted to take the kid's virginity, I couldn't very well do it on the dance floor. Well, could I?

He must have read my thoughts because he whispered, "Let's go outside, let's get some fresh air!" I smiled at him, and the music ended just in time, so I led him back to the sidelines and his friend. A few of the dancers applauded, because the bulge of his erection could be clearly seen through his loose pants.

Then he started begging. "Please, mademoiselle, ten minutes. No, five. Just five minutes, outside, please, I'm so horny, you can't refuse me."

I felt like telling him to go back to his base and think of me while he jerked off, but the fact was that I'd started something which I really ought to finish. Besides, what would five minutes mean? Moustaffa would hardly know, and I'd already told him, back at the hotel, not to get jealous. So I took the kid outside.

It didn't take us long to find a perfect rock, which was just right for him to lean back on. I had no intention of fucking him, but at least I owed him a blow-job. So, with his still-hard cock pushing against his white linen trousers, I opened his fly, and he swiftly swept it out. I even let him remove my top and feel my breasts. He pushed his cock against them, and the tip was already glistening and moist, he was so horny.

So I told him to lean back and relax. Kneeling in front of him, I let my lips just rest gently on the tip of his penis. It grew bigger and I spent a lot of time giving it little nipping kisses at the base, the head, and up and down the shaft. He groaned each time I planted one of these quick little kisses on him. Then I reached between his legs so that I could get at his balls, and gave them the kiss treatment as well. He was holding on to my shoulders and I could feel the shivers coming up from his cock, and when I had it really quivering, I began the blow-job in earnest.

Within a minute after I began sucking his cock, nibbling at the little knot where he'd been clipped, I could feel his spasm begin, ready to ejaculate into my mouth. And so he did, with deep gulps, his balls getting bigger and harder in my hand while I pushed the ridge between his ass and his scrotum with my little finger, feeling the movement of his orgasm with my hands as well as my mouth.

When it was over he laughed and kissed me again and again, thankful for what I'd done for him. He confessed that he'd never before been with a woman, and even though he'd love to fuck me, this was the greatest experience he'd ever had, and hopefully we'd get together some time and have a proper fuck.

I told him I'd like to do that, and give him a proper lesson, knowing, of course, that it would never happen, but saying it made him feel so good.

As I returned to the discotheque, Moustaffa was looking for me. He wasn't upset when I told him where I'd been and what I was up to. He obviously (thank goodness!) wasn't one of those jealous Moroccans. He knew that it was just a kick for me and that I enjoyed giving aid and comfort to young kids, even if I didn't have an orgasm myself.

Moustaffa and I fucked again that night, out on the same rock, when the club had closed and all was quiet. You should try it some time—Moroccan on the rocks. Very refreshing!

At night, my desire for sex in Ile du Levant was extravagant. Daytime, I didn't want to think about it. Strange!

I set my own schedule for my vacation there, not going to sleep till late at night, after dancing and being all pooped and exhausted, then getting up next day at seven-thirty. I'd go sit on the terrace with my notes and cassette machine, and work on my book. Around ten I'd have breakfast, then go to the beach.

There's only one sandy beach in Ile du Levant, and it's dirty, so I used to go to Les Pierres Plats, which means "the flat rocks," or literally, "The stone platform." The moment one walks onto Les Pierres Plats, it is expected that one will strip, and if you don't, you can expect a dedicated nudist to start harassing you. One morning a stranger arrived, wearing a bathing suit, and was attacked with all manner of screams.

"Get away! Voyeur! Take off your clothes or get away from here! And don't ever come back!"

The same would happen to people paddling by in a canoe, fully dressed, who would stop to take a closer look at the nudists basking in the sun. I never realized how aggressive naturalists could be until I saw one of them throwing stones at a canoeist. They let it all hang out, all right, including their anger at nearby people with clothes on.

Despite this, there's a very casual atmosphere on the entire nudist island, which I haven't quite encountered anywhere else in the world. Almost immediately, everyone is a friend, and it's like one big happy family. If someone has a bottle of wine, or Coca-Cola, he shares it. If the ice cream man comes by (fully dressed, incidentally), people treat each other. And needless to say, they respected the island, always making certain that bottles and wrappers and all items of garbage are carefully and correctly put away. I don't think I ever saw any rubbish or waste dirtying the island.

I liked the island, had a few fine times there, and it certainly helped me to relax. But I could never stay there for an entire summer. I think I'm too restless for such a peaceful place. And possibly because my relationship with Leo and Marika, and certainly with Freda, was not as strong as it had been, I was happy when we returned to St. Tropez.

SWINGING APART

Back at the villa in Ramatuelle, more and more tension was building. The time we'd spent in Ile du Levant had too often been marred by outbursts of misunderstanding, aggressiveness, and hysteria among the four of us. And things weren't getting any better, partly because of Freda's stubborn and stupid remarks. Her complete lack of a sense of humor drove Leo and me up the wall, since we're both natural jesters, and she would continually become impatient with our humor. I must admit, too, that I may have been jealous of her because Leo and Marika had accepted her as fully as they'd accepted me, and I suppose my ego was somewhat hurt.

I've already mentioned, too, how the swinging scene became progressively less appealing to me. I began spending more time alone in my room, and if I happened to bring home a date, I frankly didn't want to share him with Leo, Marika, and Freda, who always seemed to be there these days.

At least one good thing in our relationship was honesty; we never tried to bluff each other, and I never lied to them. But our relationship was unhappy, and I was reacting to it.

I moved out of the Ramatuelle house for a couple of days when I met Andreas, a really appealing man from Megeve, a ski resort in the French Alps, who happened to be a wealthy Swiss banker. (You'll meet him later on in this book.) I wanted to spend some time with him and get to know him—without sharing—so I joined him in the Byblos Hotel for a few days.

When I rejoined Leo and Marika, however, I certainly wasn't prepared for what transpired. Leo was obviously uncomfortable, and had difficulty saying what had to be said. But he stood and looked at me, and spoke firmly though without rancor.

"Xaviera, we want you to leave the house. As soon as possible."

We looked at each other, but I said nothing. Leo obviously had more to say, so I sat down and waited for him to continue.

"You're not loyal to us. Maybe you've never had true friends in your life. But when you have friends, you have roots. And you have to maintain those roots, and maintain your friendships. We came here together because we wanted to be together, and then you disappear for a few days. You walk out on us. You reject us.

"You've been on your own too long, you're too accustomed to having your own way. Do you realize that everything we've done here has been *your* choice, not ours? You've never paid any attention to our concerns, you've just decided what we'd all do, no matter how we felt about it."

At this point I had to interrupt Leo. It was my turn to take the floor for a few minutes. "Leo," I said, "I've gotten to know you two people pretty well during the past few months. You know how much I like you . . . you two received me with open arms, you've taken me traveling with you, you've turned me on to yourselves, your friends, and lots of good times. I realize all this, and believe me, I'm grateful.

"There are two things in life that you've surely noticed are hard for me to do. One is to say thank you. On June fifteenth, for instance, you brought me birthday flowers and candies and gifts . . . and I was so pleased that perhaps I never did get around to saying thank you properly. Frankly, for a long time now I haven't been accustomed to receiving kindness from others, and perhaps I've forgotten how to be grateful. I'm sorry. Please believe me, I didn't mean to be rude or thankless.

"Something else I hate to do is say goodbye. In any language, it's one of the most difficult words to say . . . because it means an ending, a loss . . . and every little goodbye adds up to a great big farewell. And I guess I don't want to face that.

"I don't know if you can accept this, but I'm afraid that's part of me . . . when I left you for a few days to be with Andreas, I didn't mean to reject you. I should have said thank you and I should have said goodbye. But it's been so long since I've had people who really cared about whether I stayed or not, maybe I've forgotten what it's like.

"Besides, to be honest—and this may just be my insecurities again—I thought that you were tiring of me, and were more taken by Freda. I felt that you wouldn't really miss me if I were to disappear for a few days with a man.

"And one more thing . . . how many times have I heard Marika saying, 'Oh, Xaviera, you're pairing off again,' when I wanted to have a date by myself with a man. Yes, I realize you've paid for my trip, and you're wonderfully generous . . . but what price do I have to pay for it? Do I have to procure bed partners?"

I stopped there. In situations like this, one starts to defend oneself and soon it begins to sound like "The lady doth protest too much." But I was hurt and confused by Leo's comments. And I guess he and Marika were hurt and confused by my seemingly rude actions.

"Xaviera, you have to sacrifice if you want to keep friends," responded Marika. "This probably sounds like a string of clichés, but they're all true. Friends have to stick together through the good times and the bad times. For all the suffering that you have to go through with friends, there'll always be more moments when you love to be with them, and when you know you can rely on them."

Leo cut in: "That's what we mean about being loyal. We want you to be our friend, but possibly you don't understand friendship. Because we see you pick people up, use them yourself, maybe have fun with them, then either drop them completely or perhaps toss them to us as leftovers, you're worse than a callous playboy. You virtually wipe your feet on men as if they were doormats. The men you've brought home lately have been attractive, intelligent young men, yet you toss them away. Is it because of your hooking days? Is this your way of revenge—picking up a man and using him, then dropping him without regard for his feelings?"

This was a question that required an answer, and I'd

never really faced it till then. But the fact is that I *had* been using men, I'd considered most of them my "victims," not my lovers.

Maybe I *was* taking revenge, maybe I wanted to be like the aggressive male animal. In order not to get hurt, I'd cut off the relationship before the man had a chance to . . . particularly in a resort area like this, where I knew we'd pass each other like ships in the night, with no real chance of a lasting relationship.

This was one of the many identity crises that we all go through, particularly when our life enters a new cycle. This was my summer of change, and I was caught between my past and my future, with a present I didn't understand.

So with affection despite our misunderstandings, I packed my bags and prepared to leave the villa. But first I biked into town and bought a cake, and some pâté which I knew Leo and Marika would particularly enjoy. I also found a card, with a funny little monkey on the front, which read, "Let's be friends and forget the bad moments of our lives." The card spoke for itself, so I simply signed it Xaviera, and quietly left the card, cake, and pâté on the dining table.

Leo seemed more than a little depressed as he helped me out with my suitcases and bags and books.

"Leo, I hope you and Marika won't mind, when Larry comes, if we all get together for dinner. I've written him about you, and I've told you about him, and I know you'd like each other."

"Of course, Xaviera," he answered. "By all means, let's keep in touch. I'm sorry things had to go this way, but, you see—it'll be best for all of us. Everything will find its place, and we'll be close again."

And in the bright Mediterranean sun, we exchanged kisses and I told the taxi driver to take me to a hotel in St. Tropez.

SEX, WITHOUT A HITCH

I needed a day away from St. Tropez, and a day alone with Xaviera, figuring out what to do with my life. So I rented a Simca and followed the Côte d'Azur through Monaco into Italy and elegant, expensive San Remo. The driving was fun and it helped clear my mind. I spent a quiet evening in the Italian town, and dined alone on delicious veal baked with cheese and prosciutto ham, and served with lightly garlicked and buttered green beans. And since I was feeling a little sorry for myself, I splurged on two different kinds of *gelati*—Italian ice cream—for dessert. My faithful favorite, spumoni, with chopped fruits and nuts hidden within it . . . and (I couldn't resist it) a tempting, rich, chocolate and vanilla combination.

And I followed a quiet evening with an even quieter night. I went to bed early, and I think that's just what I needed—a good night's sleep, alone, to sort things out. In the morning I was refreshed and optimistic as I pointed my Simca back toward St. Tropez. I was so optimistic that I didn't notice the near-empty gas tank until I passed the Italian border. The nearest service station would be Menton, so I left the main road, making a sharp right turn to go downhill to the town. It was a steep and curvy hill, so I drove cautiously. I glanced at two hitchhikers sitting by the side of the road. One was a dark-haired kid and one was blond, but I was concentrating too carefully on the driving to really notice them.

In Menton I had the gas tank filled and picked up some peaches, a bar of chocolate, and some cookies for lunch, then drove back up the hill to the main road. The hitchhikers were still there, and though I'm usually reluctant to pick up hitchers in areas that I don't know, I slowed to pick them up. These kids looked honest and tired, and as I slowed down they were obviously relieved that someone was finally stopping for them.

The dark-haired kid spoke with a trace of a Spanish accent.

"Thank you, madame. Are you going as far as Nice?"

"Sure. Jump in!" I threw open the door for them, and they piled in with their sleeping bags and rucksacks.

"This is Reinhold, he's from Germany," said the dark-haired one, as Reinhold climbed into the back seat. "My name is Miguel, and I'm from Mexico."

"Hi, I'm Xaviera, and I'm from . . . Holland, I guess! But I'm living in St. Tropez at the moment."

It turned out that hitchhiking was a tough job in both Italy and France. The two boys had been sitting at that spot in Menton for a full day without a lift. Overnight, they'd slept in the grass at the side of the road. And they hadn't seen a bath or shower in at least three weeks.

Still, Miguel was a good-looking kid with fine features and I got quite turned on to him as we drove. He was wearing purple flared pants with black and white stripes, and a pinkish shirt to match. He was about five feet nine, with long, dark, hippie-type hair, which clearly needed a good wash. But he didn't want to be considered a hippie. He wasn't particularly a love child and had no special ideas about war or peace. He wasn't affiliated with any political movement, and just wanted to be left alone, to be friendly and honest with people. He was tanned very deeply; his brown eyes were slightly slanted and he had a long, narrow nose and high Mexican-Indian cheekbones.

Reinhold was wearing what had once been a white Moroccan shirt, and a pair of gray suede pants. I was sure he must have been suffocating from the heat in those pants, but they were probably all he had. He wore thick, heavy boots, too, whereas Miguel wore open sandals that exposed his filthy feet.

But I didn't really care how dirty they were. They were good kids and I was glad to have their company and be able to help them.

"When was the last time you had a good meal?" I asked.

"Oh, wow—it's so long I can't remember," Miguel answered.

"Well, here's some fruit, and cookies, and chocolates, if you're hungry, and—" I could barely finish the sentence. They were starving, and as soon as I offered the food they ravenously gulped it down. We stopped at a roadside stand for soft drinks, and they eagerly quenched their thirst.

Miguel was quite animated, while Reinhold (who spoke no English) sat quietly in the back. The boys were friendly and intelligent, and I persuaded them to come all the way to St. Tropez rather than just going to Nice. Since they couldn't afford hotel rooms, I offered Reinhold the car to sleep in overnight. He agreed that in the morning he would lock the car and leave a note on the windshield as to where we could find him. Miguel would stay in the hotel with me.

As we entered the hotel, the concierge looked at me questioningly. I had forgotten how strange I must have looked, accompanied by a dirty hippie-looking kid with long shaggy hair and worn clothing. However, she kindly changed my accommodation from single to double, though just for two nights. The hotel was busy and I'd have to resume my single reservation in two days.

When we got to the room, Miguel disappeared into the bathroom for about forty-five minutes. He was a different person when he emerged, squeaky-clean and dripping wet. He'd not only scrubbed thoroughly, he'd even cut his hair a litle shorter, trimmed his fingernails, shaved, and brushed his teeth. But what a disaster area the bathroom was! The floor was flooded, and there was sand and hair everywhere.

Clean and fresh, he stood there grinning sheepishly at me. He had a lithe, golden-brown body with just a light band around his middle, where the sun never got through his bathing suit. He had very little hair on his body, and his penis was small and delicate.

While he dried himself I cleaned up the bathroom and took a shower myself. Then we took a nap together. The moment his head hit the pillow, he drifted off into sleep. I enjoyed watching him, asleep and content, and a few minutes later I dozed off myself, thinking how good it felt to be able to please someone not with my body this time, but with a kind word, a ride, some cookies, and a comfortable bed to sleep in.

We woke and dressed around eight o'clock, and found a message from Reinhold to meet him at La Gorille, one of the restaurants near the port. It's one of the spots where the hippies and drug dealers sometimes gather, and the two boys wanted to pool what little money they had and buy me a few joints of grass. I settled on a fruit drink instead, and in turn treated them to a good meal of steak, potatoes, and salad.

Reinhold, hungry as a wolf, ignored the silverware—he devoured the steak in a few big gulps, using just his fingers, then did the same with his vegetables.

I whispered to him in German, "Take it easy, man. Cut your meat and behave like a human being."

But it was too late; he'd finished! He still looked hungry, though, so I gave him half of my steak and my vegetables, and this time he ate them slowly and properly. Miguel took it easy, but was obviously just as hungry as his friend. Between the two of them, they ate everything on the table—pickles, rolls, even the crumbs.

Then we walked around the yacht basin and enjoyed the night sounds of St. Tropez: kids on the street playing their guitars and singing, music coming up from the discotheques, the clatter of dinner from the restaurants and yachts. Wherever we went there was music, laughter, and happiness.

And that night Miguel and I made love. There were good vibrations between us and we knew that we could be friends and trust each other. He wasn't a great lover, but we were good together, and I couldn't help feeling protective toward him.

It was the only time we made love. From then on we slept together, and hugged and talked, but without sex. When I had to move back to my single room, he slept on the floor, which, as it turned out, he preferred to a bed.

The next day it was time for the boys to move on. They had some friends in Paris, so they left St. Tropez, their sleeping bags and rucksacks on their backs, and with two hundred francs (fifty dollars), which I'd tucked into Miguel's wallet. We'd had a good time together, but like the wanderers that the three of us were, it was time to say farewell and continue our separate lives.

LOOK, MA . . . NO CLOTHES!

My final quickie romance in St. Tropez was with a square Belgian industrialist in his late forties. We met one afternoon at l'Escale, when he very politely complimented me in the old-fashioned way, and asked if I'd be kind enough to join him for dinner. I was a bit lonesome and so was he, so I gladly accepted.

He was dressed like a banker, with little flair, but he was attractive and appealing. He was very masculine and I immediately sensed that he was a real up-front man— open, straightforward, honest. His name, if you can dig it, was Ferdinand. (And that's no bull!)

Ferdinand chose dinner for us both. We began with *Crème Flamande*—cream of onion and potato soup, rich with cream and butter. It was simple and scrumptious. I was in a mood for something unusual, so for me he chose *Aubergines Imam Bayeldi*—a dish of Turkish origin, combining eggplant, tomatoes, onions, currants, and spices. It was served on couscous—ground semolina steamed over a broth. It was delightful—a different taste sensation with almost each mouthful.

For himself, Ferdinand ordered *Poulet Duc de Berri*, a combination of sliced chicken breasts with dried peaches, almonds, sultanas, tomatoes, peppers, onions, garlic, and carrots. I couldn't resist a sample taste, and it was as wonderful as it looked. For wine, he ordered a sweet white Bordeaux, Chateau d'Yquem, and was especially pleased with its vintage, which was 1967. He was disappointed when I declined to join him in tasting the wine, but when I explained that I simply didn't drink, he graciously understood and didn't try to encourage me to try just a little bit, as so many drinkers do.

We were tempted to have *Glace à la Framboise*—ice cream with fresh raspberries—but finally moderation intervened, and Ferdinand called for *l'addition* instead. Needless to say, the bill was rather steep, but one of Ferdinand's greatest pleasures was a fine meal, and he pronounced it well worth every *centime*.

We were staying at the same hotel, and since we were so comfortable together, we decided to spend the night together. He was a gourmet in more ways than one, and pleasantly surprised me with his lovemaking. He certainly didn't appear to be the Don Juan type that most girls (myself included) would fall for. Indeed, he was square, quiet, and introverted. But beneath it all loomed an experienced lover who approached sex with gusto and imagination. He brought me to climax three times during our night, which is excellent for a first-timer with me.

The following day we spent in each other's company, and he explained that his family would be joining him within twenty-four hours. "So let's make the best of the brief time we have together," he suggested, and I was pleased with his frankness and good attitude. We crammed a lot of experience and conversation—in and out of each other's arms—into our day in the sun. And in the late afternoon we bumped into a boyhood friend of his named Claude, who was in St. Tropez with his wife, son, and daughter.

The six of us had dinner that evening—considerably less exotic than the *diner à deux* Ferdinand and I had enjoyed the previous night. Claude was a short, stocky man with twinkling, laughing eyes. His wife, Annette, was tall and striking, with jet-black hair, happy green eyes, and a ready smile. Their son, Marc, about ten, resembled Claude, and their daughter, Michele, was very much like Annette.

They were a happy family, full of humor and friendly gestures, and it was a pleasure to have dinner with them. The children were bright and polite, and our meal was cheerful and animated.

After dinner, Annette took the children back to the hotel. Then, following a relaxed hour or so over drinks at a terrace cafe, we four adults went for a drive to Pamplona Beach, about a half hour from the town.

It was one of those lovely, warm summer nights in St. Tropez, the stars sharing the sky with a full moon. The unusually calm sea had been pretty rough during the day, and the waves were still higher than normal, rippling in with a soft seabreeze.

The beach was completely empty, so we parked Claude's convertible near a few other deserted cars and took off all our clothes. Nude, the four of us walked down to the shore with only towels and my pocketbook, which contained our few valuables.

There were several hippies in sleeping bags on the beach, but they were fast asleep. It was about two o'clock in the morning when we got into the water, splashing each other and frolicking. The sea was relatively warm, but the wind was chilly when we came out of the water. We swam up against the big waves and went out further.

In the light of the full moon, from where I was, far out in the water, I could see vague shadows walking on the beach. I called to Annette, who was nearest me, then to Ferdinand and Claude. We hurried into shore, but we were too late.

The shadows on the beach turned into fully dressed figures, and as we came in they began to run. And for good reason. My pocketbook was gone, complete with the key to my rented motorbike, about two hundred francs (fifty dollars) in cash, Claude's watch, Annette's ring, and about four hundred francs belonging to Ferdinand.

The two men had escaped quickly, and we weren't exactly dressed to chase after them while raising the alarm. We did shout, though, calling, "Merde, les voleurs!" which might roughly translate as "Damn those thieves!"

(*Merde*, incidentally, is handy when you want to say *shit* in polite company. Theater people wish each other merde for good luck on opening nights, and a few years ago, Canadian Prime Minister Pierre Trudeau made the headlines when he told an angry group of strikers, *"Mange la merde."* It translates as "eat shit," although one reporter suggested that Trudeau was simply reminding the men that it was their lunchtime!)

The thieves had left our towels, fortunately, so we quickly dried off and raced for the car in the hope that we might still be able to catch them. Luckily, Claude had hidden the ignition key in the glove compartment rather than putting it in my purse. But we'd left the doors unlocked, and all our clothes were gone.

Our towels were barely enough to go around our waists, so you can imagine how odd we would look returning to our hotel at three in the morning. Ferdinand had the added problem of explaining to his wife, who would arrive the next day, the disappearance of a complete suit of clothing.

The car started, thankfully, but the lights didn't work. Those bastards must have fooled around under the hood, trying to jump the ignition and steal the car. They'd failed, but in the process had buggered up the electrical system.

Fortunately we still had our sense of humor—if nothing else. And we needed it, for we were in for a dangerous drive back to St. Tropez without lights. The only solution was to do it slowly and drive carefully. We drove with the car door ajar, since the interior light still functioned and would at least make us visible to oncoming traffic.

We had a few close shaves, I must admit, and we were becoming quite anxious when finally a young man in a Renault pulled up next to us and asked if he could help. Even though he was going in the opposite direction, he very kindly turned around and guided us back to St. Tropez, while we followed closely behind him. It was a tremendous relief and we were enormously grateful.

When we reached the town square where our hotel was, the embarrassing moment arrived and we had to get out of the car, all of us practically nude. The fellow who had guided us in took one look at the four of us and broke into hysterical laughter. We told him the story and, although he was clearly sympathetic, he couldn't help but guffaw and slap his thighs and clap us all about the shoulders. He couldn't wait to get home and tell his wife about it, though she probably accused him of inventing an outrageous excuse for coming home late.

Because we weren't in the best of situations, we couldn't invite him in for a drink, but thanked him profusely and promised to make up for it, fully dressed, if we met again.

We never did meet again, so if by any chance you happen to read this, dear sir with the red 1972 Renault 12, thank you again. If your wife still doesn't believe your alibi, you now have printed proof!

THE RETURN OF LARRY

Throughout the time I'd been back in Europe, I'd been inviting my old boyfriend, Larry, to come on over, but his business didn't let him get away. In my own way I still missed his companionship—he'd been my great, loyal friend in New York—and I certainly wanted to see him again. Finally, early in July, he was able to fly over and spend a whole three weeks with me. It was his first trip to Europe and I really think I was as excited as he was.

By this time, I almost felt like a native of St. Tropez, so I was well qualified to be his guide and translator. We spent great days in the sun, exploring the beaches, sipping drinks in the cafes, and flitting around in a rented Volkswagen. At night, I'd introduce him to the delights of French cuisine, then later we'd return to our room and practice a little French cooking of our own. After all, it had been over two months since we'd been together, so we had plenty of lost time to make up for. Which we did!

Some days we'd spend practically all our time at the beach, heading back to the hotel for a noon-hour siesta (we went to bed all right, but we rarely bothered to sleep!) and then back for another afternoon in the sun.

Other days we'd tour some of the quieter spots in the town. There's an old chapel, for instance, which is now a museum and houses an excellent collection of paintings —including works by the impressionist Henri Matisse, an adopted son of St. Tropez at the turn of the century, and townscapes by Maurice Utrillo. There is also a fine collection of marble sculpture and bronze statues. Larry enjoyed the maritime museum, which is part of a sixteenth-century citadel. In addition to seascapes and marine curios, we were fascinated by the model boats and ships. The citadel also gave us a magnificent view of the sparkling Mediterranean, and the Esterel and the Maures—nearby ranges of volcanic rock mountains and forests.

The days went by beautifully. The beaches, the boats, the bodies—everything was a turn-on for Larry, and because it all meant so much to him, I found myself enjoying it in a fresh way myself. As usual, the people were very friendly and hospitable, and Larry could barely get over the change from one day being in big anonymous New York to the next day being treated as a long-lost pal by virtual strangers in St. Tropez.

I introduced him to Leo and Marika, and to Freda, and we even had dinner together with Leo and Marika, as I'd hoped for. It was a fine evening, and it helped me realize just how much I did like them. It was good that we'd had our soul-baring confrontation, and that we'd separated when we did. Daily company is sometimes too much to handle in the early stages of a friendship, and it's possible that by trying to push things too quickly, we nearly destroyed something very special.

But having gone through our valley of tears, we now seemed on our way upward again to the peaks of friendship. Leo and Marika were planning to leave St. Tropez shortly, and so were Larry and I. So they decided to have a big farewell party at Ramatuelle and of course we were invited. I knew that it would be more than just a party, and I wondered if I'd really want to share Larry at a swing when I was jealously enjoying him all to myself. And I knew how Larry disliked mass orgies. But we happily and eagerly went. And what a night!

I'd originally written several pages about this fantastic stoned swing, but when Larry, the Silver Fox, decided a few months ago to write his own book, *My Life With Xaviera,* I allowed him to use that story, so I won't repeat it here. Suffice it to say it was unlike any orgy I'd ever been to. Larry and I felt very close, and we cried, screamed, laughed, and went wild for hours and hours.

PENTHOUSE BOUND

You'd think that opening a luxury hotel and casino on a Yugoslav island would be about as commercially viable as a cat house on Fire Island. A great location maybe. But a limited market.

But breaking the rules is the name of the game for Bob Guccione, publisher of *Penthouse* magazine, and his Penthouse Adriatic on the island of Krk (yes, that's how it's spelled—pronounced *krrrrrk!*) was designed to attract the high-rolling gamblers from the United States and Europe.

The spot chosen was superb: a sheltered coastline on the opposite side from the sea, with a beach that was seldom out of the sun.

Bob had asked me to come to the opening, to which he'd invited people from around the world who were in a position to influence the movements of those jet-set gamblers who roam the world looking for where the action is.

The Adriatic Sea flows north from the heel of the Italian boot to Venice. The sea's western coastline is Italy; its eastern shores are Yugoslav.

The island of Krk is hidden in the northern tip of the sea, near Rijeka. Getting there was definitely not half the fun. Larry and I had flown from Nice eastward over northern Italy to Venice, then over the tip of the Adriatic to Trieste. From there we drove across the border into Yugoslavia.

At the end of an exhausting journey that involved a car ferry to the island, we were given the kind of treatment you find in more and more hotels these days. We were refused a room. It needed a call to Guccione's office and the intercession of one of his aides to get us a good-sized linen closet. They should have had a sign reading "No Pets Allowed" because believe me, there wasn't room to swing a cat—let alone a pussy.

The closets were too small for our suitcases and all our stuff had to be spread on the floor. Most of the room was taken up with two single beds, which were so close a snore could extend from one to the other. It was all very harassing. Not only that, to leave our room involved tiptoeing over our knee-deep knickknackery. It was the first time I'd camped out in a so-called luxury hotel.

But the public areas of the hotel were magnificent and fully made up for the inconveniences of the rooms. The huge lobby was luxuriously appointed and high-ceilinged. The two pools—one indoor, the other outdoor—were Olympic size and equipped with saunas. The hotel facade was white stone, the kind of white you can't seem to find away from the Mediterranean, beautifully set between the blues of the sea and sky.

The gardens, too, were magnificent and sculptured, obviously the work of many hands; the kind of attention that can only be afforded in a low-cost labor market. In the grounds were clay tennis courts for the energetic, and for those that weren't the hotel basement was a fairyland (no, not that kind) of pool tables, bowling alleys, and pinball machines.

Because of the language barrier the staff wasn't exactly up to first-class standards. But what they lacked in understanding they made up for with courtesy and a desire to please that has vanished, along with the Stutz Bearcat and the five-cent cigar, in the rest of the world.

You'd ask for bread, and get salt. Ask for salt and you'd get a bottle of wine. Ask for wine, and who knows, you'd get directions to the washroom. It was hilarious. But you couldn't get angry with someone whose face shone with a desire to please. We just relaxed and put it down to understanding between nations.

The gambling was done in a casino which led off the lobby and stayed open until four in the morning. Not my scene. By four in the morning I wanted a pair of something other than dice in my hands. (Or whatever.) There was roulette, blackjack, craps, and *chemin de fer,* with the business so brisk that places at the crap table were being sold by scalpers.

The croupiers were all British and London-trained, many of them women, or as Bob called his hostesses, Penthouse Pets. Their costumes left little to the imagination. Or should I say left much to the imagination. They were bursting their seams, as were some of the men who stood very erect at the tables.

At the time of the opening there was no air-conditioning in the hotel and it became unbearably hot. But the men would stay at the tables, perspiration dripping down their dinner clothes, while their wives sat outside and sipped drinks into the early hours.

The casino manager told me that they were trying to get electric fans for the casino so that they wouldn't have to wring out the dinero bills each night. Once or twice it got so hot that some men who were standing at the tables stripped to their waists, their previously immaculate evening clothes lying on the floor like so many discarded swimsuits.

But the casino was simply going through the usual teething troubles and plans for air-conditioners in every room were well underway. And they proposed getting in slot machines, and a movie program for the gambling widows on those occasional rainy days.

The beautiful beach was but five minutes' walk from the hotel, and was usually inhabited by local island people. It was placed well away from the island's nudist beach, which—would you believe?—I never got to visit. One of the reasons was the hotel pool. It was so relaxing to sit beside the pool and be served iced drinks by those voluptuous English and Yugoslav pets.

The casino was the Yugoslav government's attempt to get into the big-time tourist business. Bob Guccione was merely operating the casino and hotel, the structure itself being the property of Mr. Tito and his minions, who were very much in evidence as soon as any decision had to be made. I suspected that Bob, whose deal involved setting up and operating the casino and getting a percentage of the room money, was slowly being driven mad by the bureaucratic meetings these guys demanded every time a water faucet needed repairing.

Maybe they were being cautious. But as Yugoslavia is Communist, the only country to break away from Moscow without getting zapped, perhaps they have every right to be cautious. But it was hard to visualize these people doing business with the West—where time is money.

They'd obviously gone in with Bob because his magazine-and-club setup was an ideal way of syphoning tourist dollars into a place that isn't exactly the hub of international travel. In the way Las Vegas gives freebee flights to known high rollers, Bob's job was to attract that kind of clientele by creating an attractive package. Not only would they gamble, and occupy the hotel's rooms, but there'd be lots of financial fallout for the rest of the country when they took side trips to beautiful resorts along the coast, places such as Dubrovnik.

The idea is great. But east is east and west is west. For instance, making the beautiful local girls cram themselves into costumes that obviously owed their creation to Chicago wasn't very bright. The girls should have worn their native clothes, which are quite stunning, and much more attractive for visitors coming to the country for the first time. On the same count, their complexions didn't need the rouge and heavy eyelashes they were made to wear.

Then there was the question of money. The waiters earned about sixty dollars a month. Sixty bucks! The price of a deluxe meal for two in the hotel's own restaurant. But they seemed happy enough. Maybe they liked playing capitalist. Who knows? We discovered that if we wanted to leave a tip and ensure the waiter got it, we didn't write it on the bill. We gave it in cash. All tips charged to our bill never found their way into the hands of the staff, but probably went to the state.

The waiters were so subservient to the system that they didn't tell us this. We found out from other sources. After all the meals when we'd put the tip on the bill, they merely laughed and smiled, and said thank you, knowing that not so much as one dinar would ever pass into their palms.

By the end of the trip we learned to leave cash, as did

most Americans; the combined tips in one evening often exceeded the waiter's monthly salary. But it was a different story when local Yugoslavs came to dine. They'd eat their heads off and then leave a four-dinar tip—which comes to about four cents.

The staff was not allowed to hang around the hotel unless on duty. Fraternization was just not allowed. And even the girls who worked in the boutiques on the lobby level couldn't socialize with a friendly customer. Only the manager and top personnel could enjoy a drink, or even dinner, with the high-rolling guests.

Not that the staff had that much time off. The casino, for instance, opened at four in the afternoon and didn't close till four the next morning. When they did have an hour off, the youngsters working there usually headed for the sun and sea to recharge their batteries. Or had a swift afternoon nap demanded by the long working hours.

Many of the guests didn't hang around the casino and pool the whole time, but took the opportunity to water ski, scuba dive, go boating, fish, play tennis or ping pong. Many had even brought their golf clubs. But the island possessed only a miniature course and this was not the kind of thing they could boast about back home. And what's a holiday without a hole in one, if you'll pardon the expression.

One evening, two of the senior hotel staff—Lou and Zlatko—invited Larry and me to a restaurant in a nearby fishing village, Malinska. It was just a few tiny houses grouped around a breakwater where small fishing boats lay at anchor, and a quaint hotel, where the restaurant was located. Inside, it was decorated with wooden carvings and wooden benches topped with foam pillows and looked truly old, reflecting the peasant origins of the people who lived there. It was delightful.

Now there was no confusion over the orders. Lou proceeded to rattle off the food we wanted in the native tongue and Larry and I just sat back and waited. The restaurant's specialty was scampi—scampi which only half an hour before had been enjoying their untroubled lives on the seabed.

Zlatko was a gourmet—of wine, food, and women, as

I found out some time later, in London. But if at that point it had been a choice between me or the scampi, the shrimp would have won hands, or tails, down.

When the food came, the scampi were fat and tender and served lovingly by the waitresses with smiles on their happy Slavic faces.

Do you remember the scene in the film *Tom Jones* where Tom eats supper with his chosen bedmate, and every juicy, sucking bite they take telegraphs the pleasures to come? Well, that's the way I felt watching Zlatko.

"You can take my woman any time," he said, wiping his chin, "but never never, take my scampi."

It simultaneously turned me on and turned me off. His eating was erotic, but for some strange reason, I've never cared for the taste or smell of fish. So I sat, contented with my huge, steaming dish of chicken paprikash.

While I watched Zlatko put away the scampi by the dozen, Lou told us tales about the island, which was once called Veglia, before one of the many wars that had swept over its shores.

The Greeks had owned it five hundred years before Christ, and at that time it was called Kurikta. For the next thousand years it was ruled by Rome before their withdrawal to defend their dying capital, at which time the Slavs took over. They ruled from 500 A.D. to about 1100, when the Venetians dropped by and planted their flag firmly on the foreshore, where it remained until Napoleon swept it into the net he was putting around Europe late in the eighteenth century.

In 1814, as part of the carve-up that saw Bonaparte stick his hand in his coat for the last time, Austria took it over. Then, when Austria backed the wrong side in 1914, a post-war deal saw it pass into the hands of Italy. The end of World War II saw it returned to the people who lived there—the Yugoslavs.

But with the kind of randiness the Mediterranean sun provokes, you can bet your sweet cheeks, and theirs, that the locals have strong infusions of Greek, Roman, Italian, and Austrian blood.

At one time the island, and much of adjacent Yugoslavia, had been ruled by the conquering Franco Pani family, who went down with a nasty case of slaughter in 1739 when they were stupid enough to take on King Ferdinand of Austria. Today there are fourteen thousand people on the island, complete with a high school whose brighter pupils go to a university on the mainland at Rijeka.

I asked Lou why the island looked so barren and unattractive when viewed from the mainland. He said the sea winds carried the salt spray all over the island and the salt killed off all growth. It had once been covered with trees, which had given protection from the winds and ensured plant life. But the Venetians needed the wood to reconstruct Venice and had cut down every tree in the place—an early example of ripping off natural resources. In their wake the island became barren, though if the present state of Venice is any indication, the gods are having their own back. Venice is slowly settling into the sea.

When dinner was done and we were returning to the hotel, I asked Lou how the local Yugoslavs felt about the casino and the hotel—wide open capitalism in a Communist state. He said they didn't mind. They enjoyed making more money than they ever had before and were not envious of the rich Americans who came there. They hadn't become greedy or pushy—yet—and worked just as hard to serve Yugoslavs as they did for foreign tourists with much more money to spend. (Though Lou hoped they would eventually learn to give more attention to the Americans.)

But in the hotel itself there were also a lot of Europeans who came for a few days: Italians, Frenchmen, Germans, and the odd Russian. However, the gambling was done basically by Americans and a few rich Germans, for Yugoslavs were forbidden to enter the gambling area; indeed, their currency was not accepted. Dollars were the currency of the tables.

It was late and dark, and as we approached the hotel, near the beach, the air was full of cries, groans, and assorted huffings and puffings. Zlatko explained that late-night open-air sex was very popular, and that that beach had seen more bangs than an antique steam hammer. It may have been the only beach in the world where it wasn't the steady beat of the sea that had turned rocks into sand.

I didn't know how expert this screwing was because I'd never made love with a Yugoslav. But then I met Vladimir. . . .

VIRILE VLADIMIR

Vladimir was a photographer from Montenegro, in southern Yugoslavia . . . an incredibly handsome man, built like a bear, with jet-black hair, high Slavic cheekbones, and a smile that made any woman say "take me!" We'd gone to a remote part of the island to take some photos of the now-famous Xaviera, both clothed and nude; some for *Penthouse*, some for my private collection. (Someday I'll donate them to the Smithsonian Institution just to see their reaction.)

I was lying on the beach, naked, stimulating myself to make my nipples erect for the camera, when Vladimir looked down at me and said, in Italian, "If ever I got into bed with you I'd destroy you with my frenzy and passion."

"Lots of men have said that," I told him.

"None from Montenegro."

I looked up at him—the long, thick black hair, the strong, black, matted chest, and the always-horny-looking mouth framed by a long, drooping moustache—and wondered if this was true, or just good old Latin-lover bullshit.

I didn't realize then that the Montenegro area bred passionate people; fiery lovers who just about broke each other apart with passion. They seemed to be quiet, charming, and docile, until they hit the bedsprings—and then they went berserk.

Then, a few days later, Vladimir was sitting at the pool one afternoon when Larry wasn't about, just wearing a brief pair of trunks, making no attempt to hide the silky pubic hair that curled from his crotch. I lay beside him, sipping orange juice.

"You were talking bullshit," I said.

"About what?" said Vladimir, quivering. Women just don't talk to men like that on his turf.

"Montenegrans being great lovers. I checked with one of the girls here and she says they're all talk."

"Which one?" he said, his eyes flashing over the girls going about their jobs, as if he might detect her on the spot and show her otherwise.

"Never mind which one. That's what I heard."

"I'd break her in half."

"How do I know it's not just talk?"

"Come to my villa . . . if you dare," he replied.

With that he jumped to his feet and charged off toward his home, on the balls of his feet, as if expecting an enemy at any minute. In his mind I suppose he was. And I was it.

I thought about following him. Cockteasing was something I'd never believed in. For most women in my home country it was a national pastime. But here I was . . . if I didn't go, I'd be guilty of something I didn't believe in. If I did go . . . well, maybe he wasn't conning me, and I'd get my comeuppance.

I resolved to apologize, and tell him I was merely pulling his leg. (Oops!) His villa wasn't far—we'd been there the other day. So I walked over, tapped at the door, and called his name. It opened swiftly and he was standing inside with nothing on.

I said, "Listen, Vladimir . . ."

They were my last words for nearly an hour.

He just threw out a long, hairy arm and pulled me into the house and onto a bed. The next moments were a blurr. I remembered my dress coming off with a renting sound and this huge erect penis flashing before my eyes as he stripped me with all the dexterity of Attila the Hun. I'd always believed in the old saying "When rape is inevitable, lie back and enjoy it." So that's what I did.

I've never been one for acrobatics during fucking, but this time I had no option. I was thrown around like a rag doll. He held me upside down while he sucked between my legs. Next second I was on all fours, being driven around the tiny room like there was a bulldozer behind me. Then I was spread-eagled on the bed, taking it with great, lung-shattering thuds, then sideways while he held me horizontal with his long, strong arms.

He had a cock like a bull's and even with my vaginal capacity it was driving right into me like a stake.

Suddenly I was facing the wall, being driven up it literally and metaphorically, feet off the ground, while he roared great romantic phrases in his native language. I figured they were romantic. He sure as hell wasn't asking me the time.

Then I was looking out of the window. What was I doing looking out of the window? My head was popping in and out like a cuckoo clock gone mad. Then he rolled right over on his back, taking me with him, and we did a backward roll onto the carpet, Vladimir still driving like a maniac. A sudden flick of the body and he was on top again, not once having moved his prick out of me.

For the first time he looked me in the eyes.

"Is it bullshit?" he asked.

"Well . . ." I said. I shouldn't have hesitated. He put his hands under the small of my back and virtually lifted my hips off the ground and thrust me down onto him like a toy. He wasn't just big . . . he was *big!*

Then up. Then down. I was just this tiny thing on his prick and he was moving me up and down like a yo-yo, giving my torso a sudden twist like he was driving in a screw . . . which I suppose he was.

On and on and on. Until we came with such fury that one of the bed's legs actually collapsed, and we both slipped onto the floor, still united. I was battered, bruised, and torn apart by the time that great, gushing torrent sprayed my insides like a hose pipe.

I was totally exhausted. Vladimir pulled out his prick, and it was just as big as when he'd started.

"Do you believe now?" he said.

I was in no condition to argue.

"I believe," I said.

"Good."

Then he picked me up gently and carried me to the bed, and made love to me slowly, sweetly, and with incredible tenderness, as if massaging all the hurts I had suffered earlier.

Finally he dressed me slowly, patted me on the buttocks, and said, "If anyone asks you what kind of lovers Montenegrans are, what will you say?"

There was no way I was going to go through that again. Well . . . not right away.

"Fantastic," I said.

"Good. You'll have to go now."

The reason he wanted me to go immediately became obvious. There was a knock on the door. As I went out, he let in a local peasant girl, a wide-hipped Slav with enormous boobs.

I didn't believe it. But I wasn't going to hang around to find out. I had merely been the appetizer; she would be the entree.

I walked back to the hotel weakly . . . my knees were like jelly, I ached all over, and my clothes looked like I'd caught my knickers in a revolving door.

I flopped into my room and almost passed out. I was carrying about six gallons of sperm and every time I moved, a muscle somewhere or other screamed for mercy.

By the time Larry came in, I had my head together. But there was no way anyone would believe I'd just come from the vicar's tea party. He was mad as hell, demanding to know who it was, and why had I done it.

Would he have believed me if I'd cried rape? No way! So we had one of those stupid arguments that are part of any relationship, then we made up over dinner, which I devoured like I hadn't eaten for three days.

Later, over a cool drink on the terrace, Lou joined us and the talk turned to the men's magazines in Yugoslavia. He introduced us to the editor of one, a publication called *Adam and Eve*, who happened to be a guest at the hotel. His magazine, which he showed me, was quite explicit in its photography, and similar to *Penthouse* in format.

The editor told me that five years ago there was no way such magazines would have been allowed. But recently the regulations had been relaxed, and the authorities had become much more lenient. Now, informative columns and photos on sexual topics had become quite the fashion.

During the conversation we heard our first Yugoslav sexy joke. Very often jokes don't translate, but let's see what you think of this one:

Three Yugoslav girls wanted to be village prostitutes, and while there was lots of trade, they felt they lacked the expert knowledge of Parisian hookers. So they went to Paris to learn, promising to return with their newfound expertise.

All the people of the village saw them off, and wished them luck. Some months later, only two of the girls returned.

"What about the third?" the villagers demanded.

"She's staying in Paris for further study."

"But why, what happened?"

"She flunked her French orals!"

Oh well, maybe you had to be there!

However, I'm digressing. Our lazy idyll on the island of Krk soon came to an end and Larry and I set off in our rented car, heading north.

As we left the ferry we took one last look at the island . . . a bare-rocked Las Vegas on the Adriatic, owned by Communists, run by capitalists, and frequented by the high rollers of any nation. A strange combination that was never questioned by the poor people who lived there . . . a warm, pleasant people who seemed happy and contented with their place in life.

It had been a great holiday. Strange, but great.

As Larry drove north I thought of suggesting a quick trip south to Montenegro. Then I looked at my still-bruised forearm and had second thoughts!

We kept heading northwest, and back into Italy—first to ancient and picturesque Verona (where you can actually see the family homes of Romeo and Juliet) and then to Milan.

Larry and I spent just a few days in Milan, where my lovely friend Fiona was now living. There wasn't enough time to get to know the city, so I planned to return alone, later on.

For the moment, Larry and I pushed on to Switzerland.

XAVIERA GOES ALPINE

Remember the great Orson Welles and Joseph Cotton film *The Third Man*? Besides all that zither music, I clearly remember the character named Harry Lime dropping this *bon mot:* "Switzerland has had centuries of peace . . . and all it's ever produced is the cuckoo clock!"

That's a harsh put-down, but in it lies a kernel of truth. Like the Dutch, the Swiss are stolid; not by chance have they become the world's bankers. This has its advantages and disadvantages, though. The Swiss are industrious, frugal, and they have an awesome respect for the law, no matter how petty. And this leads to a certain lack of sparkle.

However, this is more than offset by the almost manicured cleanliness of the country and the complete absence of political disturbances such as those that periodically rip apart other European countries.

So when Larry and I emerged from the Mont Blanc tunnel, on our way from Milan to Zurich—our rented car sharing the train journey with us—we entered a new world. Ahead lay a people of upright posture, quiet manners, and charming, healthy looks.

The girls were clean, cute, and still wearing minidresses, revealing legs that were bronzed, shapely, and owed much to outdoor living. Few were fat or carrying overloaded bust-and-butt equipment, like many of the women in Italy. The Swiss men were more gentlemanly but not as charming as their southern counterparts, and they certainly weren't as pinch-happy, I'm glad to say.

The city of Zurich was bright and clean with the heady air of the mountains sweeping through its wide, handsome streets. The stores were magnificent and the prices, particularly for leather goods and anything involving clockwork, were extremely reasonable. But the women's clothing shops were keyed to rich older matrons, and lacked pizzaz.

After a few short days in Zurich, Larry had to return to the States. To be honest, I was happy to be on my own again, free as a bird, the world my oyster. We'd been getting edgy with each other since Yugoslavia, and I sensed that we were truly beginning to drift apart.

I'd made a tentative date with Giorgio, a Swiss friend, while Larry was still around, and that had led to a bad fight, and the irony was that Giorgio couldn't get away to see me. But when Larry left, I called another Swiss friend, and he thought he could spend some time with me. But there was a day or so to spend in and around Zurich, so I drove around the beautiful lakes near the city, enjoying the careless freedom of the guitar-strumming hippies (much cleaner-looking than their American counterparts), some of them trying to earn a dollar by selling their handicrafts at the roadside.

I briefly thought of going native for a while, but I knew the lure of luxury too well. Besides, I was looking forward to my date with Andreas, a Swiss banker I'd met in St. Tropez.

He's extremely tall—about six feet three—broad shouldered and well built, in his late thirties. He manages massive amounts of money for international banks and skips around the continent like a kid playing hopscotch. He has blue eyes, a fairly long Italian nose, and is half bald— the result, he thinks, of service at sea and having to wear a cap during his compulsory years with the army.

Quiet and extremely bright, he has a good sense of humor, but he's worked sufficient years in international finance so that he's cynical and tends to trust no one. In fact there's something of a wall around him, a protective wall. But once you get through it, he's easy to handle. Then the scars of his two failed marriages become less obvious.

He'd been married at twenty and again at thirty-three, each marriage ending in divorce. He was still good friends with his second wife, and very close to his son and daughter by his first marriage.

Andreas had the kind of presence you'd expect to find in someone who deals in that strange, low-key world of high finance. But this didn't stop him from being a wild and passionate lover. He conducted his affairs, both business and bed, from a palatial home high in Megeve, an exclusive and expensive jet-set hangout on the French side of the Alps.

We had met in St. Tropez, and had only known each other for a few days. Some things he told me, others I found out for myself. He was rich, an excellent linguist, and he lived well. He liked only the best places, primarily because their high rates kept away the general public.

Andreas was a connoisseur of women, literature, art, music, mountains, and skiing—probably in that order. He despised scroungers, hangers-on, and the types who frequent jet-set playgrounds looking for the good life at someone else's expense.

To make sure we had a firm date, I called Andreas when I was ready to leave Zurich.

"Andreas, it's Xaviera," I said in French. "I'm ready to leave."

"Ah, yes, madame, the portfolio for your aunt." He had the wrong Xaviera. Or did he? "I think a few days up in Megeve discussing it might be the best way of reaching a decision. Away from the office."

He certainly was cautious. Was his office bugged? Or were the operators likely to listen in? The ever-cautious Andreas wasn't taking any chances.

"I'll meet you at the President Hotel in Geneva," he told me.

"That's at least three hours drive, I figure."

"Good. I'll see you there at six this evening. And thank you for calling!"

My tiny Fiat sped south at 150 kilometers an hour (about ninety mph), whizzing past everything in sight except the odd, aristocratic Mercedes, Ferrari, or Jaguar. Suddenly, without thinking, I was two-wheeling around a bend with a thousand-foot drop. I slowed down, using the gears the way I'd been taught, the control and handling of the car bringing me pleasure of a kind I'd never experienced in huge American cars. It was giving me such a bang that by the time I drove into the outskirts of Geneva, I felt quite sensually stimulated.

Which brings me to another subject. I wonder what it is about movement and motion that makes women erotic? I've known girls who on land are about as sexually active as a washing machine, and who become raving nymphos as soon as they board a ship. One theory I've heard is that the constant rhythm of the ship's engines is synchronized with a woman's own rhythm cycle, setting off in her subconscious mind a chain reaction that releases all her inhibitions. Maybe jet engines do the same for stewardesses, which explains their legendary horniness.

But back to Geneva: I drove so fast that I arrived a full two hours before I was due. (Talk about coming prematurely!) So I parked the car and did some walking and window shopping.

Geneva is traditionally the international capital, a leftover from the days when it hosted the League of Nations, and it was thought that a central world government would stop future wars. Along with the League came many international organizations and these, together with banking, are still the mainstays of the city.

The sights and shopping were so attractive that I got bock to the hotel fifteen minutes past our scheduled six o'clock rendezvous. Andreas was waiting for me in the bar, his impatient fingers rat-tat-tatting on the bar counter. He'd already checked out of the hotel and was impatient to start for Megeve.

He kissed me on the cheek (in the cloistered halls of the Hotel President, anything more would have been considered outright sexual exhibitionism) and we both downed a drink—the usual O.J. on the rocks for me.

I was exhausted from the drive and the shopping, and was dying to take a shower and freshen up. But as Andreas had vacated his room, I had to step back into the car and head into the setting sun. It was an hour and fifteen minutes to Megeve, across the French border.

He led in his car and I followed in the Fiat, straining to keep clear of the treacherous edges of the mountain roads, and at the same time trying to keep up with his powerful Mercedes. I was in no shape for this final part of the day, and when we finally got to Megeve my nerves were twanging like bedsprings. (There I go again . . . always thinking about bed!)

But I was soothed a little by the very sight of the town of Megeve, picturesque as a postcard, but with a chic sophistication. It was poised on a mountainside with a literally breathtaking view. (If you've ever seen the film *Charade*, the opening scene was shot in Megeve.)

The narrow streets lined with houses of wood and clay in the distinctive Alpine style gave a feeling of pampered luxury. And the hotels, with their elaborate ski facilities—soon to be crowded by the winter sports set—glowed with an aura of expensive simplicity. There are no less than ninety-two hotels there, plus a casino. Some of the hotels were closed for the summer—to reopen later, during the ski season. Their owners also had establishments in St. Tropez, so they could profit from both the summer and winter seasons. Usually the same crowd patronized both towns. Megeve, though, is about twice as expensive as St. Tropez; no place to go on a pension.

Though it was the off-season when we arrived, it was a delightful place to be, the heat of the summer sun counterbalanced by crisp, tingly air so rich in oxygen that it was difficult to stay awake after dinner. And dinner was always huge because the appetite goes berserk in that kind of atmosphere. The clarity and purity of the air was to be expected. We were fifteen hundred meters—almost five thousand feet—above sea level; the kind of height where your lungs start to complain about the extra work required to suck in the oxygen.

Andreas and I stopped off for a drink at Hotel Mont Blanc (from the mountain of the same name, as they say) and the owner gave us a great welcome, kissing me on both cheeks. Obviously Andreas was well-known and respected. Although he had lived there three years, he was still considered a mystery by the locals. And quiet mystery men always seem to get the most respect. Nobody knows just how important they might be.

Andreas enjoyed his anonymous hermit's life in his mountainside chalet.

"Xaviera, there's one thing I should warn you about,"

he murmured over drinks. "My mother is staying at the house briefly. For about a week, in fact. But don't let it worry you."

"Why should I, Andreas?"

"It's just that she hasn't seen me in fourteen months. And you know how mothers are."

He said it in such a way that he obviously didn't like the way mothers are. He told me that she lived in Como, Italy, looking after her own mother, who was ninety-seven years old. He had never gotten on well with his family, particularly after his father died when Andreas was just thirteen.

"I stayed on. But I was a loner. I had nothing in common with the two women in the house, and while I'm glad they gave me the best education they could, I don't think I'll ever forgive my mother for the Catholic junk I was forced to believe. It ruined both my marriages.

"All that puritanical stuff. It took me years to purge myself of it, and I'll never stop blaming my mother."

I let the subject die out naturally as it was something I didn't care to pursue, and we finished our drinks, left the hotel, and aimed our cars toward his chalet, high in the mountains.

The winding road was lined with lovely houses owned by famous industrialists, movie stars, and others to whom land taxes aren't much more than petty cash.

Shortly we arrived at the highest and biggest of the chalets—Andreas's. As we pulled into the driveway, which already was occupied by a jeep and a white sports car, his mother opened the door to greet us. She was a healthy, friendly woman in a fresh, knee-length dress who immediately embraced her son, obviously with much love.

He was cool toward her and this upset me, for she seemed most gracious and loving. I felt he really should have let past mistakes be forgotten.

However, the chalet was perfection! There were five bedrooms on the second floor, each with its own bathtub, toilet, shower, and bidet. Each had a panoramic view of the valleys. The beds were truly king-size, something Andreas, with his height, would naturally insist upon, and they were covered with feather comforters instead of blankets. These eiderdowns, long popular in Europe, are

now beginning to catch on in North America, and I think they're much superior to blankets. They're warmer, yet more comfortable because they're very lightweight.

From the ground floor two narrow stairwells ran up to an open-sided gallery floor, which commanded a view of the sunken living room, the hallway, and the general living area. On this level were two beds and furnishings that blended with the rest of the house—a mixture of antiques and the heavy wooden tables, benches, and chairs that are traditional in the area.

There were also copper pots, candle holders, and iron washstands that were all quite old, yet they blended well with the furnishings to create a mood that was both traditionally simple and luxuriously modern.

Andreas and I unpacked, then joined his mother for late dinner—*salade niceoise* and cold cuts. Afterward, the three of us retired to the sunken living room for hot chocolate next to the fire. I could just imagine the shouts of children, the laughter of a family, and I suspect that in her heart, Andreas's mother still hoped for such a time.

Later, after a bath and a short nap, Andreas and I set out for the valley to sample some of the off-season night life, and his mother padded off to bed—obviously delighted to be sharing her son's home for a few days.

In town, we headed for Le Glamour, a discotheque owned by the famous French film stuntman Jacques Besard. There was a long-haired American kid acting as disc jockey, and he certainly knew how to "honk out the heavies," as they say in Top-Forty Land. He played a lot of Elton John and Cat Stevens, as well as two numbers which were sweeping France at the time, "Decadence" and—believe it or not—"Popcorn, Anarchist System." These two are really wild, and the only way to dance to them is pretending to be a suicidal chicken with a bad coordination problem. It was pretty exhausting, and after a while both Andreas and I were too pooped to Popcorn anymore, so we dragged our tired bodies back to his chalet, and after a tingling shower we fell asleep in each other's arms.

SKY-HIGH

On my first morning in Megeve, I awoke as the first light crept into my room. From where I lay in bed, I could see much of the mountainscape surrounding the chalet—magnificent, snowy peaks arranged so beautifully that one might imagine a Hollywood director had designed it all.

Andreas was asleep, and whether it was a piss hard-on or he was in that stage of sleep (called Rapid-Eye-Movement sleep, the cycle when we dream, and certain physical functions take place. For instance, if you were sleepwalking or having a wet dream, it would happen during the REM cycles) where men are usually semierect, the result was the same: halfway down his long body, there was a little Alpine peak underneath the covers. So I reached down and started to stroke him gently.

He groaned in his sleep and I watched his face. There's nothing more satisfying than making someone feel erotic while they're still asleep, and watching their face as they become aware of what's going on. Or coming off.

Andreas's eyes opened, and I'll swear that his prick rose in time to his eyelids. In a flash it stirred from a sleep-boner to a big, hard, fuck-ready erection. I went down on him, gobbling deep and wet, tightening my lips around an enlarged head. Andreas put his hands on my head, holding it still, and started driving his buttocks up and down, fucking my mouth. Hard. Suddenly I knew what *Deep Throat* was all about. He was quite a mouthful.

Up and down he drove, doing a grinding motion that sent the head of his prick ricocheting off the insides of my mouth with a delightful, slippery sensation.

With one great spasm he shot into me. Usually I prefer

orange juice first thing in the morning, but I certainly wasn't going to complain about this kind of room service.

We showered together, then went downstairs to greet his mother.

The day was warm, but the breeze carried the first signs of winter's chill. Happily, this was more than offset by the strong summer sun.

Over breakfast, Andreas's mother, who seemed to approve of me, suggested to her son that we take the jeep and climb the mountains, along the tracks where normal cars can't go.

The jeep, though old and beaten up, was in good mechanical shape with a high-clearance suspension, four-wheel drive, and multiple gear ratios. (Bet you didn't know I talked that language!) It could climb with a mountain goat, and I had the uneasy feeling that it might have to.

Our first stop, still on an asphalt road, was at another Jacques Besard (the stuntman) establishment, a restaurant called Du Cristomet, which has a riding school attached to it. Jacques was busily occupied with his riding pupils and couldn't share a drink with us, but Andreas had a stiff one anyway. (A drink, I mean.) He knew what was ahead.

He said we'd go up Mont Jailliet, which adjoins Mont Blanc. We drove on and on, and the road got narrower and rougher. Eventually it changed into rough wheel tracks and by then we were so high above sea level that my ears popped, just as they do in aircraft.

The higher we went, the more fantastic the view, though I was getting a little concerned about the road and the height. My viewing of the village below, with its tin roofs, was tinged with worry.

But on we pressed. When Andreas says he's going somewhere, he goes. It's that kind of determination that made him wealthy.

To take my mind off our ascent, I looked down on the workers in the fields below; small, sturdy, figures carrying tools through the fields, helping their fathers earn a living. Husky, bronzed young boys whose muscles owed much to the tremendously hard work they were expected to do on the farm. When we passed them earlier I was surprised that they waved to us and even threw friendly kisses—to us, the high livers who enjoyed the discoes, resorts, and a mode of life that they would never know. One would almost expect them to resent us.

Suddenly my reveries were ended. By a cloud.

That's right—the peak of the mountain was covered by a cloud, and we were driving into it, lurching higher and higher, a determined Andreas at the wheel. Abruptly the valley disappeared into a heavy mist and the breeze blowing up heralded an *orage*—a local storm. So here we were, two thousand meters high—sixty-six hundred feet above sea level—on a slowly disappearing cart track wide enough for just one vehicle and bumpy enough to make me feel ill.

I felt even more ill as Andreas, intent on taking me to the top, gripped the bouncing wheel with both white-knuckled hands.

I tried to cover up my fear by smiling bravely, and I forbade my mind to even consider the dangers of a high wind blowing us over the edge, or rain causing the jeep to slide sideways, out of control. Andreas tried to ease my mind by talking about the vehicle's nonlock braking system, and its very low gear, which made the engine race even when we were going slowly. And the four-wheel drive that enabled it to crawl out of trouble even if one set of wheels was bogged down.

His reassurances helped. But not much.

The jeep was open to the elements and the approaching rain would surely put the finishing touches to my flimsy summer dress, which even now was trembling with my shivers. This Swiss banker was slowly freezing my personal assets. The higher we got, the colder it became until eventually we were in edelweiss territory, the home of the flower that grows on the upper slopes of the Alps.

At any moment I expected Julie Andrews to come charging out of the mist with selected highlights from *The Sound of Music*. Instead, we got "Raindrops Keep Falling on My Head."

Eventually the road disappeared altogether, and we plunged and bucked through wet, spongy turf. My mind went back to the days in South Africa when I traveled through rough bush in a Land Rover. On that trip, too, the jeep made its own road through virgin territory.

I must say that I prefer quite a different type of virgin territory, and when it comes to climbing peaks, my favorites are those that end with an orgasm.

Still, I couldn't help feeling a certain affection for the jeep we'd entrusted our lives to, and also for dear determined Andreas, who was going to get me to the top of that mountain even if it killed him—at which point I quickly changed my thoughts.

Finally, I couldn't hold it any longer.

"Let's go back, Andreas," I said. The rain was pelting down now and I was bursting for a pee. Probably through sheer, stark terror.

The minute I said it, Andreas hit the brakes and the jeep slid sideways, out of control. I heard someone scream. It was me! And we came to a stop.

"I have to pee," I said lamely.

"Then go ahead!"

By this time I could see the humor of the situation. "Maybe I won't, after all," I giggled. "Why should I mix my golden juices with this colorless Alpine dishwater?"

At that, we both broke with laughter, and as the tension escaped, Andreas relaxed. With a touch of throttle and brake, he turned the jeep around and we headed back . . . to civilization, discotheques, and flush toilets.

We made our way back cautiously, but even so the wheels slipped and skidded and we nearly got stuck once. Slowly the road began to seem like a road again, and when we emerged from the clouds onto the main road into town, I thanked my lucky stars. I'd been a brave guest and a foolhardy passenger.

The road was so bumpy that I joked to Andreas that it would make a perfect do-it-yourself abortion trail if he knew anyone who wanted to open a Swiss "finishing" school.

He said he'd keep it in mind.

We parked the spattered jeep in front of the Mont Blanc Hotel and staggered toward the entrance looking like two water rats after a flood.

We both headed for the nearest plumbing, where I sighed with clear, unalloyed joy as I relieved my bladder. Then, because we were wet and damp, Andreas suggested we go for a sauna and massage.

His regular masseur, Nantel, greeted us. He was about twenty-six years old, muscular, groovy, and as straight as a bull. He gave us both a splendid, relaxing massage which took away all the tension from our recent expedition.

Then Andreas and I went into the sauna for some fun. All that bouncing around on the mountain roads had made me rather horny, and Nantel's firm fingers had helped even more to put me in a lovemaking mood.

Now, I've read many books where sex takes place in a sauna or steamroom, and let me tell you, it just isn't possible without planning, no matter how sexy you feel. The reason—the heat prevents a man from keeping his erection for long. It's something to do with the blood supply.

I won't say Andreas didn't give it the old college try. We spent our time bouncing back and forth to the cold showers trying to keep his hard-on so that we could enjoy sex while our bodies were running with our own lubricating sweat.

Eventually we got a good one and I stood on the lower of the two benches while Andreas stood on the floor. Because of his height, this put his cock on the same level as my cunt. Bending my knees, I eased myself onto him. I could feel his lovely sweat dropping on my back and round onto my tits, which themselves were pouring with perspiration, partly from the heat of the sauna and partly from my excitement.

But it was no go. Andreas's prick lost its cutting edge just as it was getting interesting. So it was back to the showers to revive him with a cold spray and some expert stroking. Within minutes we were back in business and we rushed back into the sauna.

This time there was no hanging about. I threw him down on his back on one of the benches and slid onto him —with room to spare.

We had to strike while the iron was hot, so I pumped up and down on him like an old maid in a cucumber patch. Sweaty and slippery, we grappled and thudded, our wetness making sucking, slithery noises which were as sexy as the fucking itself. Within minutes he came with great, writhing spasms of the body, which almost threw me off. I rode him down like a rodeo rider until he subsided into a dripping mass beneath me.

We must have made a lot of noise because at that point Nantel opened the door to see if everything was all right. I saw that he had an erection straining his trainer's shorts and suspected he'd been watching.

At that point I was sufficiently juiced to take on the crew of the Cutty Sark after three months at sea. So I left Andreas to recover while I went with Nantel to complete my massage. A quick shower and I was on my back while Nantel stroked lovely baby oil all over my body, and up between my legs; which was the last place I needed lubrication.

I reached over, undid his zipper, and flipped out his fairly short but massively thick cock.

I've seen some thick ones in my time, but this beauty was like a tree trunk. As Nantel reached over to massage my tits, I lolled my head sideways and put his cock in my mouth. It was so thick I could hardly get it in.

I was giving him the head-job to end all head-jobs when Andreas came back from the sauna. Without batting an eyelid, he lay down on the next couch, covered himself with a sheet, and played sidewalk superintendent. He knew I was playing a game and wasn't jealous. But I must admit that having Andreas watching me suck this gigantically thick prick while having my tits and cunt oiled and stroked gave me a great feeling.

Eventually Nantel remembered my clitoris and while massaging my thighs with one hand, he finger-trembled my clit with the other, giving me a great, gasping orgasm, forcing me to take my mouth off his cock before I choked.

Afterward Andreas and I lay on the same couch under a sheet, playing with each other while Nantel wandered around the room doing his thing and giving us the inside gossip of the massage business.

He told us about the movie stars he'd handled during his years in Megeve. The one he admired most was Brigitte Bardot who, he said, had the best body he'd seen for someone her age.

He also presented these hand-held findings:

Very few female film stars had silicone treatments for their breasts. Face lifts, however, were a dime a dozen.

Most French actors were gay, or at the very best, switch hitters with a preference for the left-handed path. There were the exceptions such as Jean-Paul Belmondo, who was a real woman-hungry sexpot.

(I'd met Belmondo in the Papagayo in St. Tropez. He's a fantastic man, one of the few film stars who look as good in the flesh as they do on screen. He was indifferent, rough, attractively ugly, and supersexy. What you see is what you get! At about the same time, I'd met George Hamilton, the actor once engaged to President Johnson's daughter. Beside Belmondo he was a pretty mother's-boy type. Very well dressed, very well mannered, he looked almost too good to be true. It says something for the psychology of women that they'd prefer the rough tough ugliness of a Belmondo any time. End of digression.)

After we'd gotten up enough energy to leave the couch, Nantel gave us a more than friendly farewell and we went home for dinner. Later in the evening, when we went back to Jacques Besard's discotheque, who should we bump in to but Nantel!

It wasn't pure coincidence. He'd tracked us down and Andreas, who suspected his intentions, treated him aloofly. But that didn't deter Nantel. He sat down at our table and Andreas, against his true wishes, felt common courtesy demanded that he offer the masseur a drink. Of course Nantel accepted . . . and immediately asked me for a dance.

It doesn't require much imagination to realize the kind of scene that was developing.

I got up and danced with Nantel; it was the Popcorn, and I liked it. I was grooving away, but within minutes I could feel Andreas's jealous eyes piercing my back. I turned to look at him. He was getting a bad case of the green-eyed yellow goddess.

I quickly broke off the dance with Nantel and returned to Andreas, putting my arms around his neck and asking what was wrong. He insisted that we leave, so we went out and sat in his car, where he immediately offered a value judgment on men like Nantel: "He's a parasite.

He may be a good masseur, but he uses the connections his job gives him to intrude into his customers' private lives."

He then went on to give me a most detailed lecture on how he felt men and women should act toward one another, and I realized that Andreas, for all his intelligence and charm, could not afford tolerance for other people's behavior patterns. I knew he'd felt jealousy, I loved him for it, and also realized that I didn't choose to be his captive woman. But I didn't want to spoil what had been a lovely evening, so I suggested we drive right home and make love. It proved to be one of the better ideas since The Pill.

Soon it was time to leave Andreas's sumptuous cabin in the sky and go wherever my wanderlust would take me. Andreas and his mother wanted me to stay longer, but I'd set my mind on leaving; I have this in-built timing device that tells me when to move on.

They were both in the driveway when I pointed the Fiat down the mountainside, waving and calling out their *adieus*. They'd made me promise to return for a visit in January or February to learn how to ski and enjoy Megeve at its best.

I've never skied, for the thought of breaking my legs is too much to contemplate. But, I thought, maybe I'd try.

The car slipped past the handsome young workers in the fields as I headed once more for the stronger sun of the lowlands.

ARTISTIC LICENSE

From Megeve, it wasn't a long drive southeast into Italy. So with my rented Fiat, I was on my way again through the curvy Alpine trails—Xaviera, Queen of the Road!

Within a few hours I was in hot and humid Milan. It's the country's number two city, with a population of about a million and a half but certainly not a typically Italian city—it's chiefly a business center, and practically everyone lives in apartment buildings, giving it a strange, American tone. But there are still enough landmarks and treasures to ensure a firm Italian touch. If nothing else, it's world famous as the home of Leonardo da Vinci's masterpiece, *The Last Supper*—as well as another thousand or so of the great Renaissance artist's drawings.

I called up Fiona, who had been my roommate once in New York. Unfortunately she had a date that night, then was off to Rome for a few days the next morning. But she did have time to introduce me to a good friend of hers, who is one of Italy's most famous surrealist painters, a chubby, teddy bear of a man whom I'll call Dominic.

Fiona took me to his luxurious penthouse suite, which was in almost total darkness. When my eyes adjusted, I met the maestro and his paintings. Surrealist indeed! Most of them were bizarre mutations of women.

He had shoulder-length black hair and big, dark brown eyes which always shifted nervously, never looking at me as he spoke. Because of his weight and beard, I couldn't guess his age, but put it somewhere between thirty-eight and forty-eight. He spontaneously offered me accommodation for the night, and equally spontaneously I accepted.

Because of her date, Fiona had to leave at once, and I found myself alone with Dominic.

Exhausted from the long, hot drive, I wanted to refresh myself and relax, so I went to take a shower. I was barely beginning to shed my clothes when Dominic suddenly appeared in my room and attacked me. Jesus, before I knew what was happening, he was grunting and moaning, brutally fucking me. It was most unpleasant for me, but *he* seemed rather pleased with the effort. I felt like a prostitute again, exchanging a fuck for a place to stay. Well, I thought, now he owed me some hospitality, for sure!

Of course one side of me said "Get as far away from this man as fast as possible," but I didn't know anyone else in Milan, I was tired from the drive, and besides, now that he'd acted like a typical male bastard, I felt like the avenging angel, and wanted to stick around to see what I could do to get back at him, and to deal with him in kind. So I stayed.

I felt a little better when I'd showered and changed clothes, and when I went downstairs Dominic was in the living room, having a drink and reading the papers. "How do you feel now?" he said, as though the combination of his fuck and a bracing shower should make me feel ecstatic. What a male chauvinist pig—oink, oink, you fathead!

"Dominic, was it really necessary for you to attack me like some elephant in heat?" I said sharply in my best Italian.

"Well, my dear, I knew of your reputation and I thought you might know something of me as a ladies' man, perhaps from Fiona, and I wanted you to know it was true. Why, didn't you enjoy our little lovemaking?"

"I like to have some say in the matter, and I like making love too much to have men jump me on the way to the shower." Here it was, that typical macho bullshit—all I have to do is stick my dick into you and it's supposed to be heaven—so I added, "Well, it's your loss . . . I can be a tigress in bed when I'm properly stimulated in that direction. But you just wanted to get your rocks off —you'd rather shove than love. . . ."

Dominic looked highly indignant at my pointing out

what a whang-bang ding-dong he was in bed—in fact, I wouldn't have been surprised if he'd gotten up and hit me—but the telephone rang and he got up and answered it instead. (Saved by the bell!)

It turned out to be Fiona. She felt badly about not having time to spend with me, so she'd broken her date and would join us for the evening. I was grateful to her—for more than one reason.

Dominic told her to meet us at a certain restaurant for dinner, and then asked me, very solicitiously, I thought, if I wanted to dress for dinner.

"I *am* dressed for dinner," I said. "Don't you approve of how I look?"

"I do, I do," he said. Then he added, "Look, I did misunderstand—and I'm sorry about before." I could tell he wasn't much given to apologies, so I felt much better about being there. In fact, I felt all keyed-up, ready for a most pleasant evening.

I wasn't disappointed. The three of us dined at a lovely restaurant on Via Sant' Andrea, furnished with warm woods and leathers, and an excellent kitchen. We all had linguine made with clams, oil, and garlic—bad breath be damned—and some delicious sweets—diet also be damned—and Dominic couldn't have been more charming and entertaining. His stories about the art world had us in garlicking laughter.

Dominic had to leave for a short time to attend a gallery opening—he invited us along, but we declined because Fiona and I had some catching up to do on each other's lives—and around eleven o'clock he rejoined us and invited us to his studio.

It was a studio beyond all expectations—four spacious, high-ceilinged rooms in an old Milanese building, furnished with beautiful antiques side by side with modern sculptures and, of course, his own paintings. Dominic was fascinated by animals and women (he'd had several marriages!) and he combined the two in his paintings in the most unusual fashions.

Dominic's working studio was large, brightly lit, and in its own way somewhat merry. But the really interesting room was his office: walls filled with thousands of books, mostly on art. In one corner a black, shell-shaped chair dangled from the ceiling. It was one of his inventions, and as Fiona sat and swung in it, her feet resting on a matching extension, she said it must have been made for her. In fact, Dominic had made it. I found myself in a chaise longue with a tiger-skin color, and with my beige dress, I fitted in well with the color scheme. Dominic seated himself behind his imposing desk, and we sat for hours and talked about his life, his paintings, and his feelings.

He came from a wealthy family and was able to pursue his love for art without needing to take a job to support himself. His boom as an artist began about fifteen years ago, and since then the prices for his works have skyrocketed.

I asked him what he thought of certain modern painters.

"They're fine," he responded enthusiastically. "Let them do their own thing, they're all great artists." So I pressed him for more definite opinions.

"Look, I don't want to give my opinion," he finally lashed out. "They all think they're great artists, great painters—let them be happy with that. I don't have to buy their paintings. But let me tell you one thing. I'm not interested in soup cans and green stamps as the subject of art. I'm a neo-classicist and a surrealist. Sometimes I feel like painting in full formal dress, including cummerbund, coat, and tails. And other times I feel like painting in the nude, stark naked in the moonlight! But to get back to these 'pop' painters, let me say this: sick men shouldn't use the beautiful name of art for their vulgar work."

Hell, at least that was a statement to remember! He'd finally opened up and given an opinion. But as he spoke of ugliness, Fiona replied that she couldn't understand how Dominic appreciated ugliness—ugly people, ugly situations.

"There's beauty in ugliness," he said. "It depends on how you look at it. Most artists soften ugliness when they paint it. It is good to show ugliness sometimes. It might be cruel, but show it."

His advice to young artists today is, "Forget your era and modern art. Just be academic."

Dominic earns staggering amounts of money for his work, and even has a small international staff to look after his interests. He lives an exceptionally good life, traveling a great deal, and his hobbies are classical music, tennis, and fencing—though if he did a lot more of the latter two, he would have been in better shape.

At three o'clock our evening ended. Fiona went home, and Dominic and I returned to his suite. He kindly supplied me with a comfortable room of my own, to my relief and pleasure, and explained that he would have to leave in the morning for West Berlin for a major show of his work, and wasn't sure just when he'd be back.

"That's all right," I said. "I don't mind being alone. I'd like to really explore the city and get to know it. I've only spent a few days here."

"No, no, you shouldn't be lonely. I have a young friend I would like to introduce you to—with your permission, of course—whom I think you might enjoy. His father owns some of my work, and so does he. He's a bit high-strung, but otherwise a most intelligent young man."

"All right, if you think I'd enjoy meeting him."

"Yes, I think you will. He's rather unusual for his age...."

Antonio was the young man's name, and I wondered what was so unusual about him. Did he have two heads, or what? Or did his penis have two heads? Hmmm, that would be unusual.

MILANESE MACHO

When I awoke the next day, feeling well rested after a long night's sleep, Dominic had already left. There was a note on the dining room table telling me where to find things. It also said that Antonio would be calling up around noon to introduce himself.

I made myself a late breakfast—or early lunch, depending upon how you look at it—and at almost precisely twelve o'clock the phone rang and Antonio, now just a rather elegant voice at the other end, was asking if I would care to spend some of the afternoon with him seeing part of the city.

I thanked him for the kind invitation and said I'd be ready in twenty minutes. I was already terribly curious to meet the young man who belonged to the nice, cultured voice.

As it happened, my afternoon date didn't turn out to be a matinee idol. On the other hand, he wasn't a fairy tale prince doing a frog number, either. He had an arrogant, sensitive face which belied his somewhat nervous manner. About twenty-four, he was tall, on the slim side, and very well groomed. But it was his face which was most compelling: a full, sensuous mouth, sharp nose, large, greenish-brown melancholic eyes, and thick black hair curling over his ears. Really an interesting face!

We sat and had coffee for a while, and Antonio proved himself eager and friendly. In a brief time I learned a great deal about him. For one thing, he was absolutely paranoid about police, the result of time he had spent in Communist countries. His father, who was an Italian Jew but had avoided the Nazi camps, had left Italy shortly after the war to set up a factory in Romania. Meanwhile, Antonio stayed with his mother in Milan while his father tried his luck in Bucharest. His luck included acquiring a young Romanian mistress.

At the time Antonio's father was sixty-three and the girl was eighteen. They had a satisfactory affair for several years, and then the girl began making demands. She wanted the man to smuggle her and her mother into Italy. He agreed, to make her happy, and then his troubles began.

The Romanian police descended on the man and he was constantly harassed, so he returned to Italy and sent Antonio in his stead to Bucharest to manage the business.

Antonio promptly managed to get himself into trouble, too, and lived in a constant nightmare where he imagined that at any moment Communist police would swoop down on him and throw him into prison forever. I never learned whether he had actually done something specific which he expected to get caught for, or if it was just his paranoia.

He also despised his Catholic mother for the way she had treated his father during the war—before Antonio was born, in fact. Apparently she became anti-Semitic, and nearly caused her husband to be thrown into a concentration camp.

He also said that, before the war, Milan had been one of the first Italian cities to support Mussolini, yet was one of the first to fight against the German occupation. And the city suffered great damage during the war years, losing many of its greatest buildings.

But there was still much beauty that remained, Antonio said, suggesting that we take a walk to Brera, the district around the art school and the Brera Museum. It wasn't just a cultural area, Antonio said—black market goods were sold there, as well as drugs. So the area was popular for a number of reasons, with the bars frequented by art students and chic young Milanese. The two most popular bars, Antonio pointed out, were Bar del'Angolo on Via Formentini, and Il Nero. He didn't know exactly why, but he much preferred the Bar del'Angolo, so we went there.

The Bar del'Angolo ranged over two floors. The downstairs was a restaurant only, while upstairs was both a bar and restaurant area. Entering from the street, we came directly into a large room with wooden floors and a bar across one end, and an eating-drinking area in the far corner—very small, with perhaps ten tables. It was all white stucco, covered with old Coca-Cola posters and various antique signs. There were about a hundred bodies in the place, all being well taken care of by a chubby-faced bartender who seemed to love everyone.

The place had a nice ambience, I had to agree to that. We passed a very pleasant two hours there, talking with students and a few of Antonio's well-heeled young friends, and there seemed to be nothing awkward about the mixture of poor art students and wealthy young businessmen. Well, one difference—the students drank the cheapest red wine and the others drank scotch or vintage Italian champagne —Asti Spumante Valdo Brut. Even that was cheap by North American standards (about $2.50 a liter in the stores). The inexpensive red wine—*vino sciolto rosso,* literally "loose unpacked red wine"—was available for forty-five cents a liter. People would bring their empty bottles to the store for refills.

Teetotaling Xaviera, of course, stayed with *acqua minerale*—sparkling water—or lemonade.

By now, since it was time to eat, Antonio took me to a small nearby restaurant, which was a favorite of his. There were perhaps six tables, with red and white checked cloths; the Sicilian owners and their relatives cooked and served the most delicious food. Antonio pronounced his swordfish "out of this world," while I had terrific spaghetti with *salsa verde*—a green sauce made with olive oil, garlic, and fresh parsley. *Delicioso!*

Afterward, Antonio took me to Via Fiori Chiari in the Brera district. It was a narrow street leading to a small square, where all the action took place. There were hippies of all nationalities—birds of every conceivable different feather, all in the uniform of worn-out blue jeans, unwashed hair, and sandaled feet.

Some were painting on canvas, some on the pavement; others were sketching caricatures of passersby. There were Italians peddling black market cigarettes, booze, and records; and there were beggars of all nationalities with outstretched hands, specifying, *"Cento lire, per favore!"* (Sixteen cents—the Italian equivalent of asking for a dime.)

Here and there were groups of young girls making and

selling strings of beads and handmade jewelry. Erotic posters, phallic symbols, and hash pipes were also flourishing.

Antonio introduced me to an ugly fellow named Nino who was the power in the square and the local pusher, responsible for most of the hashish and marijuana dealing in the area. Nino was cooling it at the time because the police were getting pretty heavy in their raids. They would come in with tear gas, beating the kids and destroying everything in sight.

As we left the piazza, I nearly bumped into an old lady. She must have been at least sixty-five, slightly bent and wearing baggy old pants and undersized sandals. Her hair was short, and thick glasses obscured her small, mousy face. A familiar tattoo was visible on her bare arm. She must have been one of the lucky ones who'd escaped wartime atrocities.

But she remembered them, no doubt, and found that a frequent supply of dope helped erase the worst of it. As she passed us she held up her left arm in the "up-with-communism" salute so familiar in Europe.

"A local character," Antonio commented, and we curiously decided to follow her for a while. She stopped at the kids peddling hot records, and without a word indicated that she wanted to find some grass. She pulled a pack of cigarettes from her worn pocketbook and mimed the actions of smoking a joint. The hippies laughed at her and directed her toward a trattoria around the corner. She tottered off slowly and I suspected that she was already pretty stoned. But when she went past the little cafe and disappeared down a side street, looking for her pusher, we decided to let her go and deal in peace.

We dropped in the restaurant and it was full of kids playing chess. This cafe is remarkable because it's the gathering place of artists and writers and the better class of hippies from all over the world, and although many of them couldn't speak to each other because of the language barriers, they were all able to communicate through their chess boards.

Antonio introduced me to the female bartender, a friendly chick who seemed butch. She smiled, hugged him, and shook my hand very firmly, then offered us a drink.

We sat around for half an hour and enjoyed the scene, then strolled the few blocks to Antonio's apartment.

It was a big one bedroom apartment with a marble floor, white rugs, a white leather couch, modern furniture, and —yes—Dominic's paintings on the walls. The bedroom was cozy, with a multicolored bedspread.

We watched television for a half hour or so, and then Antonio led me to the bed, just naturally presuming that lovemaking was part of our evening. I didn't mind the idea at all, since I was feeling very mellow after a lovely day.

Antonio had a nice wiry body, but because of his youth or else nervousness, he wasn't in very good control of his sexual faculties, and suffered from premature ejaculation the moment he entered me. So, in order to try and please me, he put his head between my legs and began to work on my pussy, but in such a manner that it hurt. Not only was he painfully chewing on my clitoris and sucking very hard, but his beard—ten o'clock shadow, I guess—was irritating my skin.

"Antonio, please," I said, "I don't mind fucking you, but let's do it right. Calm down, take it easy. Let's not rush . . . we can just relax together and talk for a while."

He improved slightly later that night, but I suspected I was wasting my time in bed with him.

The following day, Antonio was anxious for me to meet some of his friends, especially Ilo.

"He's my only good friend. I've known him since I was a child, and I love him. Whatever Ilo says, I'll do."

He phoned Ilo and told him we were coming over. When we arrived, Ilo was still in bed, looking like a refugee from a "most wanted" poster, scruffy-looking with long kinky hair. Ilo was an art director in an advertising agency, and though he was the same age as Antonio, he seemed far more composed, even cynical and indifferent.

Antonio had told me that he was trying to put together a business deal and this would tie up the weekend. After that, he suggested, we could go to Positano, a sea resort which he thought I'd like even more than St. Tropez. We'd even talked earlier about his taking a week's vacation during the hot Milanese summer, but now he was discussing it with Ilo, as though looking for his approval.

"Look, why do you have to go away for so long?" Ilo

responded, right on cue. "Why not just make little trips here and there?"

I was really amazed at Antonio's behavior. It was as though he couldn't make a decision without Ilo's approval, and Ilo seemed to relish the role. Some S-M friendship this was!

They continued talking, almost as if I weren't there, and then—to my astonishment!—Antonio hopped onto the bed next to Ilo and put his arms around Ilo's shoulders and gave him a more than friendly embrace. And then—to my complete astonishment—suddenly yanked down his jeans, letting his cock hang free, at the same time pulling back the sheet to reveal Ilo's nude body.

And there they were, both with their cocks out—Antonio's circumcised, Ilo's unclipped, but both a good, firm size—and this double-dork scene was sort of amusing, if not particularly sexy—kind of a three-second striptease, with all the provocative preliminaries missing.

Ilo now got up and padded off to the bathroom for his morning pee, and while he was out of the room, Antonio asked me if I'd mind going down on his chum as a special favor. Some friendship, indeed; I sure didn't want to grant this favor, but Antonio actually begged me, so I reluctantly agreed to do it. Ilo, for his part, must have been expecting that I'd help him out because when he returned from the bathroom, he had washed up and his cock, though uncircumcised, was fresh and pleasant. So I began to suck him off while Antonio sat in a chair and played voyeur.

Ilo was quite passive and it took me at least twenty minutes to make him come . . . he let me do all the work. Afterward he confessed that he'd had a busy time the night before with a hooker he'd picked up on the street for ten thousand lire (about sixteen dollars), who had spent the night with him—a bargain at that price! They'd fucked several times and so while he appreciated my expert cocksucking, he was sexually exhausted.

Thus I certainly didn't enjoy sex with him, nor, for that matter, had I enjoyed making love with Antonio the night before, and as I ask myself why I was doing all this, I really can't find a satisfactory answer. Maybe it was a neurotic hangover from my session with Leo and Marika. I was giving, and not taking. . . .

After Ilo showered, we went out to a cafe for lunch where we met a friend of theirs—Paulo, with his roommate, Vittorio. It was hot and humid, a stifling Saturday, so the four boys and I decided to drive to Lago Maggiore, where we could escape the oppressive atmosphere and get a little sun.

Lago Maggiore is a large, enchanting lake in the Italian lake district, north of Milan, in the Alps. Part of the lake, in fact, is in Switzerland. The scenery is beautiful, as you can imagine, and it's a typically popular weekend resort—nothing fancy, but pleasant and relaxing. Tragically, many of the Italian lakes, like North American ones, are badly polluted and swimming is unsafe. Even though the water here was something less than sparkling clean, it was refreshing and we enjoyed our swimming, and then relaxed over drinks at the Villa Aminta, an old mansion that's now a hotel. Paulo and Vittorio had to be back in Milan that evening, so when they talked of leaving, Ilo said he'd return with them. Immediately Antonio jumped in and said, "Fine, Xaviera and I will follow you in her car so you won't have to drive back alone."

This made me furious. "Antonio, make up your bloody mind!" I exclaimed, slamming my fist on the table. "You told me we'd stay overnight here, so let's stick to our plans. It's late, I'm exhausted, and I don't feel like another two-hour drive just to suffocate in the hot city."

Antonio looked to Ilo for advice, if not consent.

"Stay," Ilo told him. "I want you to stay here. Check into the hotel, have a good time, and come back relaxed tomorrow. Get some sun and swim some more . . . you need it, you're looking pale."

So that settled it for Antonio. As Ilo got into the car with the other two boys, he and Antonio waved tender goodbyes, as if they were lovers. By now I had suspicions about the relationship between these two . . . could it be they were both closet queers? But Antonio and I had a good time at Lago Maggiore, and his lovemaking improved a bit that night. He was clearly more relaxed.

LOVE (for sale) ITALIAN-STYLE

Sunday was a lovely peaceful day with lots of sun and swimming, and at five o'clock we left the hotel and returned to Milan. The moment we hit the city, Antonio called Ilo and we arranged to meet for dinner at nine.

It was only seven, and we had two hours before dinner. Antonio opened a bottle of vodka while I sipped bitter lemon. He would have preferred to smoke some hash, he said, but since the heat was on in the drug trade, it was difficult to get any. So instead he polished off the entire bottle of vodka and then opened a second bottle. He had said that he was afraid of turning into an alcoholic someday, and I could see why. By nine o'clock he'd passed out, drunk as a lord.

With Antonio out cold, snoring on the couch, I entertained myself by listening to music, and especially enjoyed a cassette by Nina Simone. It was called "To Love Somebody," and she sang dynamite arrangements of tunes by Cohen, Dylan, and the Beatles—including "Suzanne," "I Shall Be Released," "Revolution," and others. She's a great singer, and she put me in a beautiful mood.

It was after nine-thirty, and Antonio was still asleep when the phone rang. Of course it was Ilo, wondering where we were. I explained the situation, and suggested that he come over. Perhaps Antonio would come back to life, I said, and we could still go out for dinner.

Ilo arrived in a few minutes, along with Paulo and Vittorio, and they were in fine spirits. Ilo looked much better than he had at our first meeting—he had shaved and was smartly dressed, so I guess I'd caught him on a bad day Saturday morning. The three boys woke Antonio, and before long we were all very animated and ready to go out and have a good time.

Since it was a four-to-one ratio, I thought of calling Fiona. She should be home, after her weekend in Rome with a film producer. I called and she was there. Yes, she'd be interested in joining us for dinner. But she made it quite clear that she wasn't interested in any sex—mentioning, in fact, that her period had just begun.

I told the boys that she was going to join us, and they were quite excited.

"She's a good friend of mine," I said, "so take it easy with her. And don't try to rape her . . . skip the sex scene. If anyone has to fuck, I'll do it if I have to. But please, leave her alone!"

They seemed to understand, and so we bounced out of the apartment, picked up Fiona, and moved on to a friendly neighborhood trattoria. We all had spaghetti as an appetizer, then a great dish of veal Milanese and a huge bowl of *insalata verde*—green salad—with oil and vinegar. For dessert, delicious Italian ice cream. We ate outside, beneath a roof of wooden beams and leafy trees. The restaurant's clientele was quite varied, including quiet, romantic couples, obvious tourists, and a large, loud table of hoody types with their overly made-up wives.

Ilo pointed out one of the men, a very heavyset gent, saying that he was one of Milan's best-known smugglers, and that in earlier years he had been the city's most celebrated robber. This gangster had served plenty of time in jail, but was still in a position to conduct his underworld affairs without too much restraint, according to Ilo.

After dinner, Ilo said he had a special treat in mind for us—a trip to the Parca Ravizza, *the* center for male prostitution. Paulo and Vittorio said they would rather skip that scene, which was just as well since the car wouldn't hold six people. They said good night, and we took off. It was a twenty-minute drive from Milan, most of it on quiet side roads, so you really had to know the place to get there.

These weren't simply male homosexual hustlers, but rather transvestites all tarted up to a fare-thee-well. The "girls" really looked great, and in all honesty were a lot more attractive than their legitimate female counterparts in downtown Milan, a lot of whom were old and sad.

Ilo explained to me how the scene operated. A major difference between the transvestites and real female prostitutes is simply that the women do less for more money. The typical line from the female hookers, when approaching a man on the street, is, *"Tre mille lire col guanto oppure cinque piu la camera"*—three thousand lire (five dollars) with a rubber, five more (eight dollars) for the room. And, like their Dutch sisters, the Italian hookers are genuine experts at slipping a condom over their john's dick as they go down on him.

Incidentally, since you can't find it in your *Michelin Guide to Italy, "Vuòi che ti succhio?"* means "Do you want a blow-job?" And if you're just passing through and thus in a hurry, you can pick up a streetwalker in your car, give her three thousand lire, park your vehicle in a side street, and she'll suck you off right at the wheel. Then you can drop her back at the corner, and—whoops!—No hard feelings.

In 1948, Ilo told me, bordellos were closed down in Italy, but street prostitution remains wide open in cities such as Naples, Rome, Genoa, Milan, and Venice. And Bologna is *the* city for *poppare*—cocksucking—with both male and female prostitutes serving an ever-growing clientele.

After the antiprostitution law was passed in 1948, thousands of students and people who sympathized with the pros flocked together in the streets to protest, but to no avail. Bordellos now are underground, and found only through careful selection and word of mouth (hmmm!) recommendation. As usual, because of yet another country's unrealistic attitude toward professional sex, venereal disease has become one of Italy's leading problems.

Another difference between these female and male prostitutes, Ilo went on, is that the transvestites never use a rubber and, more to the point (ahem!), the drag acts will offer their johns an entirely different sensation. The man who deliberately visits a transvestite doesn't feel like he's being homosexual because in his mind he's making it with a good-looking woman, and often the john will make it with the queen via the rear route, or else settle for a blow-job. However, to maintain the illusion, frequently the queen will remain dressed.

It seems quite common in Italy (as well as in France, particularly in the Bois de Boulogne area of Paris) for a lot of so-called straight heterosexual men to enjoy sex with a transvestite without going through the guilt of homosexual hang-ups. Possibly the customers are latently bisexual but not liberated enough to really make it with another man. It's a curious scene.

The boys really knew their way around Parca Ravizza, and we made a few passes, jokingly, at some of the "girls." Although there were already four of us in the car, we invited one particularly striking creature to join us. Her name was Giselle and she was wearing a tight-fitting, low-cut sweater, a miniskirt, black stockings, and spiked high heels. Her tits were enormous, easily twice as big as my own. Fiona and I looked at her in fascination. She'd had a nose job, and her face was very feminine and pretty, without a trace of beard. Her hair was shoulder-length—it wasn't a wig—and held back with a pink ribbon. She wore false eyelashes, but not too much makeup; she had slim legs and a narrow waistline. What's more, she had a fascinating story to tell.

"It sounds strange, I know," she began, "but I used to be a secretary at Buckingham Palace in London. But all my life I've felt like a woman, although my body was male. I'm a transsexual, not a transvestite, and I want to continue my life as a real woman. I've been taking estrogen treatment, which is responsible for my body hair disappearing, and for my face and breasts filling out. I still have my male genitals, but as soon as I can afford it, I'll have the ultimate operation, and finally I'll have a vagina!"

I found her royal connection pretty hard to swallow—though if you're going to be a queen, what better place to start? I also resisted the urge to quiz her on the royal family's inside dope.

Giselle acted and talked like an elegant woman, and I could easily see how men would enjoy making love with her. Like so many male hustlers, she was friendly, had a sense of humor, and was considerably less hardened than the females. The *signora* (female) prostitutes were hard and bitter, always in a rush to get the trick done, while their *signori* (male) counterparts seemed to really enjoy their way of life.

One of Giselle's regular customers paid her over sixty thousand lire—about a hundred dollars—to spend two hours smoking hash and fucking her up the ass. That's not much money in my books, but for Italy it's apparently quite good, compared to the street price of ten bucks a pop.

Because she was so attractive, and much in demand, she never had to settle for less than twenty-five dollars, and normally fifty, for a routine trick. Her cottage was just five minutes from the street where she was hustling, so she normally took her clients there.

She told us that the police were quite rough at times— as ruthless as they were in Brera with the black market peddlers and dope pushers. They'd often come around and harass the hookers—especially the transvestites—but, of course, like all over the world, the right money in the right hands takes care of everything.

Milan during the summer months was not the best place for really good hustling, Giselle said, so she was planning to go to Genoa for a few weeks.

Genoa is a city on the Italian Riviera coast, and the country's major seaport. It's the birthplace of Christopher Columbus, and its history dates far back to earliest times. And these days, according to Giselle, it's really wild, with hustling of every description: transsexuals, pregnant women, transvestites, tired old hosebags—you name it, said Giselle, and they're there—standing on porches and in doorways along the steep harbor streets or else in the bars along the harbor. This area is so full of drunken, fuck-minded sailors, that it's known as the Barberry Shore— and it lives up to its name.

Each street hooker has her own appointed territory where she can solicit, but she can't move out of that area into anyone else's. It's a tough racket, controlled with an iron fist by a legion of pimps who completely take over the girls' lives. The *padroni* (pimps) can be vicious, too, and often rob and mug the customers; as a natural consequence, fights and murders occur regularly.

Giselle, however, was in the fortunate position of being able to function as a callgirl there, so she never had to get involved in the more sordid aspects of her trade. In fact she really enjoyed her business, although, she explained, she also needed the money to cover her medical bills, which could easily amount to eight thousand dollars.

We were all quite taken by her and when, after half an hour, she had to leave us, we were sorry that she had to go. Feeling warmly toward her, we thanked her for having joined us, and sincerely wished her success and happiness. What a switch, from Queen's helper to helpful queen!

Yet another interesting aspect of the Parca Ravizza is its peek freaks—voyeurs who get their rocks off through the weirdest things.

Antonio said, "Let's get out of the car for a few minutes, and you'll see something strange."

Fiona decided to remain in the car while the boys and I got out and walked into the park. Antonio and Ilo then went up to a tree and pissed against it.

As soon as they opened their flies and pulled out their cocks, they attracted a bunch of men who'd been waiting in the bushes. As the boys peed, a dozen of these men furiously began to jack off, completely turned on by the urinating duo.

Talk about different strokes for different folks!

I'd had my fill of Milan's kinky corners, so we drove back to Antonio's apartment. He still wasn't quite sober and was clinging to Fiona, who, I must say, looked great. When we got to the apartment, she agreed to come up and join us all for a nightcap.

Almost the second we got in, Antonio took Fiona by the hand and led her into his bedroom. I let five minutes go by and then, since she still hadn't emerged, I went in to make sure he wasn't trying to pressure her into sex. There was Antonio, lying naked on his bed, his body slightly burned from our day at the lake, his cock hanging limp, and his expression very vexed. He glared at me.

Fiona was standing next to the bed with a cynical smile on her face, fully dressed, while Antonio kept trying to yank her down on the bed. I could tell that Fiona didn't know how to handle the situation without getting angry, so *I* got furious instead.

"Antonio!" I shouted. "You're a real asshole! I warned you earlier not to try anything with my girlfriend!"

Then he started yelling back. "You jealous bitch! Why did you come in here, anyway, disturbing something beautiful? Fiona's marvelous, and I really dig her, and she was just about to get undressed—weren't you, eh?"

Fiona quickly indicated to me that it wasn't true, and she clearly wanted to get out of this unhappy scene.

"Antonio, you're stupid, drunk, and a sex nut," I told him. "If I hadn't taken care of you and your buddy already, I might understand. But you've hardly been deprived of sex, so why do you have to attack Fiona? Besides, look at you, you look like a pooped schmuck with your sunburn and your drunk limp cock!"

Then I called Ilo in.

"Ilo, Fiona doesn't feel well, and Antonio won't leave her alone. Would you mind taking her home, please?"

Ilo responded by pulling down his pants and coming over to me.

"Maybe if you and I gave them a good example," he leered, "Fiona might get in the proper mood."

I was so pissed off that I took Fiona by the arm, hissing at her, "Look, it's your fault, too! You shouldn't stay here in the bedroom, looking sad and embarrassed. Why didn't you simply get up and leave, and join us in the living room?"

Meanwhile, Antonio was drunkenly yelling obscenities at us and the whole scene was a mess. But eventually things calmed down and Ilo drove Fiona home. I would've gone with her, but she had no room to put me up, so I had to stay there, but certainly didn't share a bed with Antonio.

Sadly, Antonio, who had seemed so interesting to me, had turned out to be merely a spoiled, immature boy, and neither his money nor his education had taught him much about respect, decency, and personal relationships. So in the morning I told him I'd be moving along. He looked at me like a sad little puppy, but I quickly packed my bags again and went to find a hotel for my final day in the Italian city.

A FRIENDLY FINALE

I checked into the Excelsior Gallia Hotel, in Piazza Duca d'Aosta. It was a large, comfortable hotel, and best of all, it was completely air-conditioned. Then, because I'd be flying out of Italy, I returned my rented car. When I checked into the C.I.T. office (the Italian equivalent to Hertz or Avis), I was faced with another happy surprise.

There, behind the counter, with a little sign saying "English Spoken," was yet another girl I knew. She was from Chicago, and everyone used to call her La Divina—she was short and pretty with lovely eyes and dark flowing hair, and although she had a tendency to gain weight, she was one of the happiest and most sought-after callgirls in the Windy City. She always used to delight everyone with her fantasies about becoming a European princess or Frank Sinatra's next bride, and she knew everything about every movie ever made. She was also extremely capable between the sheets, I'd heard.

She took one look at me and just squealed with delight.

"Xaviera!" she cried, her face lighting up. She hugged me and said, to use her own words, how "thrilled to the titties" she was to see me. It was just the kind of reception I needed after my depressing night, and I was thrilled to see her, too. It was also great to be speaking English again. She quickly checked in my car, then informed her supervisor that she would be taking off a few hours.

"Oh no, you're not," he snapped in Italian. "We're too busy. It's out of the question."

"In that case, I'm taking the entire week off. You'll have to replace me."

This took the man quite by surprise, and while he seemed to be figuring out how to react, she quickly put the "closed" sign on her counter, picked up her purse, linked her arm with mine, and we strutted out.

It turned out that she'd saved a lot of money and gone straight. She'd moved to Montreal and then to Toronto for a while, and now she'd come to Milan with two girlfriends.

She took me to their apartment—a tiny place on the top floor of a building off Piazza Piemonte. There was a wide living room with French windows leading to a Mussolini balcony—a stone balcony with room for perhaps three people. Then there was a small kitchen with a cozy table in it, and another set of French windows leading out to a larger balcony. This one had a big yellow whale, a purple octopus, and a big blue fish painted along its solid stone edge—the handiwork of Louise, one of the girlfriends who shared the flat. The third girl was Lena, a native Milanese. The three of them had met while working at a television station in Toronto, and had each saved enough money to take a year off and spend some time in Europe.

Their little apartment—they laughingly called it Casa Tarta—was neat and warm. Because the three girls shared a bedroom, it was also perfectly equipped for orgies, although La Divina admitted that she'd actually been on the wagon for a few months.

Lena and Louise were both out, so La Div left a note for them, saying there'd be a fourth for supper, and took me for a personal tour of the town. Besides Brera and Parca Ravizza, I'd seen some of the city during the few days I'd spent there with Larry between Yugosalvia and Switzerland. But La Divina was anxious to show off her new town, and so enthusiastic that she made it all fresh for me.

We walked along the Via Manzoni and had tea in the Grand Hotel Continental, then wandered down Via Monte Napoleone, the home of the great stores—Cardin, Dior, the exclusive boutiques and the antique shops.

And there was La Scala, of course, which I hadn't seen before . . . the most famous opera house in the world. Unfortunately the season was just over, but La Divina raved about it. She and Louise had been to a few performances there, although each time they'd had to stand and had been in constant fear of falling into the orchestra pit or else suffocating. We went inside, and it was just indescribably beautiful and opulent, all cream and red velvet and gold leaf. I had a quick fantasy of sitting in one of the box seats a hundred years ago while the Grand Duke of Blah mistook me for the Duchess de la Pompa, flirting with me from across the hall, sending up flowers and chocolates, and begging for my favors!

Then we cut through the parking lot and entered the Galleria, a shopping arcade under a huge glass dome, leading out to Corso Vittorio Emmanuele. In the Galleria are excellent cafes, ice cream parlors, a superb restaurant (Savini's) and one particular shop featuring Leonardo dresses. I'd already fallen under their spell with Larry, and I couldn't stop myself from going in again with La Divina and buying another. (It's the one I'm wearing, in fact, on the cover of *Letters to the Happy Hooker*.) We arranged to pick it up on the way home, and in the meantime made our way to Piazza del Duomo.

Ah, *che bello Duomo!* Imagine an incredible Gothic cathedral built of white marble, bristling with belfries, gables, pinnacles, and statues. It's one of the world's largest churches and took five centuries to complete. Standing majestically at the end of a great paved esplanade, with the sun reflected by the golden Madonna, it's an amazing sight, and it made me wonder at the faith and devotion which must have gone into building this magnificent house of worship. Since the fourteenth century, thousands and thousands of craftsmen had devoted their entire lives to constructing the Duomo, and it stands today—in a considerably less devout world—as a monument to their art and talent.

It also stands as a gathering point for pigeons, balloon vendors, chestnut hawkers, and souvenir peddlers. There are, apparently, over two thousand statues within its walls, and some of the world's finest stained glass. La Divina, who'd been brought up a Catholic, also showed me a curious statue of St. Bartholomew, who, she told me with some bizarre glee, had been martyred by being flayed alive.

It was getting late, and besides, there's only so much history and beauty you can absorb in a day, so we headed back to Casa Tarta, with quick stops at the Galleria and my hotel, where I freshened up and changed clothing.

Louise and Lena, La Divina's roommates, were home

when we arrived, and curious as hell to learn who the mystery guest was. Lena was a tiny bundle of Milanese joy—less than five feet tall, with thick, curly black hair, fantastic boobs, and an amazing voice. She sometimes sounded like an Italian soundtrack for a Mickey Mouse cartoon. She had been raised in Milan but had also lived in New York and Toronto; when she was in Italy she longed to be in North America, and vice versa. The girls introduced her as the Milanese junkie—she'd taken to fooling around with drugs and dope, but she was bright enough to know what she was doing and how to handle them.

The third girl, Louise, was a slender five feet six with a pert, pretty face under flowing reddish hair, a perfect ass, and laughing eyes. She was a sophisticated, liberated country girl from near Toronto, and the artist in the trio.

All three girls were about my age. The best thing about the three of them was their contagious *joie-de-vivre* and sense of humor. They were celebrating life in almost every move they made, and I just fell in love with them.

While La Divina and I talked about old times, Lena and Louise disappeared into the kitchen and created dinner ... a huge salad with mushrooms, and *Pollo Stephania,* a delicious chicken dish, baked in garlic, soy sauce, and lemon, with buttered mushrooms. For dessert we had apple crisp, with second helpings all around. During dinner we chattered like schoolgirls, just having a fine time, as if we'd known each other all our lives.

After all my mistakes in Milan, I'd finally found three people who were genuine, and it made the whole trip worthwhile. They asked nothing from me, and I asked nothing from them, and because there were no pressures, we found that we had everything to give to each other. We ended the evening grooving on their good records, a bit of dope, and the good feeling of friendship.

The next morning, it was off to the airport again, bidding *"Arrivederci Milano!"* Airborne out of Milan, I checked my notes about some of the odd things I'd heard.

One was about prostitution in Rome.

On a winter's evening en route to Rome, near the Via di Tor de' Conti, field fires can be seen near the highway ...

and it's a fact that a gentleman can warm more than just his hands wherever he sees this glow.

The fires are called *bivacchi*, and they're set and maintained by the hookers' pimps. The girls live in small cottages nearby, and the drivers just pull up (pardon the expression) at the sign of the fire. They warm their hands, then get the heat they're really after either in their cars or in the girls' cottages.

Among other things, it's apparently quite picturesque.

The human touch to this is that sometimes the girls then arrange to meet their drive-in clients on a different level. Instead of a quick fuck, the girls then offer the men a lavish meal with wine, in the cottage—all for a fee, of course—and absolutely no sex involved. Some men simply need a woman to talk to sometimes, someone who knows how to listen. And the pimps don't object, as long as the money comes in.

Other notes I made covered ribald Italian sayings. One goes this way:

Cazzo dritto non conosce ragione.—A stiff cock doesn't think.

Another one:

Quando il vigore va bene, avanti con il pene. Quando il vigore diminua, avanti con la lingua. Quando il vigore è quasi finito, avanti con il dito. Quando il vigore è nullo, avanti con il cullo. Ma sèmpre avanti: questro l'importante!

Which means:

When the power of the cock is strong, go ahead and fuck with it. When its power lessens, proceed with your tongue. When the power's almost gone, go ahead with your finger. When there's no cockpower at all, then try with the arse. But always ahead and ahead, that's what counts!

Oh well, I bet "a stitch in time saves nine" doesn't translate that successfully into Italian.

Otherwise, Milan to London was a blur. Not a long trip, but I dozed off in my seat . . . and awoke only as the flight touched down at Heathrow Airport.

LOVERLY LONDON

My crazy summer in Europe had come to an end. After several months of traveling through France, Yugoslavia, Italy, and Switzerland, I was ready to settle down in one place—London. And September is perhaps one of the nicest months to spend there: the tourists have gone home, leaving England only slightly crowded (its normal state) and the weather is mild—either mildly sunny or mildly wet.

To visitors from harsher climates, the English autumn seems no different from the rest of the year. A man I met once told me he'd spent two years in London waiting for the season to change! Not that the weather really mattered to him: he saw the world from the inside of bars and bedrooms—both at once if he could manage it. He was the only man I've ever met who could perform with a bottle in one hand and a buttock in the other. But that's another chapter and another book.

One of the main reasons for my stay in London was Bob Guccione and *Penthouse* magazine. I had joined the editorial staff as a regular monthly columnist, writing an advice column which I wanted to call Hang Up Your Hang-Ups, but Guccione, with his unerring eye for the market, named it Call Me Madam.

I was anxious to begin my sexual advice column because I considered myself a pretty good lay analyst. Compared to many psychiatrists, sexual advisers, and marriage counselors who depend on their experience in the field, my experience is where it matters—in the hay.

I answer the letters as honestly as I can, hopefully with a sense of humor, an ingredient too many people leave out of their love lives. In my view, sex can only be enjoyed to the fullest if there's no tension, if both parties are completely relaxed, and humor is the sure way of relieving tension. A woman told me that a much-anticipated evening with a new man was completely ruined when her date farted. If only she could have seen the funny side—he only broke wind once rather than farting up a storm—and laughed off the farting incident!

But back to London, everybody's favorite city. I love London's smallness . . . not its overall size, but the smallness of its parts. To eyes accustomed to North American streets, even most of London's major thoroughfares appear small.

As an example, take Threadneedle Street, which is in the heart of The City (the term Londoners use to refer to the mile-square financial district). It's barely wide enough for two buses to pass each other and yet Threadneedle is a major street, connecting Mansion House, the official residence of the Lord Mayor of London, and Liverpool Street railway station, Petticoat Lane, and the East End. (Threadneedle Street, by the way, is where you will probably find one of the London branches of your national bank. A walk along that narrow roadway is like a quick trip around the world.)

In the West End the small lanes are sometimes called mews and were, in long-ago London, the back alleys to horse stables behind the master's house, which fronted on a dignified square or stately avenue. Now those alleys are intriguing, well-kept lanes—some still with cobblestones—and the stables have been turned into very desirable flats.

The best area for this "mews watching" is Mayfair, bounded on the west by Park Lane, on the east by Bond Street, on the south by Piccadilly, and Oxford Street to the north. I've walked this area for hours and still haven't covered the hundreds of little streets, lanes, and mews. Perhaps the fact that this area has some of the finest stores and boutiques in the world slowed my pace a little, but they helped to make my walks in this area, on warm sunny days, some of the happiest experiences I've had in any city.

Another delightful aspect of England, for me, is the way the English woman ages: beautifully and gracefully. She accepts aging as a part of life, to be not just faced, but welcomed as one of life's stages. And with this attitude she creates an attraction all her own.

In contrast, the North American has been brainwashed to venerate youth, as though that were the only worthwhile stage of life. Constantly fighting the clock, the North American woman is a sad spectacle. Is this because aging has been linked with sexual fading? Is it because they still think that once you've reached forty you have to take up knitting needles instead of kneeling positions?

Thankfully, sexologists and their recent research into the subject of geriatric sexuality are finally putting an end to this outdated thinking. And more and more newspapers and magazines have given space to the subject. Their conclusions almost unanimously show that there's no reason why a healthy sex life can't be enjoyed well into one's eighties.

Perhaps the English have known this all along. What else do they know about sex? Read on. You'll find, like I did, that there's more to the English than a stiff upper lip.

HOT BUTTERED RUMP

Within a month I had pretty well covered the major spots and was considering London my hometown. I was fortunate to have the right connections and know the right people; I even became a member of Tramps, London's most elegant private club, restaurant, and discotheque. This was quite an honor—to get membership in four weeks when there's a tremendous waiting list and most applicants have to wait at least a year to get in.

The London nightlife scene is strange—pubs still close at eleven P.M. and the underground closes at midnight; even the buses only run a skeleton service after the witching hour. But for those with the right money and connections, the night lasts much longer, with plenty of places to go: Annabel's, Playboy, Truffles, Penthouse, to name just a few.

However, you didn't need afterhours clubs to have a "different" evening in Londontown. I remember one Saturday evening I spent with Vincent, a handsome brown-eyed friend I'd met through one of the girls at Penthouse. He was just over six feet tall and had a muscular, long-legged body. There were wrinkles around his eyes whenever he flashed his happy smile—which was often—and though his hair was brown, his moustache and sideburns were ginger.

His family was titled, but he worked for his living—as assistant headmaster in a Manchester high school. The school term hadn't yet begun, so we were able to enjoy a few weeks' romance in London before work would take us apart.

We were invited to the opening of a new art gallery, the invitation coming from Maria and Casimir—a beautiful young Polish countess and her equally delicious Russian duke. To open the gallery, they'd chosen an exhibition of morbid works by a Danish artist—Dirty Danish Oscar, as they called him. We were invited to go down to the basement of the gallery where they were about to show a movie Oscar had made. We spread out on the carpet, Maria, Casimir, Vincent, and myself, together with a bunch of well-to-do conservative men and women; some were collectors, others were dealers, and still others, like us, were just friends of friends.

The film, which from the opening shot was very surreal, began with a shot of two cruddy-looking men sitting on a table, one of them barefoot with a loaf of French bread under one foot. The next shot was of a woman with short curly hair and 1930s type makeup. She was lying on the table with the two men standing behind her.

Then there were several close-ups of the loaf of bread, which moved from under the man's foot while he had gone to lie in the corner of a bathroom whose walls were splashed with urine. By this time I didn't know whether we were watching a movie on hygiene or The Galloping Gourmet Gone Mad.

The next scene showed the woman lying on her back with the loaf of bread like an erect penis on her belly. The two men were now watching her closely. One was wearing a monk's hat, shading his face and eyes.

The lady turned over, onto her stomach, and one of the men stepped forward, forced apart her buttocks, and shoved the long narrow loaf up her ass. No, it couldn't be the galloping gourmet—wrong end!

The other man stepped forward and with a sharp knife cut open her back. A blubbery, liverish mass dribbled out. The two men then proceeded to eat this sauce—this human sauce.

At first the two men ate with fork and spoon; then, realizing that niceties would never get them a Hollywood contract, they dug into the morass of flesh with their hands, digging deeper into the woman's body. This was followed by a close-up of the woman's anguished face and then the final award-losing scene: one of the men rolled up his sleeve and, digging deep into the woman's body, extracted the loaf of bread. I felt at this point that somebody had told the Danish filmmaker about the expression "bun in the oven" and something had gotten lost in the translation.

The final shot came up—and if you have a weak stomach, close your eyes while you read this. A knife flashed into view, cut the bread in half, and a mass of human liver and intestines spread slowly out on the table. Finally and thankfully the words *the end* appeared on the screen; not inappropriate, I thought.

What an ugly, morbid attempt at art. To sum it up critically in one word: Yech!

The silent, slightly greenish-hued audience moved out of the basement and Vincent and I hurried to his red sports car. We put down the top and zoomed off along Park Lane, the fresh breeze helping to restore a little color to our faces.

With the wind blowing my hair, we wafted south down Park Lane, Hyde Park stretching out in the blackness to our right and the famous Dorchester Hotel standing majestically on our left, a landmark of a hotel that has been world-famous since the early thirties. And then the new London Hilton drifted into view, its thirty stories towering over Hyde Park, much to the dismay of many traditional-minded Londoners.

We turned right at Hyde Park Corner (on Sundays the free speech center of the world) and continued along Knightsbridge, past some of the finest department stores in the world, into Brompton Road, branching right into Cromwell Road, zoomed by the magnificent Victoria and Albert Museum, past the Museum of Natural History, and then we turned left into a series of small roads, the bit that Vincent liked most of all: shooting along narrow streets and squealing around tiny squares until finally we'd arrived where Mary Quant started the whole miniskirt fad, King's Road, Chelsea. This is a great spot to be on any evening, where any self-respecting up-and-coming swinger has got to be.

Chelsea was once the artistic center of London but now it attracts the "trendies," TV types, ad agency people, film extras (and the occasional film star), and, of course, the clothes horse: the guys and dolls whose only claim to fame is that they're wearing the very latest fashion. I always feel that these latter are never completely secure, fearing the fashion may well have changed that afternoon, and the skirt may be the wrong shade of magenta or the trouser cuffs just a half inch too wide. But that's their problem. I long ago discovered that the person has to wear the clothes, and not the other way around.

Resisting the desire to have a restorative drink at the marvelous old Six Bells Pub, Vincent decided to take me directly to a nice little Czechoslovakian restaurant where, with our appetite restored, we ordered their version of goulash. Afterward we walked along King's Road again, just people-watching and digging the scene.

That night Vincent and I went back to my place to make love. After the first time, which was fairly straight—any missionary would have approved wholeheartedly—Vince let himself go, showing himself to be a well-educated lover. As square as he may have seemed to his students, at heart he was a lovely, kinky Englishman.

Indeed, in the few weeks that I'd spent in London, I'd done quite a bit of research on the mythically cold-blooded Englishman of the upper-class variety, and found out that at least one of every four Englishmen is slightly kinky. They're very big on the bondage scene and are definitely partial to a nice, healthy spanking on their well-bred derrières. There are two theories about this.

One says that this love of spanking comes from their home life, where their nannies administered this kind of discipline. But Nanny was also the provider of a great deal of home affection, Mater and Pater being too busily engaged with other things and unemotional toward their offspring. So in adulthood the spanking and affection are psychologically linked.

The other theory says that it comes from the upper class Englishman's schooling. He was usually sent to an all-male boarding school where the cane was administered on the bare buttocks by both masters (teachers) and student prefects. Many of the pupils also indulged in homosexual activity, which isn't surprising for youth going through puberty without any real access to girls.

Now, while many men who go to prison indulge in homosexuality—again because of the lack of females—being mature, with their tastes already set, they can carry on in a normal heterosexual manner when they get out. But for schoolboys whose first taste of sex is homosexual, the effect may be much longer lasting and bondage scenes —so goes this second theory—help them to sublimate their homosexual tendencies.

As for Vincent, all evening he had been strangely intrigued by the gold chain that I was wearing around my waist. After our first, gentle fuck, he took the gold chain and tied it around my breasts and started sucking my nipples. As he sucked, he tightened the chain, and as it bit deeper into my tits, he got more and more excited.

He moved to my clitoris and I was really enjoying myself, especially after I told him exactly how I liked it: not to suck too hard but to move his tongue quicker up and down the clitoris. I felt the orgasm start its early building stages and wound my legs around his neck. He suddenly stopped his delicious cunt-licking and turned me over on my front, instructing me not to ask questions.

I was still very aroused and eager to achieve a climax. Looking over my shoulder, I saw him take his tie and belt, and with obviously practised hands, he used them to bind my ankles to the legs of the bed. For an instant I experienced a pang of fear in the pit of my stomach—the fear of not knowing what was coming next—but actually it only served to add to my already excited state.

Vincent walked away from the bed and I wondered what exotic object he was going to use for the beating. The exotic object in this case turned out to be a half pound of New Zealand butter, salted. He slowly peeled off the paper and, holding it in his right hand, rubbed it slowly up and down my "curple" which, he said, is the word to describe the cleavage between my buttocks. Not surprisingly, the butter melted pretty fast and as it did, being tied at the feet, I began to feel like a trussed butterball turkey.

With a glazed look in his eyes, Vincent put down the butter, climbed on the bed, and slowly began to rub his engorged cock up and down between my buttocks, very slowly, very gently. It was terrifically sensuous and I felt the excitement mounting all over my body.

Then he moved to a squatting position, one knee on either side of my hips while his hands clutched my shoulders. He started the same movements again, but with more urgency. I could now feel his tight scrotum rubbing my thighs and pressing against my ever-moistening vagina.

Vincent's pace started to mount and the strokes became harder and harder, and now the movements of my buttocks were stimulating my clitoris. I tried to move to get an even greater charge out of it, but with my legs tied and his body and hands pinning me down, it was almost impossible. I struggled in an attempt to ease my position, and that's what really turned Vincent on.

He was now clutching my shoulders, his fingers digging in really deep, and on his upward strokes he seemed to pull my body to meet his. The pace quickened and he was grunting and moaning—he still hadn't penetrated me— when suddenly the climax was upon us. It was just too fantastic and as I jerked to the spasms, halfway through the orgasm, Vincent rammed his already spouting prick deep inside my cunt.

It was unbelievable—the climax seemed to start all over again. I was jerking so hard now that the tie holding my right leg gave way; but it didn't matter anymore. Vince suddenly flopped down, exhausted, on top of me and we lay like that for what seemed hours before either of us had the strength to move. He untied my other leg and we managed to climb under the covers before drifting off to sleep. Here was one man who knew on which side his broad was buttered!

The next day was Saturday and it was Vincent, hungry as a wolf, who started on the eggs and bacon. It was a lovely sight to wake up to in my tiny apartment in the Chelsea Cloisters. There, in the kitchen, was Vincent, bare-ass naked, with his gorgeous young body and strong buttocks, looking like Nureyev in a modern ballet. With the eggs and bacon going in one pan, and the tomatoes and onion in the other, all looked set for a gourmet breakfast. Vincent turned around and smiled at me.

"There's only one thing, ducks," he said. "We seem to be all out of butter!"

SPIRO'S STORIES

The Reader's Digest used to have a monthly feature called "The Most Unforgettable Character I've Ever Met." Well, the most unforgettable character I've ever met in London was a gentleman named Spiro. But I really don't think I could write him up for the *Digest*. I'm afraid the editors would find him a mite indigestible. . . .

Spiro is not an easy man to describe. He looked neither young nor old, yet he was at least in his early forties since he had a son aged twenty. And his appeal was unlike anything I'd come across before.

I'd heard a lot about Spiro from Vincent, who had met him during a stay in Australia, where Spiro had been born of Greek parents who'd emigrated there after World War I. When we set off to Spiro's duplex in one of the nicer parts of London, Vincent kept building him up so much that by the time we reached the place, I expected to find a true Greek God with eight penises. Imagine my surprise when the door opened to reveal a man who barely reached higher than my shoulders. I looked at Vincent to see if he had been joking or whether this was the right man. Vincent didn't understand my look and bubbled on with the introductions.

However, it didn't take me very long to see why Spiro had the reputation he did. He was the type of man who, within minutes, makes you feel you've been friends for decades.

He may not have been tall and good-looking—the usual cliché image of a sought-after man. But he was an artistic and considerate man with a tremendous sense of humor. He was, all in all, a beautiful person . . . and all this is worth ten times as much as good looks, which is not to say that Spiro wasn't enormously appealing to women.

Part of Spiro's extraordinary charm lies in the fact that he has to be one of the world's most gifted storytellers. That first night he had me rollicking around his living room, laughing—I believe "pissing in my pants" might be the vulgar way of describing the devastating effect on one's person of Spiro's stories—at his recollections and anecdotes.

Then, too, he is a consummate host. You immediately feel that there is nothing in his kitchen or in his liquor cabinet that is not yours for the asking. And he always offers, so you needn't ever ask. . . .

And perhaps most important, Spiro gives of himself— the truly great gift—which is what I mean when I describe the instant sense of long-lasting friendship with him. And from that first night he made me feel welcome in his home, and I knew I would continue to be welcome whenever I cared to visit him.

When I visited Spiro—which was often—he always seemed to have some girl (or bird, as they say in London lingo) around the house, cooking and cleaning and doing general domestic things for him and his son. Not that Spiro needed domestic help—he was a fantastic cook, Greek cuisine being a specialty, though he could handle his way through cuisines of other countries as well. His other loves were chess and the guitar. In his huge, modern living room he had two superb Spanish guitars standing against the wall. He treated them like precious women . . . not to be touched by anybody else.

As for women, they, too, were precious to Spiro, who had once been an ardent group swinger, but now discovered more pleasure with just the one girl at a time. A different one each night if possible, but still, just one at a time.

Vincent, who still kept his hand in at orgies—and not only his hand—kept his eye open and if he met a suitable girl at a group swing or orgy, sent her over to Spiro. From there things would take a natural course—Spiro's personality would be enough to get the girls to recommend *their* friends to go to Spiro's place.

As for me, however, it was strictly friendship. I loved

being around him as he shared his company, grace, charm, and, most of all, his delightful stories.

Here, for example, are a few of Spiro's stories, just as he told them to me.

"In Australia I once knew a sweet, not too pretty, rather innocent-looking girl. I knew her for many many years—we used to see each other on the beach, in the coffee bars, and what-have-you. But I never dated her. Well, finally, due to circumstances in life, we got together a few years later and, to my surprise, we wound up in bed. I tell you, she was a pure, butter-wouldn't-melt-in-her-mouth type. But the fact that we were in bed together was only half the surprise. During our lovemaking she came out with the most fantastic, wild, ribald stories I'd ever heard in my life. And remember, I haven't led a sheltered life. When we finished lovemaking and sat drinking coffee and smoking, she said to me, 'Of course, I didn't mean any of what I said, you know.' So far, so good.

"The next night—exactly the same thing—more lovemaking, another load of stories. Seven months later . . . still the same thing. And the amazing thing is, this girl never repeated herself once! And always the same disclaimer: 'I didn't mean any of that, you know.' Well, I got so used to the routine that if she hadn't said, 'I didn't mean any of that, you know,' I would have fainted.

"Of course, she was kind of pleased with herself as a sex symbol because after all these months I was still anxious to get her to bed. But what I never told her was this: I was fucking her simply because I was hooked on her stories!"

"This was also back in Australia, when I was living in a very compact flat with paper-thin walls. We knew an Italian who used to fuck anything on two legs—we were truly glad that he'd never come across a dancing bear! But his real peculiarity was the noise he made when he reached a climax—a real racket. And he often used to make love in *my* apartment.

"Well, there was no way we could let the din of his comings seep through the walls for the neighbors to hear and so the only thing that we could do—the 'we' being Mark, another friend, and I—was to play both guitars in a frenzy of flamenco and as the cacaphonous come happened, we would stamp our feet and sing at the top of our voices to drown him out.

"A neighbor finally knocked on our door and complained, 'Too much fucking noise, mate!'

"My immediate reply was, 'But what did you think of the guitar playing?' "

"There was a pretty Australian girl who was a deafmute. And a nymphomaniac. We had a very unusual arrangement going; whenever she felt horny, she'd call my house. Obviously she couldn't speak on the phone—or even hear when it was picked up, so she'd wait a few seconds and then scratch on the mouthpiece with her nail. This was my signal to jump in the car and go and pick her up. She lived about thirty minutes' drive out of town. She would always be waiting outside her house, summer or winter, sunshine or snow.

"Anyway, one night—in the middle of winter—I was having a blackjack party with about eleven friends. We were all gamblers and we'd all been drinking and were horny as hell. They kept asking if I could get some broads over so they could get some action, but in those days I wasn't too well connected. I was in the kitchen getting some drinks when the phone rang. It was picked up by the nearest guy—my friend, Mandrake, so called because he was a great fan of the American comic strip about the Magician. He was a fat jackass with a cock the size of a horse. Well, almost.

"All Mandrake could hear when he answered the phone was some scratching, and thinking it was some idiot who couldn't get the coins down the pay phone, he slammed the phone down. We got on with the cards and drinking and about an hour or two later, I started to tell them about her. Halfway through the story, Mandrake jumped up. 'Holy mackerel, that must have been her . . . on the phone . . . before . . . all I heard was a scratching. . . .'

"I lost no time and got straight into the car and zoomed out to her place. She was there, all right. Almost frozen stiff, having waited outside in the cold for at least two hours. I hugged her and hurried her back to my place where I knew she'd get warmed up in no uncertain way. The Dirty Dozen were waiting, horny and hot. It was a sight that gladdened her eye and in no time at all she was being screwed one by one in my bedroom.

"Mandrake, however, wanted to be different. He was going to be last. And he stood there with his hard-on in his hands with a mischievous grin on his face. Because so many others had been in the front entrance, he figured he would do it the Greek way, and, when his turn came, the poor girl was turned onto her hands and knees on the bed and before she knew what was happening, Mandrake rammed his huge dick up her virgin ass. Her face turned white with pain and she let out a moan, 'Aaaaaagh!' The first sound we'd ever heard from her.

"Mandrake, without missing a stroke, yelled 'There you are, I've gone and spoiled her. The next thing you know she'll be gossiping all over town'!"

Anyhow, that's the flavor of Spiro's storytelling. And he never repeated a story, either.

ROLLING STONED

In late August, when Vincent had to spend a few days in Manchester, preparing for the school year, a man called Eric—to whom I'd previously talked only by phone—invited me to join him and a few friends for Sunday lunch. It all fitted perfectly. Vincent was gone and wouldn't mind that I was about to embark on a new trip with some newly gained acquaintances. Little did I know when putting down the receiver, after talking to Eric, what kind of trip that would turn out to be.

Eric was a friend of Adriaan, a groovy forty-five-year-old Austrian who, together with Leo and Marika, was known throughout Europe as a society swinger. Adriaan and his entire family—including his seventeen-year-old son and his daughters—were swingers. It seems to prove that the family that lays together stays together.

In my experience, Adriaan had introduced me to nice people only, so I'd no qualms about Eric. I seemed to like him just by his telephone voice. At one that afternoon, he picked me up.

His thick, brown, bushy hair topped a rather drawn face, contradicting his big, laughing brown eyes. He was dressed smartly: brown velvet trousers with a white belt, white shoes, a brownish voile shirt with a flower motif, and a cognac-hued suede jacket. He smiled at me through his dark-rimmed glasses. When he later took them off, he reminded me of Warren Beatty, whom I'd met a few nights earlier at Hugh Heffner's party in the Playboy-owned Claremont Club. Warren was with his girlfriend, Julie Christie, one of my great movie idols. The guestlist also included Peter Sellers, Michael Caine, Bernie Cornfeld (before he went to jail), George Hamilton, and Huntington

Hartford, who seems to appear at every party anywhere in the world. Even Tom Jones showed up with a bunch of his hairdresser girlfriends.

But back to Eric. He was both friendly and businesslike. He was taking me to Hampstead to lunch with some friends of his and talk about his plans to open a new business, with me as the London director.

The basic idea was that businessmen in the United States would pay his company a fee of five hundred dollars, for which they'd be guaranteed a girl in London to escort them or their wives on shopping trips, antique hunts, or a visit to the hairdresser. Or just generally show them the town. My part of the deal would be to supply the girl with no promise of anything other than escort duties. If, however, the man, on his own, wanted to take the girl to bed, he'd have to make his own arrangement with her.

Eric wanted to use my name on one of his brochures in America and of course wanted me to supervise the escort service in London. For better or worse, nothing came of it.

We discussed the deal as we drove from Chelsea Cloisters to Hampstead, a very fashionable district of London. After a leisurely twenty minutes' drive, we reached our destination to be greeted by two very attractive girls. One was about five feet nine, blond, with classic Nordic features; her name was Joyce. She really was a stunner, with very smooth skin, palish face, false top and bottom eyelashes covering clear blue eyes, and teeth which looked like they were capped. Her naturally blond hair reached the shoulders of her burgundy sweater and snakeskin vest. What was interesting was that her age was really indefinite—she could have been twenty-five or thirty-five.

The other girl was Gabriella, Gay for short. She was about five feet three, with a pretty, roundish face, big greenish brown eyes (very much like my own), marvelous long lashes, and long, light red hair. Her lush body was all encased in black, sweater and pants, apart from her broad belt, which was part gold. She had a sensual mouth, a perky nose, and a very warm, humor-filled personality. She proudly introduced me to her frisky dog—a collie named Doxy.

Then we met Patrick—tall, handsome, with small, reddish-brown eyes and gray hair. He was president of a large company and owner of the five-bedroom house we were in.

I didn't find out the exact relationship of these people until sometime later. All I did know was that Patrick was living in the house with the two girls, and that Eric visited them frequently.

However, Joyce, I soon enough learned, was Patrick's steady girlfriend, and was extremely jealous. Although she may have been ten times better-looking than Gay or myself, she lacked one thing we had—a sense of humor. At one time she'd been a dancer and now she was working as a model. Gay, who'd been appearing in porn flicks until recently, was now helping her boss fill other kinds of cavities, working as a dental assistant.

As soon as we entered the living room, Patrick put on some good jazz. Joyce then appeared with a partially cut fruit cake and almost mystically offered us all a slice. This struck me as a strange piece of cake until I took a really close look at Joyce's eyes, after she'd confessed to having eaten four slices already. She was stoned out on a baked fruit and hashish concoction, and seeing how she was just grooving away with that big baby smile on her face, I could guess it was potent.

Eric and I decided to get off on it, too, and we each had one slice. Patrick and Gay, apparently still grooving on the hashish they had ingested hours earlier, now declined even a small bite of the potent pastry.

We then all climbed into Patrick's car and he drove us full speed back into the city, to the Hot Rock, across from Hyde Park. The Hot Rock is one of those places you'd expect to find in New York rather than London—a cross between Maxwell's Plum and P.J. Clarke's—filled with young, hip people. It was a large place, with wooden benches and tables, some of them on a podium, others in gallery fashion along the sides. And the big deal was American-style food. The waitresses were pretty English girls, running their cute rear ends off serving hamburgers, T-bone steaks, and spare ribs.

It was then that I felt that special tingle and realized I was stoned. The room began whirling around me.

Gay was on the other side of the table with Eric and Joyce, and all three were drinking huge chocolate milkshakes. The rest of us were having hamburgers.

I was concentrating on eating my hamburger, or to be more precise, I was going crazy over it. I plied it with mustard, tomato sauce, onions, and every type of barbecue sauce within reach. I talked to it very firmly and slapped it around before topping it with a piece of bread that didn't seem to be doing anything important. Then I stuffed the whole spicy chunk into my mouth and bit into it.

I decided to order a strawberry milkshake to go with it, and the mixture of different tastes going across my tongue and down my throat was unbelievable. My tastebuds were ten times sharper than normal, and I was freaking out, loving every morsel of this huge, fantastic hamburger and milkshake.

I looked across at Joyce and saw that she now had her own thing going: potatoes. She was gorging herself with one big boiled potato after another. She, who was so slim and obviously on a strict diet, had let go, too. She put three pats of butter on top of her potato, plus sour cream and pepper and salt and anything else which came to hand. As if this wasn't enough, a giant potato was served and placed in the middle of the table for all of us to dig into.

We all sat there eating and eating and eating, nibbling and noshing away as though the world would end tomorrow. And I couldn't have cared less, because the more I stuffed myself, the wilder I felt.

And then dessert! I devoured a banana split with chocolate fudge and all the trimmings. When you're stoned, there are no such things as calories.

Joyce had ordered another chocolate milkshake with double scoops of ice cream, Eric got a Hot Rock Parfait, and Patrick went for the apple strudel with ice cream. Gay had a hot fudge sundae. The calories went into the millions, but we were above figures.

Finally, we were simply stuffed and decided to head back to Hampstead before we literally burst.

We squeezed ourselves into the car, with Patrick again in the driver's seat and Eric next to him, holding lovely, lush Gay on his lap. Joyce and I shared the back seat. That arrangement obviously wasn't my idea since Joyce was now giving off bad vibes and I was feeling light-headed and giddy.

As we drove along I kept getting wooden stares from

Joyce, but good, warm vibes from Gay, who kept turning around to smile at me. I was dying to touch her, to kiss her yummy mouth; but that would have to wait until we'd arrived at the house.

Joyce suddenly spoke in her Scandinavian accent. "Dahlink, ver ahr vee go-ink to?" Her accent approached Zsa Zsa Gabor's.

"We're going to Regents Park, dahlink," Patrick replied.

"Vhat ahr vee go-ink to do in Regents Park?"

"We're going to drive through it and watch the people go by."

"Vhy?"

"It's a beautiful afternoon, isn't it?" Patrick was sounding slightly exasperated. "It's autumn, remember? It's warm and pleasant, so vee ahr go-ink for a drive."

"Vhat ahr vee go-ink to do aftervards?"

"We're going to the house to have a good time."

"Have a good time? Vhat do you mean?"

"I mean grooving on each other. Stoned as we most certainly are, we might as well groove on each other."

"Oh . . . and then vhat?"

"Then," Patrick said slowly, as though addressing a child, "then, when it's all over, Eric and Xaviera will take a taxi and go home. But first we'll spend an afternoon at our house."

In his last words was a finality that Joyce clearly understood. And I was beginning to understand what the unstated plans might involve. Patrick had a swing in mind, and we weren't heading for the playground.

My time sense was so distorted that I can't remember how long it took to get back to the house. It seemed like forever. And when we did get back, without realizing what we were doing, we all ate more cake . . . and Betty Crocker it wasn't.

It began to seem that this was a familiar pattern in the household. Gay and Eric were clearly ready for a stoned swing, and Patrick was more than interested. Joyce, however, had very different ideas, and as we all stumbled into Gay's bedroom and began to undress, Joyce whispered a few choice words into Patrick's ear. I don't know what she said, but it certainly did something to him. He paled slightly, pulled his sweater back on, and left the room with her, visibly dejected.

Gay had a double bed with a light eiderdown cover ... no need for sheets and blankets. Gay, Eric, and I simultaneously dove under it, all marvelously starkers (as they say in England), to warm each other up.

Eric had a beautiful body—not a big cock (about five erect inches) but firm, strong, and circumcised. And Gay looked luscious—definitely good enough to eat. We just started feeling, touching, squeezing, and kissing each other, without favor or design. It was just a lovely, warm, womblike feeling, sharing love with these two friendly people.

We were both working on Gay, leaving no part of her body untouched, when Eric suddenly climbed on top of me and started to fuck. I lay back, passive for a change, and just accepted the pleasures they were both giving me, for Gay was kissing my ears and neck while Eric was on his knees, my legs around his neck and a pillow under my ass.

His pumping action was getting frantic now and Gay leaned back to just watch and masturbate. I watched her watching us, and got turned on even more.

Eric just kept fucking, fucking, fucking, rocking into me, and each time I thought he couldn't go any deeper or harder, he did. And I was actually getting more and more stoned with each thrust.

The bed now joined in, rattling in rhythm, and the sound of the bed combined with the pounding of Eric deep inside me and the increasing sensations from the hashish made me completely lose control and I drowned in the incredible climax which finally came. It was tremendous! I flew. I soared. I seemingly couldn't stop coming.

Eric may not have been the subtlest of lovers, but for me, at that stage, he most certainly was a fuck for all seasons. He also was somewhere on a plane by himself and after a brief rest he started up again. This time I had my legs wrapped around his, giving me freer movement. My hands were clutching his hips, pushing back and forward, controlling his lovemaking.

Suddenly Eric started laughing hysterically and began his second orgasm, bouncing his head against the wall.

Even after he'd stopped ejaculating, he continued his insane behavior. I was beginning to get scared, watching him freaking out, tripping higher and higher.

I slipped from underneath his body and Gay and I both tried to calm Eric down, but it was difficult. He just kept experiencing various peaks of ecstasy, each more violent than before.

We finally managed to place his head on the pillow and covered his body with ours. We were his blanket, and finally he acknowledged our presence. We smiled at him in relief, and he said that he couldn't believe what a trip he'd gone through. It was the most divine, astonishing, and devastating experience, he said, that had ever happened to him.

Gay and I covered him up with the blanket and held on to him, but he couldn't lie still—he simply had to move around. Finally he popped out of bed and left the room.

While Eric was gone, Gay and I made love very gently, very affectionately, and then tried to nap. Suddenly I got a mean, dry taste in my mouth. I had to get up to rinse out my mouth with something cold and wet. As I stood upright, my head swam and the dizziness made me feel nauseous. Don't ask me how, but I made it to the kitchen, and just as I was reaching for a glass, I was sick all over the sink.

I must have made some considerable commotion in the kitchen because Eric stumbled in from somewhere or other and, taking one look at my face, politely apologized for giving me too much cake. He really was a darling, and he took me in his arms and held me tight. He put the kettle on for a "nice cuppa," and in the meantime gave me a large glass of orange juice to quench my thirst.

I went to the bathroom and washed and brushed my teeth, then went back to the bedroom where Gay lay, half asleep and yet aware of everything that was going on around her. The light from the hallway illuminated her face just long enough for me to see her smiling face and childlike, wondering eyes.

I quickly got into bed with her, telling her how ill I felt, and she responded by holding me close. We lay that way for what seemed like hours.

At some point in the day—or night, since I'd lost all

track of time—Eric came back to the room and joined us in bed. Still very much flying, we all made love again—or at least we tried; but we were still all too stoned to know who had to do what to whom and where and why. Everything seemed uncontrollable and lacking in logic.

At one point I found myself thinking sadly that poor Eric had been castrated, and then gradually realized I was staring into Gay's vagina. Eric had my left breast in one hand and Gay's right breast in his other, and couldn't quite work out how one woman could have boobs so far apart. Gay was still very high and had the lips of her cunt spread apart while she kept saying, "Xaviera, come on out. I know you're in there." Finally we all collapsed into uncontrollable giggling.

Eventually we all slowly semi-passed-out, hands over breasts, legs in crotches, arms intertwined. We lay there, limp, breathing softly, hearing and feeling everything, it seemed, but unable to move a finger.

I woke up some time later, next to Gay. Eric, to my surprise, was standing beside the bed, fully dressed.

"Do you want to go home or spend the night here?" he asked softly.

"I'd like to go home, if you'll give me a hand."

I got up feeling almost normal, but still a little weak at the knees. I dressed and gently kissed Gay on the forehead. She was still sound asleep. We pulled the covers up over her shoulders and crept out, closing the door gently.

Joyce and Patrick were still up watching television like a square, homey couple. He looked unhappy, she was triumphant. Otherwise, it was as if nothing had happened in the house. We said goodbye, and just to drive the point home, my parting shot at the door was, "Thanks for a lovely evening."

When I got home it turned out to be just past midnight. It felt like a week later. I slowly undressed, took a hot bath, and got into bed, trying to sort out my fabulous London freak-out. A scene, hopefully, not to be repeated very often. As Gay had said to me at one point, "It's good to get out of yourself, but how often can you look into your own soul?"

THE SENSUOUS DRILL

When Vincent got back from Manchester, we went out to dinner with our storytelling friend, Spiro. To make the evening even more international, we ate Italian.

London, interestingly enough, is one of the best cities of all for Italian restaurants. There are an astonishing number of them; in Soho alone there are streets lined with Italian eating houses, one next to the other!

Throughout dinner Vincent was touching and titillating me. He was obviously trying to tell me something. Unfortunately, I knew exactly what the message was, which made conversation with Spiro difficult and, at times, absurd.

"Tell me, Xaviera," Spiro asked, "can you really put up with this awful English weather?"

"Of course. When you're in a city as stimulating as London, who minds the leather?"

"The leather?"

"What leather?"

"Xaviera, you said *leather* instead of *weather*."

"I did? I can't think why. This minestrone is delicious, don't you think?"

"Yes, quite delicious."

"You can only get fingers like this in London."

"Fingers?" Spiro looked a little alarmed.

"Fingers?" I repeated, removing Vincent's from a place about a half inch from my vagina. "Sorry, Spiro, I meant noodles."

Vincent held my hand in a tight grip under the table.

"Xaviera, you don't seem to be with us tonight." Spiro looked concerned.

"I'm fine, Spiro. Just thinking about the next course."
"Have you chosen?"
"Yes. I'm having their delicious—er—cock."
"Cock?"
"Cock? Cock—oh, yes—the . . . coq au vin," I mumbled, giving Vincent a vicious glare.

"But it's an *Italian* restaurant," Spiro pointed out. "They don't *have* coq au vin, Xaviera!"

Vincent smiled at me angelically and from the movement of his body above the table, I could tell that he was zipping up his fly.

As Spiro and I tried to continue our conversation about his years in Australia, I saw Vincent reach into an inside pocket and take out a small piece of suede, one end of which had been fringed. Holding it in his right hand, he nonchalantly started to stroke it across his left. I then saw that it was a kind of miniature cat-o'-nine-tails.

After that, conversation was almost impossible and the effect that this gentle whipping had on my stomach made eating just as impossible. I gave Vincent a brutal kick under the table and he lovingly smiled back at me.

Spiro sensed that something was wrong but assumed I was feeling ill. I agreed that I felt slightly beat—with a quick glance at Vince to make sure he caught my double entendre—and perhaps I should go home and get to bed. At this last word, Vincent produced his biggest smile of the evening and very courteously offered to drive me home. When we left Spiro, he and Vincent exchanged conspiratorial winks. Hmmm . . . I'd *thought* he'd been acting a little naive.

Back at my flat, Vincent opened a valise he had brought with him from the car and carefully laid out on the floor a series of leather belts, thongs, straps, and whips. I was mesmerized and stood there watching him, still in my coat.

Just as carefully, he undressed me. As he slid the dress off my shoulders, he saw my nipples were hard and extended—more from fear than anything else. He couldn't resist a quick nipple-nibble.

I was ready for action then and there. After all, the foreplay by now had been going on for two hours and my lower orifice was flowing quite freely. But fucking wasn't in Vincent's immediate plans and, from the look in his eyes, his plans were the only ones which were being followed tonight.

He laid me gently on the bed, on my side, and with the expertise of a naval officer (or advanced boy scout), tied my hands behind me with some soft chamois leather thongs. He reached down for a leather strap and as he stood up, he gave me a hard slap on the bottom with his hand. It was the unexpectedness of the blow as much as the pain which made me yelp and lose my temper.

I started to struggle and kick my legs, which was just what Vincent wanted. He dove on my legs and, holding them under one arm, roped my ankles like a cowboy roping a calf at a rodeo. With my legs tied, he took another long thong and connected the ankle bindings with the hand bindings. This, I thought, is going to make fucking very difficult.

Then he took out an electric drill! Really frightened, I tried to speak. But my throat was too dry and no sound came out. He took something like a long chopstick and fixed it into the drill and began tying pieces of narrow leather thongs along the length of the stick.

He plugged in the drill, put a leather glove on his left hand, and took the drill in his right. He pulled the trigger on the drill and the stick started to revolve, whirling the leather thongs around in circles. Using his left hand to slow the pace of the revolutions, he held the drill about a foot away from my body and the leather thongs started to strike my buttocks.

It was a soft, sensuous, almost gentle feeling, a leather massage. He moved slowly down my legs until the thongs were hitting the underside of my feet. Vincent allowed the machine to go a little faster and then faster still, then took his hand away altogether so that the drill was turning at full speed. The thongs started to bite into my soles and the sting was becoming quite painful.

Vincent was very erect now, and I could see his prick throbbing as he watched the pain on my face. Just as quickly, he slowed the machine and moved it over my breasts. Once again the thongs started their electric massage, slightly stinging my nipples, which began to grow and grow, causing my desire to become even more urgent.

He increased the machine's speed, then slowed it down. Vincent again and again repeated this slow-fast treatment until the drill's motor sounded like a police siren. The rhythm was the same as a good rhythm for fucking, and my body was really beginning to ache for his cock up my cunt, but vicious Vincent had one more trick up his Freudian sleeve.

He squeezed his right hand between my thighs and took the drill again, his hand pressing against the lips of my vagina, the thonged stick pointing toward my head. He pulled the trigger and the vibration of the motor went through his hand onto my cunt. The thongs were slapping around against my belly and breasts and I began to squirm in earnest as I felt the world move down to my pelvic region.

I started to push against his hand with shivering, uncontrollable thrusts. As he saw me approaching my orgasm, the middle finger of his hand began a forceful massage of my sphincter muscle. I no longer cared that my hands and feet were tied. I no longer cared about anything except that magic force which took me toward the climax.

The drill was going full speed, the thongs whipping the length of my torso while Vincent's hand was pushing harder into my ass. The orgasm was almost on me and I gave a final squirm when Vincent stopped the motor, put the drill aside. Forcing my knees apart, he stuck his head between my thighs and started tonguing my clitoris the way I'd taught him.

His dripping prick was next to my face, and without the use of my hands I managed to get it into my mouth and sucked like I'd never sucked before, moving my head backward and forward to the same rhythm as his tongue. I started to come before he did and it was so intense that I wanted to yell, but I didn't want to open my mouth and let his prick escape. So I yelled with my mouth firmly gripping his prick—a long, hard yell, the vibrations of which were transmitted to Vincent via his bone-a-phone.

I felt his body tense and a huge thrust of his penis into my throat, followed by what seemed like an endless series of violent spasms as his jism spurted out. At the end of his orgasm, Vincent was still erect—well, at least his prick was; the rest of him was limp.

I persuaded him to undo the leather bonds, which he did with some effort—the physical and mental stimulation had been too much for him—and without pausing to rub my wrists or ankles, I turned him on his back and sat astride him, forcing his erect penis deep into my cunt. I started to slowly revolve my hips so that his prick gave my clitoris a lateral massage.

I love this superior position because it gives me a chance to move exactly as I want, to get the stimulation I enjoy most. It's also best for the deepest penetration. I could feel the desire flowing back into me, but Vincent was still far gone and not at all responsive.

Now while I like this position, if the man isn't responding, I might as well be astride a vibrator. Something had to be done. Then I remembered the well-known golden rule: Do unto others as you have been screwed by them.

I eased myself forward until I was lying over Vincent, then straightened my legs and with a quick roll had him lying on top of me—still connected at the crotch. And without him noticing what I was doing, I picked up the heaviest of the leather straps which were still lying on the bed.

I brought it down as hard as I could on his buttocks. His eyes jerked open and so did his mouth. He was about to speak when I gave him another good whack, hard enough to make his buttocks clench, sending his penis straight up my vagina. Now this was a discovery that made sliced bread look feeble. I tried it again. Yes, there was something to Newton's third law: for every action there *is* an opposite and equal reaction. I bet they've never proved it this way in a lab before.

My legs were now curled around the back of Vincent's legs, just behind the knees, and I was holding him tight. I started a rhythmic spanking on his buttocks and found that I didn't have to hit too hard because now it was the thought that counted. But who was counting? I had other things on my mind. And on my chest, my belly, and most of all, deep, deep inside me. And Vincent was going strong, his whole body now arching and straining to every lash of the belt.

As I increased the pace, he began to lose control. His breathing became a rasping exhaust as he tried to drive into me deeper than before. He began to quicken of his own accord as he strained toward his climax. Without realizing what I was doing, I dropped the belt, grabbed his buttocks, one in each hand, and dug my nails in hard.

He came almost immediately, with me a millisecond later. It was another intense orgasm, one of the fiercest I've ever known. We thrashed and yelled and strained, rolling over and pushing at each other as though survival were at stake. But through it all I kept hanging on, my hands never letting go of his lovely, firm buttocks. When it finally subsided, Vince kissed me tenderly on my lips.

"Xaviera," he said softly, "if all women in the world were like you, psychiatrists would be out of business."

I kissed him back, and we were both too exhausted for anything but sleep.

A night together like that is pretty hard to beat (sorry!) and we never managed an encore. Vincent's school responsibilities soon took him to Manchester permanently, and he was as devoted to his career as he was to his pleasures. There was a time and place for everything, he felt, and during the school year he wasn't prepared to come to London for wild weekends.

So that was the last I saw of Vincent, and his kinky equipment. Which is just as good, because I'm sure I didn't have the strength to continue a relationship like that. And "whipped cream" is really not my cup of tea.

I LOVE PARIS IN THE FALL

I hadn't seen Larry since we'd parted about six weeks earlier in Switzerland. He was in New York, attending to business, and we continued to keep in touch mostly by mail. Theoretically you can dial New York directly from London, but by the time you successfully get a call through England's inept phone system, you can have written the letter, mailed it, and received a reply. Except from Larry, whose strength didn't lie in letter writing. What was obvious, during the time Larry and I had been apart, was that distance—among other things—was putting a severe strain on our relationship.

Also, my leaving New York (and prostitution and America) was more than simply going to a different country. I had left behind a lifestyle, and after three years was beginning to discover myself again in Europe. I think that the woman Larry loved, and the woman who felt she loved Larry, was The Happy Hooker . . . not necessarily Xaviera Hollander.

Our time together in St. Tropez, Yugoslavia, Italy, and Switzerland had mostly been fine—barely an argument until the last week. Which right away should have tipped us off that things were changing!

Nevertheless, we'd still created a lot of good times and good memories together. So impulsively I called and invited him to join me in London for a Penthouse press party, inaugurating my first "Call Me Madam" column.

We had a whirlwind time in London. Larry had never been there before, so I tried to show him several centuries of style, beauty, and tradition, all within a couple of days. The pace was unbelievable, but fun. He was so overwhelmed by it all that I couldn't resist showing him

Paris, too. After all, we were so close to the French capital, and we might never get to see it together, otherwise, so off we went, up up and away to the lovely city on the Seine.

We had a wonderful time together. I showed him all my favorite spots, and we really had a ball. Which reminds me, our sex life was booming, too. I'll never push an exciting new body out of bed, but there's also a lot to be said for a favorite, familiar one. And Larry was certainly that.

One night we got together with my journalist friend, Max. He worked for one of the major wire services, and at the time was covering the Kissinger Paris peace talks. He was established in the city, and I'd known him a long time—dating all the way back to the good old days when I was still a straight chick in New York City. An American, Max had lived in several European cities and was a very sophisticated man. He's also a swinger from way back, and in fact we'd attended a few orgies in New York.

We'd also been given an introduction to a girl named Cecile, who turned out to be a tall, charming, French girl —part-time callgirl and part-time fashion model. She was a perfect lady, and equally at home at the theater, in a restaurant, or at an orgy. In fact, she was a continental queen; charming, elegant, and bright. Larry was very much turned on to her, and I must say she was great fun to be with.

Max took us (Larry, Cecile, and me) to a groovy restaurant called La Grenouille (The Frog), at 26 Rue des Grands Augustins. It's an uninhibited little place, hidden away on a short street near the Seine, and it's known for its unique ambience. The proprietor kisses you, and the waitresses grab the men's pants and pinch the ladies' bottoms the moment you walk in. If you're wearing a low-cut dress or blouse, you take the chance that sometime during the meal, your boobs will be plucked out of your bra, and your nose decorated with ice cream!

Needless to say, the atmosphere is casual, and although it's known to worldly tourists, most of the couples there were native Parisians. The food was fine but it was the atmosphere which really made the place. I'd never heard so much laughter, nor had such a good time, in a restaurant before. During the two hours we were there, people were playing musical chairs and just having the time of their life.

The only exception was a square couple who just sat morosely at their table, quietly nibbling at their frog legs and scampi, with barely an expression on their lips. Every now and then one of the waitresses would approach their table and try to make a little joke, or perhaps flirt with the man, but it didn't help at all. As soon as the bill was presented, they got up to leave, but all the waitresses gathered near the door and held out their hands very provocatively. The poor man had no choice but to flash a weak smile, and press an extra tip of a few francs into their outstretched hands.

For dessert that night, I'd arranged for *partouze*. I'd hoped to be able to introduce Larry to Chateau Roger, since he'd heard all about my dance-floor dong-along there, but alas, it had just closed following the owner's fatal misfortune.

But I knew of another swingers' club in the *sixieme arrondissement*, and it turned out to be just a short walk from the restaurant. It was supposedly a private house, but it looked more like an old-fashioned brothel. Our hostess (a perfect madame from Central Casting) and three giggling maids discreetly asked us to identify ourselves, and extracted our "membership" fees—two hundred francs or fifty dollars for the four of us. We were shown to the cocktail lounge, where one of the maids asked us to take off our coats and leave all valuables with her for safekeeping. We then proceeded upstairs, and she followed us with our tray of drinks. We had all chosen fruit juice, to keep our heads sober.

Larry describes this evening, as he remembers it, in his book, *My Life with Xaviera*. But since he wasn't participating, let me share with you my feelings.

Upstairs, the mingled smell of sperm and sweat permeated the air. Larry wasn't as turned on as I'd hoped. Apparently he would have preferred a private orgy with just the four of us. Max and Cecile didn't feel that way, however, and since I was an exhibitionist and voyeur by nature, I was sure I'd enjoy myself much more if there were a lot of people all fucking together.

Looking around, I saw plenty of attractive men and some really humpy-looking girls. A number of the girls I'd already met in France were bisexual, and I knew, at a glance, that I was going to be a satisfied swinger that night. We walked into one of the changing rooms, where several people were casually undressing, while on a double bed in the corner, four swingers were having a fine time screwing and sucking away. There were three other bedrooms, all similarly inhabited by happy gangbangers.

Larry and Max had shyly stripped down to their underpants, but Cecile and I were already naked. We finally persuaded the boys to let it all hang out, and Larry became very embarrassed, displaying a shy, shrunken penis. Max, however, was strutting around with a good randy hard-on, ready to make it with Cecile. The three of them stuck together for a few minutes while I wandered around, always on the lookout for titillating titbits to tell you about.

The moment I walked into one of the other bedrooms, an older man, in his late fifties, spotted me as a newcomer, flipped me onto the bed, and started giving me such a slobbery tongue-job that I was just revolted. He'd barely begun that when he plopped himself on top of me and started humping away. I let this go on for about five minutes, when Larry walked in and became instantly jealous. I pushed the man off of me, got up, took Larry's hand, and walked back to the room where Max and Cecile were embracing on the couch.

With me stage-managing the little tableau, Cecile began to suck Larry's cock while Max fondled her tits and I went down on her delicious cunt. She had a bushy, untrimmed beaver, yet her clit was easy to find and she was perfectly clean. Her body felt soft and smooth under my face, and her milky-white skin smelled of clover and honey. I was concentrating on making love to her, just the two of us, but soon realized that we'd attracted quite an audience. At least a dozen men and women were circled around us, watching eagerly, and vicariously enjoying our lovemaking. Some of the men had their cocks in their hands, while others were diddling their girls' crotches. Before long the dozen doubled, and soon there must have been forty people watching our performance. Cecile, with her eyes closed, was enjoying every juicy minute of it, moaning and groaning under the spell of my magic mouth. The more she moaned, the more excited our bystanders became, and they were all touching themselves or Cecile or me. It was too much for some of them, and there were people standing there masturbating and going down on each other.

Larry grew rather uneasy with all this, and was upset at me for putting on such a show. But Max enjoyed it every bit as much as I did, and whispered in my ear, "You're still the great Xaviera I've always known. You've started another riot, and that's why you'll always be the best, baby!"

By now my mouth-to-muff motor was really purring, and I'd been chowing down on Cecile's pussy for about fifteen minutes when I felt a woman's body huddle close to me, her hot cunt actually wetting my thigh. At this point I turned Cecile's sopping snatch over to Max, so that he could finish with his cock what I'd started. I gently pushed the two of them together, and made room on the bed for the recently arrived lady. She was a gorgeous brunette with a magnificent body, and I was eager to give her a good licking. Larry was still annoyed and limp-limbed, so I maneuvered the brunette into his lap and suggested he play with her tits or something while I went down on her, hoping it might turn him on.

But no way. He got even more upset and eventually stood up, swearing that I was a bloody exhibitionist putting on a cheap floor show for a lot of sex-starved voyeurs. I told him in polite English to fuck off, and took my brunette between her lovely thighs. Some of the girls who were watching even said they wanted to be next in line for my rapid tongue, but at the moment she was all I wanted. She'd gotten so excited by now that she was on her hands and knees, doggie-fashion.

"Eat me, eat me," she begged in French.

I was already sucking her cunt and licking her rosy little ass but she obviously wanted more. I thrust my tongue deep into her cunt, then stood behind her and almost instinctively pushed my entire groin against her cunt and thighs.

"By God, if only I had a cock," I was thinking, and she must have read my thoughts.

"Fuck me, fuck me," she cried. "Be my man, explode me!"

I didn't have a dildo with me, of course, but luckily one of the girls watching—she looked pretty butch—reached under the bed and produced an enormous rubber dildo with a strap around it. She handed it to me, and helped me tie it around my waist.

My lovely brunette was already well lubricated, and had her ass in the air, so I slid the dildo into her vagina, doggie-style, the way I love being fucked myself. I thrust my pelvis back and forth, back and forth, jamming the phony phallus into her again and again while fondling her clitoris with my one hand and fingering her puckered asshole with the other.

This three-way thrill attracted even more bystanders, but Larry was furious now and stomped out of the room. What a party pooper! He almost turned me off completely with his jealousy. This made me pump even harder, which drove my brunette lover into ecstasy and she came with a groan which seemed to come from terribly deep within her.

She was so grateful that she wanted to go down on me, but as you know, that's not my style, so I kissed her goodbye and returned the dildo to its owner.

Naturally, I was hornier than a two-peckered billygoat (as they say in the States), but not for long. Three men had been hovering around me while I'd been fucking my lady friend, pushing their cocks against me, sucking me, and fondling me all over. So now I lay back on the bed and they took turns, giving me one, two, three delicious fucks, as I made them come, one by one by one, into my supercharged cunt. Each of them was an experienced lover and while none had a particularly enormous cock nor a fantastic body, they certainly knew how to satisfy me with what they had. And that, of course, is what good lovemaking is all about. Quantity is nice, but quality is always better. Although, I must say, a combination of the two is irresistible!

This was certainly the last time I'd go to an orgy with Larry. The Silver Fox was turning into a silver fuck-up as far as I was concerned, pouting and looking at me with childish disapproval. I rejoined Max and Cecile, who, it seems, had already shared two good fucks, and asked her if she would be kind enough to take care of Larry, since he'd been so impressed by her during dinner. But nothing helped. Whether I was in the room or not, Larry just couldn't get it up.

I was disturbed by this, and was almost ready to leave when I saw the butch girl whose dildo I'd used. She was finger-fucking another lovely blond . . . although actually I should call it fist-fucking. She was virtually jamming her entire hand into the girl's twat, spitting on it occasionally for lubrication, and stimulating her clitoris with the other hand, or else giving her a slight spanking. The sight and sound of this gentle little tableau got me all juiced up again, and as I approached the bed they were cavorting on, the audience from my earlier performance greeted me with a cheer, urging me to go down on one of the lesbian ladies. As it turned out, Butch was only interested in hand-jamming the girl, and refused to eat her. So again I got into a double-header, Butch using her hand and I using my tongue on the little blond. Eventually the dildo made another appearance, and I fucked the girl up front, strapping the thing very tightly around my upper thighs so that it also stimulated my clitoris. This way, I fucked her and we both got off.

Then someone produced a huge vibrator, and a double dildo—two big rubber pricks, end to end. Suddenly there were four girls on the bed, vibrating and fucking away with every combination of fingers, hands, tongues, and appliances. I managed to have one end of the double dildo in my pussy, and the other end was in a nice-looking brunette's cunt. We were both well juiced up by spit and natural lubrication, and as we jumped up and down together, we both got caught up in a super tidal wave.

By now I was quite exhausted, thank you. That last scene was really something, and if I'd been Larry I would have been too horny for words. But he was totally turned off by it all. Fortunately, when we got back to the hotel he was his normal self and we managed to go half 'n half on some dynamite sex. But that was just the two of us, alone together in our hotel.

We left Paris early the next morning: Larry back to New York, and I to Amsterdam to see my parents for a few days before returning to London.

HAPPY HOOKER'S HOT SEAT

I was firmly back in the groove with my life in London when the telephone call came through from Canada:

"We'd like you to appear on a television show called *Under Attack*," said the voice.

"What is it?" I asked.

"The guest sits in a bear pit," explained the caller, who I later learned was the producer. "And gets grilled. By a panel of students."

I then remembered seeing the show during a visit to Canada. It was a toughie. The questioners didn't pull any punches and those in the crossfire had to move fast and think on their feet.

I asked the producer if I could call him back, and he agreed. This wasn't the kind of thing to jump into without some thought. So I sat down, looked at a wall, and weighed the pros and cons.

The audience, according to the producer, would be composed of college students, who, I knew, would be sympatico to me. The invitation also came with a free transatlantic ticket and this was as good a reason as any for some travel... an activity I love.

And let's be honest—television is the fastest way to fame, and the best way to maintain that fame once you've gotten there.

The exposure wouldn't do my career any harm, I thought, and it could result in new avenues opening up.

There was also the fact that I'd made some very good friends in Toronto in the past. And in that city I was treated as a celebrity... not just because of my book, but also because of a TV talk show I had done there with Elaine Callei.

She'd invited me on her show, *Call Callei*, to give explicit sexual advice to listeners calling in. And was I ever frank! I told it like I knew it was and the proverbial shit hit the fan. I had touched on something sacred and unmentionable and the amount of hostile, neurotic reaction it stirred up was remarkable.

I mentioned such things as "going down on your husband in the bathtub"; and when a woman called up and asked, "Miss Hollander, what do you have that we don't?" my answer was; "I have the quickest tongue in town, and a snapper." Believe it or not, I then had to explain what the word *snapper* meant.

I fully expected these words to be bleeped off the air. But they weren't. They went out loud and clear. Neither were the other words I used: masturbation, clitoris, orgasm, penis envy, closet banger.

This last term I'd invented to describe those couples who fuck only when the lights are out and they are tucked safely away from each other's sight under the sheets.

I guess there must have been lots of those in the audience for the telephone didn't stop ringing from the second I began to speak.

Boy, were they angry!

The press picked up my comments and everyone and his brother let fly at dear old honest Xaviera.

As if the first show wasn't enough, Elaine invited me back the next day for part two. By this time, however, the producer had started to back off. The public pressure was so great that he'd warned Elaine to cool it in the calling-a-spade-a-spade department. The angry complaints had not stopping flooding in overnight and the station was beginning to get a little nervous.

One woman called in, mad as hell. She said her twelve-year-old daughter had come into the kitchen and asked her, "What is masturbation and what is a clitoris?"

The mother dashed into the TV room, saw me on the program, switched off the set, and immediately called the station to complain of the "foul" program on the air.

I find that regrettable, for I'm sure the girl would have heard more wisdom about sex from me than she ever would from her old-fashioned mother.

After these shows my career as a celebrity in Canada

took on a new dimension and I was invited to lecture to women's groups—the more open-minded kind—colleges, and even all-male clubs.

So it didn't take much of a skull session with me and me to reconvince myself that Canada would be a nice place to be, and I flew to Toronto for *Under Attack*.

Toronto, I soon discovered, was the best place for me to be just then. Not only did it offer interesting work, but it was within easy calling distance of my publishers in New York, without the high cost of transatlantic calls from London or the bothersome inefficiency of the British phone services.

It also meant I was within a few hours of my editor, who was now working on the final manuscript of *Xaviera!* He flew up from New York and after the very successful *Under Attack* show we spent several weeks putting the finishing touches to the book.

By the time the book was finished I was feeling more than a little pooped. I needed a vacation. While on the move for months, I'd also been working constantly, and the TV show had taken quite a lot of my energy.

The show had been taped at a university not far from Toronto, with an audience of surprisingly uptight college kids. The panelists were students and included one nineteen-year-old boy who'd been married for two years, and a pseudoliberal chick who blushed and stammered when I asked her if she was a virgin.

They began their attack with variations of "dirty" and "degrading" as adjectives for both my book and my lifestyle. They were textbook examples of the sexual repression that a puritanical upbringing causes.

But obviously I knew my subject better than they did— I'd certainly done my share of homework!—and I think by the time the hour ended, I'd scored a few points for sexual liberation.

During the closing question period, one cute young guy said, "Miss Hollander, now that you're here, are you planning to open a whorehouse?"

"Definitely not," I told him. "I've found I can make more money vertically than I could horizontally. Why do you ask?"

"Well, to tell the truth," he confessed, "I'm tired of falling in love with my right hand every night!"

I would have told him to try his left one for variety, but I never would have been heard through the roar of laughter.

Among other things, I was in the mood for some sun after weeks in London and Canada, and once again a fortuitous phone call made up my mind for me. A hotel in Nassau, which I'd stayed in several times before, was willing to trade two weeks in the sun in exchange for the publicity I might bring them as a result of my new celebrity. Would I like to do that?

Does a Hungarian fart? Does a squirrel eat nuts?

THE CATAMARAN CAPER

An expense-paid holiday in Nassau!

I called Larry in New York, told him where I was going, and invited him along. I followed this with another call to an old New York girlfriend named Kirsten, and asked her along, too.

I was assembling the action and I figured Kirsten would be a good addition to the group. She's a Scandinavian beauty who at that time had just had a new breast operation. Not a silicone treatment, just a lift. It was a minor operation but she felt she needed time to recuperate. So my invitation to Nassau fitted in perfectly with her plans, and she agreed to see me there.

When Larry, Kirsten, and I finally met up at the Nassau hotel, it was like old home week. We greeted each other effusively, and in no time at all a pattern developed; Larry, Kirsten, and I would go each day to an island that belonged to the hotel, and just bask in the sun.

Our activities together don't need to be described here, but let's just say they were up to the usual Xaviera standard. Except for one thing. Larry once more began to be a pain in the ass. And no—I don't mean *that* way!

I don't know if it was jealousy of Kirsten and me, or whether he just wanted me alone and felt thwarted. Anyway, I wasn't disappointed when he announced, after a few days, that he had to return to New York. He'd started to watch me like a hawk and I can't take that kind of treatment.

So Larry left, and Kirsten and I got on with our wonderful life in the sun.

The Bahamas comprise seven hundred islands in the Atlantic, starting just east of Miami, and dotting the ocean for about six hundred miles southeast. There are perhaps twenty major, inhabited islands. Nearly half of the Bahamas' 131,000 population lives on the island of New Providence, where the capital, Nassau, is situated. This island has little to offer in the way of exportable goods, and its revenue comes almost exclusively from tourism.

Every kind of hotel from the humble pension-type residence to the palatial international pleasure house competes for the overflowing dollars that come from Americans and Canadians seeking solace from their harsher climates.

The hotel we were staying at was no exception. It was grandiose, superbly run, and got quite a play in the press over my visit.

Shortly after Larry left, Kirsten and I met an attractive blond English girl called Anne, who was enormously and proudly eight months pregnant. She was the kind of woman that got turned on by being with child and gave not a damn about how she looked or what she did while carrying it.

She'd run around in the smallest of bikinis with her huge swollen tits peeping out over her bra, almost dropping down onto her blown-up belly, which was hardly contained by a handkerchief-size swimsuit bottom.

I found her attitude quite groovy and I really took to her. Her boyfriend, and the father of her upcoming child, was a banker by the name of Brian, also an Englishman. They'd met a year previously in London where Anne had been a hooker. For six years she'd been in the profession, making money to keep her illegitimate boy who was now twelve.

She was still legally married to somebody, somewhere, but her husband had left her long ago, and now she was married, in all but law, to Brian.

The moment that Brian and Anne first met, they fell instantly in love.

"Give up what you're doing," he had told her. "Pack your bags and let's leave."

Anne had needed no second bidding. She had grown weary of her life as a hooker, and Brian represented the kind of life she had always wanted to lead. She packed her bags in record time and, as they say in the movies, headed into the sunset with the man of her dreams.

The sunset had led to the Bahamas, where Brian had lots of banking business to attend to, and about eight months before I met them, their liaison had reached that fulfilling stage where they decided they wanted a baby: Brian's first, Anne's second. They also considered that it might be her last; she was thirty-three years old.

Brian was the object of Anne's constant attention. She would take him to the office in the morning, pick him up at lunchtime, drop him back at the office . . . and be there to pick him up again when work was over.

In an intimate moment, Anne told me they'd fucked continuously, at every possible opportunity. Now, however, she was so far pregnant that their activity had been reduced both in frequency and intensity.

I believed her because whenever I phoned I always got the feeling that I was interrupting something. I told this to Anne, who let it slip to Brian, and from then on he did a number every time I phoned.

"I'm taking her," he'd pant and groan the minute he heard my voice. "My God, I've got her up against the wall giving it to her . . . we were doing it on the kitchen table but this is much better. . . . We just got out of the back of the car, where I gave her head . . . *wow* . . . can you hang on a minute?"

When he first started doing it, his acting was so convincing that I believed him. But soon I realized that he was putting me on, so then it turned into a private joke among the three of us.

Kirsten and I enjoyed the company of Anne and Brian and we'd spend days on the beach together . . . the four of us often stripping naked and going skinny-dipping in full sight of passersby. Mostly they were tourists of both sexes, and they'd interrupt their promenade to watch three women—one quite pregnant—and a man braving the waves in the altogether. Kirsten, proud of her newly raised tits, used to run in and out of the water as if no one were there . . . just to shock. And maybe it did her ego a lot of good, too.

However, Nassau did not have the tolerant sophistication of Ile du Levant or St. Tropez, and if a policeman had come by in mid-dip, we probably would have been arrested immediately and thrown into jail. Such were the risks we took.

We would sit on the beach with Anne, when Brian was at the office, and watch the young studs pass by. She had lived in Nassau for over a year and would point out some of the more attractive young men and tell me their backgrounds.

Those with mixed blood were called "conchie Joes," and many of them looked white, with blond hair and big blue eyes. Yet at the same time they displayed certain black characteristics. They were very good-looking young fellows.

Xaviera, needless to say, was curious!

Because of Anne and Brian's particular closeness, I hadn't gotten into a swing with them, and old reliable Larry had been back in New York for a few days. So I'd been celibate for longer than I cared to be; calling myself horny would be a major understatement.

I particularly lusted after a conchie Joe who operated a marina on one of the beaches. He was a tall, slender blond with intensely sexual green eyes and dynamite features. But his business was booming, and he chose to resist my "come hithers" one day when Anne and I rented a catamaran from him. I'd been hoping that he might be able to come out in the boat with us and give me a few tips (or at least the one tip I wanted), but he had to decline. He did, however, offer one of the boys who worked for him—Colin—to teach us how to operate a catamaran.

And so Anne and I, suited in scandalously cut bikinis, headed toward the deep and open sea with Colin, a beautifully built deep-black Bahamian whose red, white, and blue trunks and white shirt set off his blackness perfectly.

Covering his crinkly black hair was a big white cotton hat to protect him from the sun. Out of its shadow glowed two big black-brown eyes, full of life and mischief. His face was constantly creased into a smile, his sensuous purple-brown mouth opening to reveal perfect white teeth and a tongue of delicious pink.

As the boat glided onto the water, he guided it easily with his muscle-knotted arms and his—bingo!—huge hands. It didn't take long for my regret at missing his boss to leave me. The stand-in was just as gorgeous. As we skated at high speed over the water—catamarans, I discovered, really move—Anne found herself the most comfortable position in the boat and lay down to enjoy it, her pregnant belly up in the air like a human mountain.

Colin told me to sit between his long brown legs, so that I would come to no harm. (!) And also, he said, so that he could reach around me and teach me how to control the boat.

After sailing for about fifteen minutes, Anne and I decided to take off the tops of our swimsuits. As they came off our breasts tumbled into the free air, mine nice and easily, Anne's with a great gazonk, as the milk-heavy mammaries suddenly lost their support.

At this point Colin moved up tight behind me and hung my bra on a rope so that it wouldn't be blown overboard. I turned around and saw his pearly white teeth and sensuous mouth right on top of me, so I snuggled in and let what was gong to happen just happen. As I did so, I could feel his member snap to full attention inside his swimsuit and I heard his suppressed sigh of relief. It couldn't have been easy to hold down what he had inside that swimsuit. My God, it was almost nudging me on the back of the head!

I was about to turn around and fondle it, when Colin, whether intentionally or because his mind had wandered, let go of the control ropes and the boat spun out of control into the waves.

Both Anne and I shouted.

I yelled, "What the hell is happening?" and turned toward him. Colin wasn't listening. He was too busy trying to cope with his brief swimsuit, his monstrous cock now peeping out like a one-eyed python. Within a second it was displayed for us to see . . . a monument to physical engineering and the power of the human mind.

Anne looked up with surprise, and then I saw another emotion take over as her jaw sagged. She started at it with amazement, wonder, and more than a touch of envy.

"By God," said Anne, "no one can be that big. I thought Brian was hung . . . but Christ. Look at it, Xaviera!"

"I'm looking," I heard someone say. Maybe it was me.

Colin was just standing there, looking down at it himself, the ever-present smile on his face. Now, I thought, there's nothing worse than a man standing on a deck at sea with a monumental erection. My mind told me something had to be done. But what? The answer was blowing in the wind.

I reached over and touched it, and gently tugged Colin toward me. But the minute I did, he leaped on top of me, obviously intent on making his own hole.

"Easy, Colin," I said. "If you're going to take me, it'll have to be done the right way, or you'll never get in."

The minute he realized he wasn't getting any opposition —at least, not from me—he eased off and let me handle it. I took off my panties and rubbed some suntan oil into my vagina as extra lubrication. Talk about carrying coals to Newcastle, I was just about flooding the deck with horniness.

I eased Colin onto his knees and put his cock between my lips, just the head, and only to moisten it. Trying to blow Colin would be like trying to blow a telephone pole. When he was good and moist I put my legs astride him and started to ease the head of his penis inside my cunt.

God, it was big . . . so *that's* what taking a horse feels like! But I felt the lips of my vagina open and the head make its way in with a slight plop. Then came the stalk, thicker than the head, and I made my strokes easy so that only a modest millimeter more went in each time. Slowly up and down, lower and lower, until, after about twenty strokes, his prick was right inside me. I was very, very full. And it couldn't have been anything I ate.

I let it stay there, still and bursting, for a second, then eased myself onto my back, braced my feet against the seat, and said, "Go!"

Colin could have been an Olympic sprinter, the way he got off the blocks. He was thrusting in a flash, his huge prick making sucking noises as it throbbed into me. My cunt must have been the widest it had ever been and by now I was taking him easily . . . mind over matter, as they say.

Meanwhile, the water lapped gently against the side of the boat as we sailed, controlled, through the gently swelling sea. Wow, did I feel good! I felt I could have fucked for hours, but with the kind of load Colin was carrying, I knew we weren't going to copulate anywhere near that length of time.

I pride myself that Colin's big cock would have resulted in extreme pain for most women; but I had used patience and knowledge to ensure that it was done right, and it was turning out to be the fuck I wanted it to be. No pain, all pleasure.

This was obviously Anne's estimation, too. She was lying there, eyes glazed, not believing what she saw.

The kid humped himself silly and I took all he could give me and even gave some back in return. Then the minute he came—a copious coming, it was—he quickly whipped out his prick, pulled on his bathing suit, and stood there, embarrassed. After all, he was only seventeen, and wasn't quite sure how to handle situations like this.

By now Anne had regained her power of speech, and said: "Colin, would you let me see your prick again? I want to see if it's still big even when it's small!"

Colin just didn't know what to do with himself. So I tried to help.

"Come on, Colin," I said. "Let's see it again."

Anne suddenly had second thoughts, however . . . she was afraid he might want to fuck her, and that cock wouldn't do much good in her delicate condition.

"J-j-just show it to me, Colin," she said. "Don't come any closer."

Shy and embarrassed, the kid once more pulled down his swimsuit to show us his prick, with just a little help from Xaviera. It was soft now, hanging down shyly. But it was barely an inch shorter than when it was inside me! Anne and I admired and petted it with a funny mixture of delight, desire, and incredulity. At full tilt it must have been eleven thick inches.

Holding wonder-whang respectfully in my hand, I asked Colin, "How come you're so well hung?"

He answered with the funniest thing I'd heard in a long time.

"Because," he drawled triumphantly, "it's not circumcised!" And with that he flipped it inside his swimsuit, folding it back so that he was almost sitting on it.

Then, with a beautiful, arched leap, he dove into the water to cool off.

Shortly (time-wise, I mean!) he returned to the boat and we set sail for the coast. Anne and I were still topless when we got to the beach, and Colin asked us to cover up our breasts. I think he was shy, and also a bit scared that his boss might see us and suspect what had happened.

Afterward Anne and I couldn't wait to tell Kirsten what a sight she'd missed. We now realized why chicks come down to the islands to get banged by the Bahamians. If Colin was typical, there was a hell of a lot of hot cock up for grabs!

A RAVISHING RECOLLECTION

My escapade with Colin had repercussions. With the bravado of any seventeen-year-old, he had told the beach boys that he'd made me, and the word was spreading. Wherever Anne and I went we could feel the eyes of the natives boring into our backs, and I'm sure that if we'd happened to come across some of those gentlemen on a lonely beach some night, we'd have been in for a very unhappy surprise.

There had been some brutal black-white rapes on the island recently, which forced me to think about the attitude of the island's blacks toward the whites.

Though usually friendly with me, occasionally some blacks had been nastily aggressive. Even some near-white conchie Joes were bitchy toward white tourists. And if you went into a store and offered U.S. dollars, very often the person serving you would get awkward, for no good reason, and refuse to accept them.

When you consider that tourism is their main source of income, this attitude is insane. It's forcing whites to leave in droves, taking their money with them. The situation has become worse since independence in 1973, and rape is becoming a national sport. It's not as bad in Nassau as it is on other so-called holiday islands . . . but the fact is that the islanders are simply screwing themselves. If they continue like this the flow of tourists will dry up completely. This will give the natives the islands to themselves, and abject poverty to enjoy them with.

Nassau may eventually lose its prized position as a paradise in the sun, but when I was there it was still the watering hole of the international set. There were many Americans and English people living there—I met young people from all over the world who'd come there as teachers, nurses, or government employees just to enjoy the beautiful climate, and the tax-free salaries. I sure couldn't blame them, although life there would be too uneventful for me over a long period of time. However, these were a glorious two weeks. Sun 'n fun and friendship between we three females.

Anne, Kirsten, and I would sit looking out at the sea and swap yarns from the past . . . mostly sexual stories. Considering that Anne and I had both been hookers and that Kirsten hadn't been living in a nunnery, they were quite spicy.

Inevitably, our conversation came back to the local rapes.

"Why don't we try our own rape?" said Kirsten.

"How?" asked Anne, not with too much interest, for she was *hors de combat*.

"Let's entice some young stud and rape him."

"Who's going to be so reluctant that it'll turn into rape?" I wondered aloud.

"Him," said Kirsten. She nodded toward a British boy we'd seen around the beach who was as queer as a duck. A gay duck. We'd often seen him with his male lovers.

Anne and I laughed, but Kirsten was serious. I was beginning to wonder what made the girl tick.

We had rented a beach tent to provide Anne with some shelter from the sun, and Kirsten suggested that it would be ideal for the action.

"How are you going to get him in there?" I asked.

"Just watch," she said. She sprang to her feet and headed for the faggot.

Anne and I watched them talk from a distance, and eventually the man swished along with Kirsten toward us.

"He says he'll have a look at it and see if he can help," she said, winking and pointing to the tent entrance. I never did find out what she'd told him.

"Only too happy to help if I can," said the gay guy, who was very finely spoken.

I'm generally game for anything, so as he went through the flaps of the tent, Kirsten and I piled in after him while Anne quickly closed the flaps and kept watch.

Inside the tent, we went at him like tigers, me sitting

on his chest while Kirsten tore at his trousers. At the first attack he started to shout, and then cooled it suddenly as he realized what was happening.

"This is very naughty of you," he said. "Honestly. Very naughty."

I lowered my crotch slowly onto his face, while behind me I could feel Kirsten whacking him off nineteen to the dozen. Then I turned so that I was still sitting on his face, but looking toward Kirsten, who was now slipping herself onto his suprisingly firm cock.

She was bouncing herself to a fare-thee-well while I sucked at her tits, and underneath I could feel our captive gay boy start to give me a tongue job.

Then Kirsten changed over and started to suck my tits, which turned us both on and she came within seconds of me. We'd almost forgotten the boy when this voice said:

"All change!"

So, being well-brought-up girls, we changed places with each other and I slid onto the cock, which was still hard. It fucked me most beautifully to orgasm number two ... also experienced by Kirsten, now sitting astride the anonymous gentleman's face.

At this point we felt a trifle obligated and both of us eased ourselves off him in the small space allowed by the tent.

He was quite charming.

"Thank you, ladies," he said.

He slipped on his pants and light-footed his way gracefully out of the tent, tipping his hat to Anne in a most courtly manner.

"Any time you wish. Just let me know when you're interested ... *or* your husbands!"

And with that he walked off down the beach, mincing slightly as he went.

The three of us watched him go in amazement. Then we realized the ridiculousness of the situation and broke into bursts of laughter.

It was only later that we learned the gentleman's name: Switch-hit Sid.

SQUARE PEGS IN ROUND HOLES

Too soon, my fun in the sun was all done, and it was time to leave Nassau. I had to be back in Toronto to read my galleys. At the same time, I still had to flit back and forth across the Atlantic, completing European publishing arrangements. This also allowed me to see my parents and to resume my friendship with Leo and Marika.

After that awful day in St. Tropez when they asked me to move out, we'd continued to see each other. For starters, we'd had dinner together when Larry arrived, and later we'd had a fine time at their stoned swing in the Ramatuelle villa.

During the months since then, while they'd returned to Holland and I'd continued traveling, we'd kept in touch if only with a post-card just to say we were thinking of each other. And, of course, whenever I was in Amsterdam we got together. Our relationship mellowed once again, and we were able to look back on those bumpy days during the summer as part of the pain that's sometimes endured en route to a lasting friendship. On only one occasion did we discuss Freda; they had continued to be intimate with her sexually, but she still had enormous problems in this area. Then, too, they finally realized—they conceded—what a bothersome creature she was.

During the visits to Amsterdam, besides spending time with my mother and father, and Leo and Marika, I'd occasionally look up some old acquaintances whom I'd missed during the spring. Thus, months after my return, I finally caught up with Frank, who had been my friend for years—since I was sweet (and sexy) sixteen, as a matter of fact.

It was really great to see my old pal again. We had

been close buddies—and occasional lovers—with never an argument. I'd called him immediately upon my return, but he'd been out of the country at the time.

But he was home now, and it was his birthday, so he asked me to come along to his party, and to invite a few friends if I wished. Even though I knew it was to be a straight party, I asked Leo and Marika if they'd care to join me, and they did.

Frank was now thirty-three years old, his thick black hair streaked with silvery gray. He stood about six feet two, every inch of him charming and attractive—the exception to so many Dutch clods. During the day he worked as a car salesman, but his real vocation and main love was his night-time occupation—drummer in a New Orleans-type jazz band. He also still played soccer, so it wasn't surprising to find that many of the men at the party were either from Frank's football team or the jazz band.

The party really got started when out came the instruments and the jam session began, the musicians relaxed and grooving as they do when they play purely for their own enjoyment.

It had been a long time since I'd been at a Dutch party. The jazz was great fun but it was strange, in fact, to be at a party with everybody fully clothed. It reminded me of my high school days, particularly when a few people at this party, who'd gone to school with me, called me Vera—my highschool nickname, which I hated.

How much I'd changed, and oh!—how *they'd* changed! For instance, one man, almost completely bald and wearing thick glasses, turned out to be the kid who had been the Don Juan of the year, when he'd had thick bushy hair and no glasses. I only managed to recognize him by his voice and eyes.

Another guy at the party who looked five years younger than me turned out to be an old school chum who was in fact two years older than I. He was a professional musician now and looked the role—shoulder-length wavy hair, a raggedy sweatshirt over a pair of blue jeans that looked as though they could stand up by themselves. Although I didn't mind, he did look very out of place among the crowd of well-dressed men and women.

I was wearing an "eat your heart out" ensemble of tight black crepe pants and a multicolored silk blouse with short, puffed-up sleeves. Almost a peasant-girl look. But—and this is where the tease came in—the blouse was held together at the front by just one tiny button and when the party got hotter, I opened the button, and with no bra on, there was no doubt that things were swinging. It was this mixture of peasant innocence and purple Jezebel that blew a lot of minds that night.

It didn't seem to affect Leo and Marika, however. They seemed bored, although Leo perked up when the jam session started; like any musician, he always appreciated good live music.

Marika seemed to be having a decent time. She'd met a girl who was working as a receptionist for KLM, and since Marika herself had flown as a KLM stewardess, they were quickly on the same wavelength, talking about the airline and mutual acquaintances.

The girl's name was Hetti and she was just stunning! She was about twenty-six and had superb reddish-brown hair flowing halfway down her back. A tight green sweater indicated that she had good, upstanding tits, and her tight black pants revealed the kind of ass which would get her gang-pinched in Italy. Her almond-shaped eyes had a childlike expression in them, but if you got very close you could detect that she had some Oriental blood in her—her eyes were slightly slanted. She was a very, very sexy person, seemingly cool at first but actually very warm-hearted.

As we talked, I found that Hetti was the girlfriend of Hans—Frank's brother. As a mere callow youth, I had been to bed with both brothers and knew that while both boys were fairly well equipped, they were not the world's greatest lovers. Hans was also very immature and—in those days—used to jump around from one girl to another. So I was pleasantly surprised when I found out that he had been living with Hetti for about two years. She could only be a good influence on him.

While Leo and Marika continued talking with Hetti, I continued to survey the party. I noticed an extremely good-looking man sitting on a bench near the band. He must have been about twenty-nine, with long, straight, thick dark hair falling over his face and almost covering one eye. He had high cheekbones, giving him a Slavic look—a look enhanced by his outfit: a black sweater with a checkered jacket over it and a pair of black velvet pants.

He noticed me studying him and stood up to get a better look at me over the dancing couples. I smiled at him, he returned the smile, and he moved with ease through the couples and came over and sat next to me. I've found that men who move well and gracefully usually have good bodies. Well, this man had a fantastic body; without touching him I knew it would be a pleasure to have him close to me.

He introduced himself as Sergei, a name which suited him perfectly. It was his father, a Russian, who had given him the Slavic look and name, his mother being Dutch. We got up to dance, and I was aching to confirm my body theory. I put my arms around his muscular shoulders and pressing close to him as we danced, I felt the muscles moving in his thighs—not the overdeveloped muscles of a body builder, but the muscles developed over a long period of regular exercise. I couldn't resist the temptation any longer and let my hands slip from his shoulders until they were resting on his ass. Just beautiful—shapely, firm buttocks that immediately reminded me of Rudolf Nureyev. (Only seen him in ballet tights, folks.)

When I complimented him on his excellent physique and the way he moved, he explained he had been a jazz-ballet dancer for seven years and now had his own dance school. He offered to give me lessons, but I explained that I would be a peripatetic pupil.

Sergei and I danced for about a half hour. Leo and Marika were also dancing, as were Hans and Hetti. Soon we were all dancing together, three couples in a tight-knit, intimate group. But now Sergei was steering us away from the group, toward a fairly dark corner of the room. I sat on his lap and could feel his cock growing, pushing up into my derriere. I squeezed even closer and slid my hand onto his lap, arousing his semisleeping beauty even more. Then I let my hands crawl up inside his sweater until they rested on his hairy chest. We were both getting very excited in a gentle way.

Marika danced by, spotted us, realized what was happening, and smiled her encouragement. Hetti danced by several times and blew affectionately kidding kisses at us and, I felt very warmly toward her. She had a very sensuous way of dancing, almost a snakelike movement, and it seemed she could sway any part of her body while keeping the other parts perfectly still.

When the music stopped I gestured for Hetti to come over and join us. She approached rather shyly, not quite knowing what to expect. I could see from her nervous movements, when she sat down on my lap with my arms around her, that she had never been with a girl. Which is not surprising—most of the people I knew in Holland were superstraight. I had already whispered with Sergei about the possibility of a swing, providing we could get the right people to agree. He was all for it—and why not, since he already had two women sitting on his strong legs.

The swing would be at Leo and Marika's house, naturally. It was just a matter of talking Hetti into joining us. I didn't figure Hans would have any objections to the swing since he and Frank had been pretty wild boys and had fucked around quite a lot. But then, I hadn't been around Amsterdam for a while and they might have turned middle-age serious. Who knew?

When I suggested to Hetti—who had taken a liking to both Leo and Marika—that she come to the house after the party, she seemed very eager and curious, not realizing precisely what we had in mind. While the discussion was proceeding I caressed her back under her green sweater and soon had her flimsy, strapless bra unhooked. She giggled, looking around to see if anyone was watching us, and Sergei silenced her soft protests with a gentle kiss as I slipped the bra from under her sweater and dropped it on a chair. As I continued caressing her back, he ran his fingers under the front part of her sweater from her navel to her titties, gently but persuasively massaging her nipples.

It was all very erotic, but we realized we couldn't fulfill any of our fantasies until we got out of the party. So I decided to be open with Hetti, telling her of our plans, and to my delight she agreed to join us, although she confessed it would be very new to her. At that moment Hans came searching for her. He seemed more than a little tipsy.

"Hans, I'm going with Xaviera and these other people to their house for a . . . a . . . swing."

His drunken eyes narrowed. "You are not. I don't want to hear about it."

"I want to go, Hans."

"You are not going to an orgy, Hetti. We've never done anything like that before, and we don't want to now. I will not have my girlfriend fucked by another man"—he looked angrily at me—"or woman."

Hans must have known that I was pretty good at changing ladies' appetites—from boys to girls. Hetti was obviously very keen to come along, liking Sergei and also wanting to experience something new with me. But she also wanted her boyfriend's approval and went to get him another beer while we worked on him. I tried my best rational, diplomatic approach.

"Look, Hans, we've been good friends. That's why I feel I can talk to you. I really dig Hetti, but I certainly don't want to offend you. It's all going to be a harmless sex game. No emotions involved."

He still shook his head. I tried another approach.

"If you want to know more about swinging, why don't you talk to Leo and Marika? They've been married for quite a long time and they've been swinging for some time, too. And you know what? They're still together. Maybe it will loosen you both up and make you both less jealous."

He started paying attention to me, which was a good sign. I talked to him for twenty minutes and finally he agreed to come along. I thought of asking Frank along, but didn't—it was, after all, his birthday party, and he would want to stay and entertain his guests.

Around two in the morning we left the party and went on to our own special type of amusement. Just before we split, Sergei finally introduced his date, Nadja, who couldn't have been a day over twenty-one. Her face wasn't too pretty and the dress she wore—a loose-fitting number—didn't tell us too much about her body, but although Nadja looked innocent, I sensed that going with a supersexy man like Sergei, she had to have something going for her.

When we arrived at Leo and Marika's house on the Prinsengracht, I was glad that it was truly beautiful. I don't know what the others expected of people who believed in group sex, but they were all very surprised at the artistic way Leo and Marika had decorated the canal house—the huge room with the wooden ceiling beams, the many objets d'art, the multicolored lamps and the erotic paintings and sculptures. The large leather couches and the cozy bar put the finishing touches to a very lovely house.

Drinks were served and then Leo sat down behind his favorite piece of furniture—his Steinway piano—and played some of his own compositions. Then I gave our new guests a guided tour of the entire house. As we passed the bathroom with its blue and white tiles, large bathtub, and wall-to-wall carpet, I laughingly said that in order to join the swing, they each had to take a bath, either alone or with their partner.

Well, I was only half-serious, but before I knew what was happening, everybody was stripping. So I ran the bath—adding Badedas, as Vitabath is known in Europe—and was confronted with Hetti, Nadja, Hans, and Sergei, all wearing their birthday suits. Naturally I couldn't stand there fully clothed, so I followed suit. (Or is it unsuit?)

We stood there, ogling one another for a while, then Nadja and I were the first to hop into the tub. Hetti quickly joined us, making a nice cozy crowd, so I took a big bar of sexy-smelling soap and started lathering her body. Good girl! She came to swing and she wasn't going to miss a thing.

Both girls had beautiful tits. Hetti's were particularly firm and stood up like rocks, her aureoles and nipples very dark, showing her Eurasian background. Nadja's breasts were softer but still very attractive, her nipples almost the same color as the rest of her virgin-white skin.

The soap-sudsing was very sensuous and Sergei couldn't remain on the sidelines. He came over to the tub with a tremendous erection. He really had a fantastic body, from his toes right up to his neck. But I was busy playing around with Hetti's bushy black pussy and kissing her nipples, which made her giggle with delightful excitement. Meanwhile, Nadja, that sexy, uninhibited young thing, was gently touching and exploring my ass—it all made a great water ballet.

But I was their host, after all, so I stepped out to make room for Sergei to join the ballet corps and, as I did so, he brushed his prick against my tits. That was too much and I couldn't resist kissing his beautiful dong for a few seconds before finally pushing him into the tub. He kidded around with Hetti and Nadja briefly, but now it was the men's turn to bathe and suddenly they became embarrassed, frightened to accidentally touch each other's pricks and, funniest of all, covering their crotches with their hands as they stepped into the tub.

It didn't take them long to lose their inhibitions and they were soon splashing around without worries. Meanwhile, I'd located a bunch of large beach towels and soon we were all drying each other. Leo and Marika came into the bathroom and told us the bedroom had been prepared with soft lighting and good music. With the bathing over, the reality of the swing at hand must have settled into everybody's mind and suddenly everyone became uptight. Hans was even putting on his underpants and Hetti slipped into her bra.

Leo leaned over and whispered in my ear, "This is going to be amateur night."

"What do you mean?" I asked, ever the optimist.

"You'll see. This isn't going to work out the way we're used to."

"They were great in the bathtub, Leo."

"Just wait and see."

I playfully got Hans to undress again and then led them all through the long hallway to the master bedroom now lit by two red phallus-shaped candles. It was time to divide the boys and girls from the men and women.

SWINGUS INTERRUPTUS

The flickering shadows on the walls, the moody music—very rhythmic and yet calming—plus the overall sensual feel to the room combined to create an atmosphere for relaxed sex, and I think this atmosphere served to reduce everyone's anxieties and we all wordlessly arranged ourselves somewhere on that giant bed. Hans and Hetti remained together, both lying in the middle of the bed, her legs spread slightly apart, but his locked together. I couldn't wait any longer and just dove in between Hetti's legs and started eating her with real passion. I'd leave Hans to other hands.

I needn't have worried. A second or so later Marika started sucking on Hans's cock, which had what I can describe as a polite erection. After about five minutes of this Marika straddled Hans, grasping his prick firmly in her hand and guiding it into her trimmed cunt.

While Marika was riding him, Hans had his head turned to the right, looking into Hetti's eyes, as though he were saving his love for her. On another part of the bed, Leo was playing with Nadja's tits and nibbling her earlobes, while Sergei was at base camp, his mouth glued firmly to her very edible pussy. Marika's action on Hans, and my tongue, which had long since fought its way past Hetti's pubic hair to her lovely moist cunt, seemed to bring the two young lovers closer together and they were kissing each other.

I didn't want to be rude—or unromantic—but Hetti's clitoris was becoming more swollen and I knew she was close and without thinking too much about it, I excitedly pushed Hans out of the way, climbed on top of Hetti and, holding her closely, rubbed myself against her until I felt myself shuddering into orgasm. Yet Hetti still hadn't come, so I soon enough went back to eating her kinky pussy.

Marika had moved off Hans and with a curious detachment he was watching me eat Hetti. Intent upon one thing, I continued driving my tongue inside her and now Hetti's moaning was out of control, her pelvis thrusting against my face, her hands behind my head, seeking to pull me deeper and deeper into her until I felt almost suffocated. Then, with a final gasp of gurgling pleasure, she fell back on the bed, drained for the moment, looking a little lost and disconnected from reality. Hans immediately moved over and took her in his arms. He seemed distressed at the violence of her reaction to my lovemaking.

To be frank, I was too aroused to be concerned with his distressed sensibilities—there'd be time for talk later. Having pleased Hetti, I was more than ready for my next playmate—Sergei. He was sitting in the middle of the bed, looking undecided, which is a fate that shouldn't happen to a man with such talent, such machismo, and such an incredible hard-on. He'd been watching my performance with Hetti and now he moved toward me, obviously in a fucking mood. But I was in a sucking mood that night, and while I would have loved to feel that Russian missile inside me, I wanted Sergei to have the best blow-job of his life. I moved between his legs and got his cock in close-up, as they say in the movies. Wow—what a cinemascope! It was swollen and really straining at the skin—the blue veins were standing out.

Getting my message, Sergei propped himself up against the pillows and watched every movement of mine, as though checking out some piece of choreography. I began as if I were doing the Nutcracker Suite, taking fluttering steps with my tongue from left to right, then around the head, then back down to its hairy base and a long, slow, slick slide up to the blood-flushed head. I then plunged his whole cock into my mouth and performed a solemn suck from the base all the way up his stem until I reached the circumcision edge. Now it was time to change roles—I would be a musician and play the skin flute.

Sergei could no longer act the disinterested spectator.

He was caressing my head and pushing his cock all the way into my mouth until I almost consumed the whole thing. I was chewing and licking and sucking it, all the while playing with his balls with one hand and my own clitoris with the other. Sergei suddenly slammed himself back on the bed and let nature run its course—which it did, all at once, first with a loud yell from deep within *his* throat, then with a deep thrust into *my* throat and his hot sperm shooting into my mouth.

Nadja looked up from her place on the bed and her expression indicated surprise that Sergei had come so fiercely in my mouth. I don't know *why* she was surprised, since that was the general idea, but there was temporarily no one with her and she'd been playing voyeur and perhaps left lonely. But not for long. Hans, at last turned on by the action, gave up his spot adjacent to Marika's paradise and moved over to settle down on Nadja, who happily spread her legs for him.

Moved by the pioneering spirit, Hans shoved his cock into Nadja and began exploring her vaginal canal like a runaway land rover. She showed her appreciation of his hot vehicle by a series of frantic motor responses and loud moaning noises—and she meant every sound. This scene worked as a turn-on for all of us, except Hetti, who looked as though she'd been stung by militant bees. And when Hans started yelling for Nadja to take all his cock, and to wrap her legs around him, Hetti jumped up, pushed Leo —and his nearby cock—away from her face, and ran out of the bedroom. Not everyone had noticed this drama, being involved in each other, but I did . . . perhaps I was half expecting it.

I walked over to the bathroom and found Hetti, her makeup smeared all over her face, tears running down her cheeks. About two minutes later Hans himself dashed out of the bedroom, very upset, and apologized to his girlfriend for what he had done. At the same time, Hans was upset at her for having had sex with Leo and me. A fine pair of hypocrites!—but this was no time to tell them that. I suggested that since this was their first time together in a swing, this jealousy was normal.

What really upset Hetti was the fact that Hans was getting the same pleasure from Nadja that she thought only she could give him. How naive could she be! And by now everybody else—the whole bloody lot!—had joined us in the bathroom. Marika, never the greatest of diplomats, said, "Come on, you two, it's not that bad. We'll probably never see each other again after tonight, so don't take it so seriously."

Nadja was also angry at Sergei for having such a good time when I blew him . . . what did she expect him to do —suffer?

Okay, gang, time to let it all hang out—this time with words instead of music. Best not go stomping out of the house without any better understanding of their hang-ups and even though it was nearly sunrise, Leo persuaded us all, still stark naked, to go down to the kitchen while Marika brewed coffee and served cake.

"Okay Hetti," Leo led off, "why are you crying? What upset you?"

"I don't know. I thought Hans and I loved each other. I didn't mind him fucking Marika, because he was holding on to me. But then with Nadja—he wasn't holding me then. . . . You see, as long as he doesn't come inside another woman, it's all right, because that's actually the height of the relationship—the climax together."

"Bullshit," Marika interjected. "You don't really believe that 'coming together' bullshit. If a man fucks another woman, he can still love you. It's just a sexual act, not emotional, particularly in a swing, with everyone there . . . how could it get emotional? A swing is a very honest way to live up to your sexual desires."

"I don't think God made man and woman to do this," Hans proclaimed. "You should love your woman and she should love you and respect you and be faithful. One should apply the Ten Commandments. One shouldn't cheat. This is a sick situation."

Leo was incredulous. "You must be crazy, Hans! What's this got to do with Christianity? You mean that a man and woman should stick with each other whether they get bored sexually or not? Look, what is really wrong with another sexual relationship, eh? Be honest now . . . have you ever cheated on Hetti in the two years you've known her?"

"Well . . . yes. But only once! And she was nothing but a whore. It was a one-shot deal, no emotions involved. And it all happened out of town, when I was on business."

I certainly wasn't going to let that one slip by. "What do you mean 'nothing but a whore'? You know I was a prostitute for two years. And I was also a madam and had a first-class house. Why do you say 'nothing but a whore'? They're human beings, too. And are you trying to say that if you pay for it, it doesn't count, you're not cheating?"

"Yes, more or less. There's no involvement," he answered.

Marika took the words out of my mouth. "Let me understand this—if you pay for it, you don't feel guilty, but if you get it for free, you do feel guilty!"

The discussion was interrupted by another outburst from Hetti, her hazel eyes blazing, confronted with the fact that her lover had gone to a prostitute. It turned into another screaming match between the two of them before Leo stepped in and calmed them down.

Marika was still after Hans's illogical track. "Let's get back to Hans's point about Christianity," she said. "You knew what was going to happen—we told you, as honestly as possible, at the party. And do you mean to say that while you were fucking me and Nadja, you weren't enjoying it?"

"Yeah, what *about* that?" Hetti wanted to know. "You're contradicting yourself, you lousy bastard."

I tried to calm her. "But, Hetti, don't get so mad. You made it with me, didn't you? You enjoyed it and you came. . . . You didn't fake it. So why are you so angry at Hans for doing the same thing?"

"But that's *entirely* different, Xaviera," she said. "Another woman with me, that's something new and exciting. That's not like fucking another man. When Leo came close to me I almost puked."

"Did it ever occur to you," I responded immediately, "that a man can sometimes be more jealous of another woman pleasing his girl than another man? He knows how to compete with another man. But I don't think a man can ever compete with another woman. So conceivably it may be that my pleasing you is far more dangerous to your relationship with Hans than him going with another woman."

Sergei chimed in to agree with me: "If you reach an

orgasm by Xaviera kissing your cunt, Hetti, why shouldn't Hans be able to reach an orgasm by fucking my girlfriend? He does it the normal way, you do it the homosexual way. Everyone has homosexual tendencies. If Xaviera brings this out in you . . . well, who knows—maybe one day you'll find yourself enjoying women more than men."

His girlfriend, Nadja, wanted to amplify this point. "Let me tell you about my relationship with Sergei," she said. "The most we would ever do is take in another girl and have a threesome . . . because I don't usually feel like fucking another man. I dig Sergei more than any other man and for me there's no reason to fuck around. I enjoy making love with another woman, but ultimately I most enjoy getting fucked by Sergei. I think the most perfect relationship is the happy threesome."

The discussion wandered, as discussions often do, into tangents off the main topic of swinging. We went through marriage and what it was, women's liberation, and other related man/woman topics.

Soon the morning sun had brightened the room, and it was time to leave. It was enjoyable, but as I'd been through these debates many times before, I would have preferred to spend the time doing rather than discussing it.

DANISH DELIGHTS

Leo and Marika had a good friend named Hendrik—a swinger, naturally—who had to go to Denmark for a day or so. He was one of those people who hate to travel alone, so he invited me to join him. He was offering return air fare and hotel accommodation—plus a trip to a country I truly wanted to visit—in exchange for my companionship. He let me know that sex was not part of the deal, and since I'd done much more for much less in my New York days, I naturally didn't refuse.

Denmark actually consists of about five hundred islands, with perhaps only a fifth of them inhabited. As we began our descent toward the island of Zealand, where Copenhagen is situated, the beautiful Danish countryside came into view. There were miles of fields, forests, and flowers, dotted with attractive cottages and farmhouses, divided by gentle streams and crowned by ancient castles . . . rural Denmark is nothing less than magnificent.

Copenhagen, loosely translated, means commerce harbor, and it's the nerve center for this nation of nearly five million . . . a nation which has contributed more to the world than you'd expect from such a small population, especially in the realm of sexual freedom.

As we drove to our hotel, the Kong Frederik, I wondered what surprises were in store . . . after all, the Vikings were always front-runners in the rape and pillage department. (Not that pillage appealed to me.)

While Hendrik began his round of business calls, I took a basic tour of the city. I knew I wouldn't have time to see everything, so I didn't even bother trying. Copenhagen's zoo is among the finest in Europe, I understand, and of course the Tivoli Gardens is an internationally known potpourri of pleasure . . . a beautiful amusement park filled with fine dining, concerts, and attractions for all ages. But instead of touring the major spots—I wasn't in the mood for obligatory tourist sights—I simply walked around the city and got my impressions that way.

What I remember best are the people . . . clean, happy, attractive people. There are no slums, no racial tensions, and a very low crime rate, and the population seems cheerful and untroubled. Practically everyone in Copenhagen speaks some English, incidentally, and you can always rely on a gracious welcome wherever you go—hotels, stores, restaurants, even the porno shops!

Danish men are remarkably handsome and, young or old, they keep themselves trim and healthy. The women are pretty and wholesome. Cleanliness is almost a national fetish (there must be some Danish blood in me!) and sex and humor rate high among the great Danes. Altogether, the people are warm, helpful, and superfriendly.

Hendrik and I met for dinner in the hotel's comfortable Queens Restaurant at six o'clock, and he arrived with a friend. Inga was a jolly blond extrovert in her forties who owned a bookstore. Hendrik hadn't expected to see her this trip—he'd thought she was in Stockholm—but by chance he'd passed her bookshop and spotted her. She kissed me on the cheek and seemed quite thrilled to meet me, which of course flattered me tremendously. She had read the Danish edition of *The Happy Hooker*, which in fact she stocked in her store, and felt that she already knew me.

During dinner—Danish beef and ham, with crisp, tasty vegetables—I asked Inga about Copenhagen's sex scenes. I hadn't realized that it was a subject close to her heart.

She told me that the city's erotic night life had changed considerably in recent times because of police harassment.

"In what way?" I asked.

"There used to be live sex shows, quite well done. In some of them the audience would participate. But they've almost all been closed down now."

Inga was proud of her country's reputation for sexual freedom, but quite despondent over the closings. She was divorced, supporting a daughter, and the increased competition in the porno book trade—a thriving industry in Denmark, where books banned throughout the world are sold openly—was slowly driving her broke.

Before the nightlife changed she had made a lot of money arranging visits to sex shows for the package tour organizations. And this major source of income had now dried up. The bookshop, once just a sideline, was now her mainstay.

Now things were getting more and more difficult, she explained. Although there was no explicit law against sex shows, the police were clamping down on the little sex theaters. Apparently, many were not paying their taxes, and others failed to meet the fire department's safety standards. Another reason for the police crackdown was the fact that some of the performers were selling drugs to the audiences after the shows. In addition, officials were now insisting that anyone entering these theaters had to be a member of the club for at least twenty-four hours before admission.

This was obviously bad for tourists, who were only there for a short stay and wanted to be admitted immediately.

Most of the theaters were tiny, and only seated a few dozen people. So when the police started closing them down two and three times a week, there was no way they could cover costs.

Inga knew a girl who worked the clubs with what's known in showbiz as a "specialty act." And that's an understatement! Hendrik had once been visiting Copenhagen with a friend, and Inga had arranged for this girl to give them a command performance.

"She showed up at our hotel suite with a bucket of live eels," he recalled. "And much to our horror, she made love to these aquatic snakes . . . swallowing and fucking them."

"Oh, Xaviera," chuckled Inga, "it was unbelievable. She'd put them deep into her cunt, take them out and caress them, suck their heads and their tails and then wrap them around her body so that she was covered with a writhing mass of slithery eels. The following day she'd kill them and eat them."

Hmmm . . . Eels à la Quim, anyone?

"Every time this girl got fresh eels," Inga continued, "she would perform at a private home or on stage. If people wanted to see her perform with animals, they could go to her farm! She'd do anything, but eels were her favorite."

I wasn't too disturbed to hear that she was out of town at

the time; she'd gone to Stockholm to shoot a porno flick. With eels, no doubt. But her act isn't the kind that turns me on. And I've never liked seafood anyway.

After dinner (which ended with fabulous Danish desserts), Inga took us to Club 25, a tacky but busy sex spot.

As the curtain raiser—as they say in the theater—a couple of lesbians entwined themselves and gave us a definitive lesson in the multiple techniques of mutual masturbation.

One of the girls who followed, a voluptuous, buxom beauty, put everything imaginable into her cunt: first a single candle, followed by eleven more—the last of which she then lit. I was waiting for someone to sing "Happy Birthday."

After that she started tucking away things like vibrators, cucumbers, bananas, cigars, and anything else that came to hand. Meanwhile, back at the tits, she was using her free hand to squeeze and slap them like they were personal enemies. At one point she had another girl tie them down. Maisy Masochism was probably her stage name.

The next act was a scene in which a small woman—who later turned out to be a man in drag—dressed in leather pants with a bikini top to match and thigh-high leather boots came on and asked members of the audience to participate in a playlet.

She, or he, or it, or whatever, finally revealed a prick, and the chosen member of the audience administered a heavy beating on his ass, which produced huge welts. It took away our breaths, for we didn't believe that this skinny little faggot was capable of taking such heavy punishment.

I'd watched the show so far without much involvement. But when the next act came around, it really turned me on. Up to that point the onstage balling had been done by bored-looking Scandinavian blonds. But the ultimate screw saw a lovely, olive-complexioned young man with a superb physique and shoulder-length hair making love to a supple, long-legged honey. She wrapped herself around his body with rhythmic movements that blended with the background music, Beethoven's "Eroica Symphony."

Their gyrations, their changes of positions and subtle interrelations were artistically right on with the music. What was happening on stage wasn't just screwing; it was a sexual ballet. Their bodies moved in time with the undulating tempo of the music, gathering speed as the finale approached and the young stud, with a great shuddering movement, achieved his climax with the final notes of the musical masterpiece.

It turned me on in a way that was quite compelling. The boy literally dripped off stage and I realized that this was not one of the fake acts that often occur in these shows. That boy was faking nothing. He was a sexual musician.

I was now so horny that I could hardly wait. He came out from behind the curtains, smartly dressed and looking rather aloof. I approached him and whispered, in English, "That was truly magnificent, sir. Do you think you have another emission in you, for myself, this evening?"

He gave me what used to be called an old-fashioned look.

"What is your name?" I asked. "Where are you from? May I say that you made my evening worthwhile."

I was babbling on. I do that when I'm horny and not sure how to handle it.

He looked at me with those big brown questioning eyes and for the first time I noticed his Indian features. I hadn't taken too much notice of his face during the performance.

"My name is Rasheed," he answered in a soft, low voice.

"Are you Indian?" I asked.

He looked at me indignantly. "Do I *look* like an Indian? I beg your pardon, I am a West Pakistani!

"Of course I can perform again this evening. And will," he said with a strange smile. "But unfortunately not with you. I have to take the ferry over to Malmö to perform in another live sex show tonight."

A double-header! I asked him why.

"There's not so much work here in Copenhagen these days and I need the money. However, perhaps we could meet later this week. Are you here with your parents or friends?"

"Friends," I said.

"Well, I can't imagine your friends would wish to see the show again, but perhaps *you'd* like to accompany me . . . ?"

"I don't think I should leave them."

"Of course. I understand perfectly."

"Well, I'll ask—see what they have in mind for the rest of the evening." I went over to Hendrik and Inga—who was eyeing Rasheed with more than audience interest—and explained that I thought it might be a lark to go over to Sweden with Rasheed. Would I be spoiling their evening?

"No, not at all," Hendrik said generously. "Enjoy yourself."

"Enjoy that gorgeous young boy, too," Inga added with a wink.

Rasheed said we'd have to dash to make the ferry, but we got there in time and about twenty minutes later, had crossed the straight and were in Sweden.

SWAN DIVE

As soon as the ferry docked in Sweden's Malmö harbor, Rasheed and I raced for the theater where he was due to perform. We got there in time for me to witness a remarkable act involving a love scene between a girl and a long-necked white swan. It opened with a beautiful girl lying languidly on a couch, where she was approached by the swan, whom she petted, putting its head against her belly, then moving it up higher, to her tits. Then the bird began nibbling her earlobes, just like a lover. A swan obviously can't kiss with his beak, but it sure looked like it from the audience.

The girl, who was fully dressed, suddenly stood up and started doing a wild, seductive striptease, with the assistance of the swan, who, with great precision, picked off each piece of her clothing one by one. First she unrolled her gloves, and the swan took them delicately in his beak and put them aside. She unzipped her dress and started to step out of it, and the bird again carted it away in its beak. Then she sat down and lay back as the bird, with a clever snap of its beak, whipped off her brassiere with the speed and ease of an underwear salesman.

All she had left on was a small black G-string, and this too proved no problem for our feathered friend. With two swift pecks, he disengaged the clip on each hip and the G-string fell away to reveal a pussy all ready for the *coup de grâce*.

By this time the girl seemed really turned on to her bird and began caressing him again, only this time more erotically. She wrapped both her legs around his brilliant white body and wings and started to writhe against his neck, like it was a long, white, feathery cock. Meanwhile, his little head peaked out, almost with a wink, every time a space opened up between his body and hers.

Slowly she started to move his head down so that it was on the same level as her cunt. Obviously it was impossible for the swan to eat her. But she was so horny she used her hand to put some spit on her already wet cunt, and slipped the bird's beak inside her.

The bird seemed to have no qualms at all about this little trick and before an amazed audience, he sank his head up to the eyes, and then continued, piercing the girl with his entire head. The head-job of all time!

Then she squeezed its neck and it started to disappear inside her. The bird, well trained as a lover, started to move his head backward and forward, coming up for air between strokes, as the girl writhed in obvious pleasure. As she got carried away, so did the swan, going faster and faster and obviously getting worked up himself, in his own birdlike way.

I was amazed at this, for the girl was surely risking serious injury from that beak. However, as in the way they file down bulls' horns in bullfighting, I'm sure that something had been done to that bird's beak to avoid damage to her ovaries or womb. This act was really far out—exotic . . . much more interesting than the usual man-woman or lesbian scenes. For this alone I was glad I'd come to Sweden!

Rasheed then gave another virtuoso performance, which nearly had me fingering myself, just to relieve the incredible sexual excitement he'd created.

The evening ended with a gorgeous tall black girl, her skin the color of light chocolate, who possessed a superb pair of tits with enormous nipple rings. And her act was . . . fucking a pillow. That's right, folks, the common house-and-garden pillow. Well, not quite. It was man-sized, and could be reshaped into any form at will.

This sounds tame, but believe me it was a sight to behold. She banged it to distraction, hugging, kneading, gripping, bending, tossing, turning . . . wham, wham, wham. She could make it into anything she wished, so that when she finally came, sitting astride it, like a man was underneath her, the object had ceased to be a pillow, but a great muscular horny machine capable of giving an endless fuck.

As the black girl pounded to a final orgasm, a woman in

the front row seemed to go out of her mind with desire. She leaped onto the stage and started pounding away at the pillow, at the same time screaming and yelling and ripping off her clothes. At first I thought this might be part of the act, but no, the black girl was even more turned on and, anticipating the appreciation of the part-lesbian audience, she grappled with the woman and the pillow simultaneously, rubbing herself up and down on the now-screaming woman. Then she literally ripped off the woman's bra and panties and began giving her head. The woman went crazy and her screams rang through the hall until she too leaned over and started to eat the black girl's purple-lipped cunt.

By this time not only the lesbians in the audience, but the men too were going bananas with lust and three of them actually went up on the stage and began balling the women and the pillow, working themselves into a multiple fuck that thrashed around the pillow like a shark shoal at a shipwreck.

By this time I was a wreck too, washed-out and quivering. Rasheed joined me and I needed his steadying hand as we walked into the cool night air.

What an orgy! So far as I knew, the show went on, and on, and on....

Rashy and I talked about it on our way back to Copenhagen on the late night ferry. He explained that the show I had just seen was the kind that used to take place in Copenhagen until the Danish police started cracking down.

However, to change the subject from sex shows at least for the rest of the evening, I asked Rasheed how he'd come to Denmark in the first place, and as we sat on the ferry, watching the ship's lights shimmer over the sea, he told me about his background. He was West Pakistani and had been trained as an engineer. But he preferred sex and travel, so decided to strike out on his own. In Denmark he had struck it rich. His dark looks had made him eminently bedworthy to the light-skinned Danish women, and just about any woman in Copenhagen was his for the asking. Well ... let's say he'd maybe done the asking in the right places.

He was addicted to fashionable clothes and out of his briefcase took a series of photos, each showing him stylishly garbed in a whole range of clothing.

You might get the impression he was a little conceited. It's not a false one. But if he thought he was a gorgeous, smart stud, he wasn't kidding himself. He was. He couldn't have been a day over twenty-five but he acted with the maturity of someone who knows just how good he is.

He was a Moslem, and believed in their sexual traditions. For instance, Moslem men and women are not supposed to see each other's sexual organs. Fondle them by all means, but no peeking. According to tradition, this makes lovemaking more exotic and mysterious. And sperm—because it is the seed of human life—is not considered edible under Moslem dietary laws, so fellatio is not allowed.

Moslems must also wash their genitals before sex—presumably an ancient way of minimizing disease—and must take a bath within four hours of copulating. Otherwise they are unclean and not fit to pray to God. They even wash their anus immediately after going to the toilet. As a hygiene freak, this is fine with me.

Far be it from me to enter the field of comparative religion, but to one of my background, some of this seemed rather bizarre. However, seven hundred million people believe in it, so who am I to question their beliefs?

As for his stage act, Rasheed explained, "It's not very romantic, I know, but it brings in the cash and where else can you combine business with that kind of pleasure?"

"That's exactly the way I felt when I was hooking," I said.

"The only other way to do that is to become a gigolo. But I could never do it with older women. This way I get young gorgeous girls and can fuck twice a day without it costing me a penny."

At this point I still didn't know how good he was in bed—though I must say the stage performance was a fair indication that he wasn't deficient.

RASHEED + XAVIERA = 3

Rasheed and I were soon back in Copenhagen. We got off the boat and walked to my hotel room, his hand delightfully fondling my ass, guiding me toward our destination: bed.

We'd hardly stepped inside the room when I almost came from sheer horniness. But I held it back and took a steaming-hot shower . . . in world-record time. Rasheed was lying on the bed, fully clothed, when I got back to him, and slowly, surely, I undressed him, a kiss here, a suck there. When I came to his last piece of clothing it would hardly come off because of the load of bursting flesh pushing against it.

When I finally got his underpants off I was confronted with a crotch completely devoid of pubic hair. Nor had he any hair on his chest. Or under his armpits. This wasn't the result of nature . . . shaving his hair was part of his religion. He saw my smile and started to go into an explanation, but I quieted him. I'd had enough religion for one night . . . although I *was* planning to get down on my knees, and I wouldn't object to a few ejaculations.

We started to kiss and caress, and he covered my face and neck with his mouth. I moved his head down to my left nipple, the more sensitive of the two. Within seconds both left and right were standing up like cherries and I began to slowly press his head toward my crotch.

"No," said Rashy. "My religion forbids."

"For me," I said.

"No, I can't."

"Just this once."

"No. It's no good."

"It's an appetizer for the real thing, and I'm squeaky clean."

"Sorry. But I'm not allowed to. I am a Moslem and we do not do such frivolous things. Please forgive me. But I would like to have intercourse with you."

I felt all nice 'n warm inside. But only for a second.

"You don't have VD, do you?" he asked.

"That's bloody insulting."

"Our upbringing demands that we ask these things. It is nothing personal."

"Well, I don't! Wow! . . . if you were Jewish, at least I could say I was half kosher, and you could go for either milk or meat. But what can I say to you except . . . go ahead and fuck! Come on . . . I'm plenty lubricated. Since we've been talking religion, let's go for the good old missionary position."

No second invitation was needed. He was inside me in a flash, his cock the way I remember it from the stage show, long and hard.

As he was thrusting into me, my mind wandered for a moment when I caught a glimpse of his hand. It was slim and dainty. This destroyed my theory that men with small hands have puny cocks. His cock-hand relationship definitely didn't fit in with my observations. He was a biggie!

As we'd dispensed with the hors d'oeuvres of oral sex, I wanted to make the most of our plain, old-fashioned fucking and started to make passionate yells and screams, hitting him with dialogue that went roughly as follows:

". . . marvelous . . . that thick hard cock . . . all the way up . . . stirring my juices . . . pounding against my clit . . . I've been oozing . . . just waiting for this moment . . . the moment you'd bury that stiff thing inside me and never stop thrusting . . . ahhhh . . . go, baby, go . . . do it to me, Rasheed, all the way . . . agggghhhh . . . you turned me on so much in that club, you sexy bastard, I almost raped you . . . y'hear . . . *raped* you . . . while you were fucking that gorgeous blond . . . oooooohhhhhh . . . how I envied her . . . I'd have balled you all fucking night.

"Squeeze my ass . . . go on . . . bite my tit . . . go on, bite it . . . aaahhhhhh . . . ."

Our bodies literally flew off the bed into a surging mass of heaving flesh as we came together, mixing our juices in mid-air. My cunt milked every last drop out of him, and we sank back with a thud onto the bed, spent, our bodies moist and slithery from perspiration.

The room was now heavy with the scent of our union and as I slipped out from under his beautiful body he, without a word, rolled sideways and in one action picked up a cigarette and lit it. He turned his head away from me and was nodding slowly. Was there something wrong?

"What's the matter, Rasheed?" I said. "Are you all right?"

"I'm fine."

I put my arms around his neck from behind. "Then why are you shaking your head?"

He laughed. A brief, almost embarrassed laugh.

"You talked so dirty I couldn't believe it," he said.

"But—"

"And I liked it. Every word of it. Not just liked it. I *loved* it. In all my years on stage I haven't come across one girl who enjoys fucking as much as you do. That was truly exotic."

I told him he was welcome to come across me anytime. I didn't have to repeat the invitation . . . before Copenhagen saw the morning sun, Rasheed and I scored a hat trick (hockey talk for three in a row—but we were counting fucks, not pucks!). That almost made it a six-pack (if I can mix my metaphors) for him, when you include his stage acts. Now *that's* performance!

The following morning I called Hendrik's room to see if he wanted to join Rasheed and me for breakfast, and to my surprise, Inga answered! I hoped her night had been as exciting as mine.

We did meet for breakfast and Inga and Hendrik ordered kippers. I don't eat fish, so I went for delicious Danish bacon and fluffy scrambled eggs. Rasheed wouldn't have any of it, so he ordered lots of warm Danish pastries and fresh fruit. He had quite an appetite for food as well as sex, but I suppose his athletic performances help keep him trim.

During breakfast we talked again about (what else?) sex, Danish-style. Rasheed maintained that the government's sanctioning the sale of pornography had done much to bring down the incidence of sexual crimes. And at the same time, it had done much to create a whole new awareness of sexuality, even spawning a "Dear Abby"-style newspaper column written by a husband and wife, which answered sexual questions explicitly, without the kind of pussyfooting (oops!) the North American press gives to such subjects.

The Danes' opinion is that anything enjoyed by consenting adults should be permitted and, furthermore, regarded as normal.

Another newspaper's Monday edition carried a weekly two-page "Sexual Merry-Go-Round," in which people from all walks of life wrote about their desires and experiences in sex, inviting readers to reply and share their own such tastes.

Inga told us that books on sex were being published by the score, and about one hundred films a year were produced on the subject. Many deal with specific minority tastes . . . as do the very specific photo magazines, all with high quality reproduction. They are sold in special pornography stores, though most of them can be obtained on newsstands.

"In the typical porno shop," she explained, "you can buy anything: erotic post cards, lewd pencils, matchboxes, many things—all with drawings and reproductions of the most explicit nature." They apparently had everything but suggestive cutlery and a naughty kitchen sink.

The shops are quite liberated and cater to women as well as men, selling a wide range of vibrators and massage machines in all kinds of exotic and lifelike shapes to excite the female fantasy and give satisfaction through self-stimulation.

There are pubic rings, Inga said, which slip over the prick and prolong erection, many of them with knots, spikes, and ferrules that excite the clitoris during sex. For men who find the chase a little too fatiguing there's even an ersatz vagina, complete with hair and a built-in vibrator. For visual stimulation the range of made-to-measure sexy garments is endless. High-heeled shoes, straps, feathers, chains, handcuffs, crucifixes (see what *The Exorcist* did for sex?), whips, and any other piece of equipment you may need to turn on, are readily available. And again, such equipment can be made to your specifications.

To go along with such tastes, there's undearwear in every substance known to man, the accent of course on the traditional turn-on materials—rubber and leather. But if you get a charge out of wood, they could probably meet your needs. These shops, said Rasheed, are seventh heaven for flagellants, masochists, sadists, and transvestites.

But perhaps the most interesting piece of information to come out of this conversation was Rasheed's recollections about a sea-going sex club. While cruising the strait between Denmark and Sweden it offered sex, porn, and, for the bored, gambling. Onboard was a shop which sold and rented photographic equipment so that you could take your own shots of the multisexual activities taking place onboard. You could also enjoy live sex shows, films, stripteases, some very tricky massage, or any other activity you came across during a tour around the ship.

"The weirdest act I ever saw," said Rasheed, "involved a couple playing tormentor and victim roles. He was dressed in rubber panties and a leather mask and sported an artificial penis strapped to the front of him. The girl was tied to a crucifix, and during the act the male pulled down the girl's rubber panties and forced the dildo into her gaping vagina while he whipped her mercilessly with a cat-'o-nine-tails . . . sometimes even drawing blood.

"Then he took her down and put her on a piece of equipment that was once used by Louis XVI of France. It's shaped like a horse's back except there's nothing immediately below her vagina . . . but her legs are arched as though she's on a horse. Her lower parts then moved up and down on the artificial penis while she was whipped into an orgasm, which came with a scream. Then she was chained to a pillory in a stooping position and tightly gagged, while the man entered her anus to get his orgasm. It was all too incredible to believe."

He then went on to reminisce about some of the recently closed clubs, and said he believed they were still operated secretly for members of the city's diplomatic corps. This kind of show usually starts with free drinks served by naked girls, followed by stripteases, pornographic films, a lesbian love show, and general intercourse for all the guests. Later a sex lottery was arranged, followed by dancing with the naked waitresses, who were available for sex at a reasonable price.

"Well, I hate to see you go," Rasheed said when breakfast was over and it was time for Hendrik and me to leave. "Sure you won't stay?"

"No," I answered regretfully. "I don't know what lies ahead, but I've got to find out. My life is in something of a turmoil right now and I have to sort it out. Maybe travel is the answer. And I won't know until I finish going everywhere I want to go. But some day soon we'll get together again."

He kissed me, quietly and sweetly, and wished me good luck.

I miss Rasheed, though we have kept in touch. As I write this chapter, I have his most recent letter on my bedside table. At the end of five closely written and intimate pages it says:

"It's four-thirty in the morning and I'm now going to bed. I am tired, but I wish you were here beside me at this time. Wow!! Love and kisses . . . *everywhere*. . . . Rasheed."

I read it again and touch myself and find I am moist. Such was the effect of Rasheed, a lover in a million.

THE FLYING DUTCHGIRL

I was in Holland, and the first gray signs of a dreary mid-European winter were beginning to show. After a beautiful summer tooling around Europe and two happy months in Toronto doing TV and personal appearances, I was in no mood to accept the winter delights of North Sea fogs.

Like most people stuck in that kind of situation, my mind started wandering . . . to some place in the sun. Anywhere, as long as there was sun, a beach, and some interesting sex. (Give me the first two and I'd provide the third!)

For some reason my thoughts kept turning to Acapulco. It's a famous haven for the jet set, and has that good-living fiesta ambience that Mexico provides so well.

Another reason was its lack of gambling. The loud clientele, noisy and money-oriented, who jumped from casino to casino throughout the world would give Acapulco a miss. And that was fine by me. I don't find the high-pressured gambling life to my liking. Maybe I was getting a little like Andreas in my desire to stay away from the common herd. Who knows?

But I did know I had this burning desire to catch the first plane to Acapulco and enjoy Christmastime there.

So once more, I said goodbye to my mother and father and boarded a jumbo jet at Amsterdam's Schiphol Airport, heading for the sun.

Well, not directly. For some reason known to God and the airlines (they're much the same—anonymous and all-powerful) the flight took me via Montreal and Houston. Even after arriving in Mexico City I had to change planes for Acapulco.

As the huge aircraft lifted out of Schiphol I got to know the passenger next to me—a cute young guy in his twenties from Washington. He had unfashionably short blond hair, yet he was dressed in worn-out blue jeans and carried a heavy, rolled-up carpet.

He explained that he was on his way back from Afghanistan—the reason for the carpet—and that he'd recognized me at the airport, as his brother had given him my book *The Happy Hooker* in Istanbul. That book really travels all round the world, as do I!

The young man's name was Foster, and he had an intriguing story to tell.

It all come out when, in the course of our conversation, I asked him for his number to put in my address book. He refused. I asked him why.

He became very hesitant, as though he didn't want to impart the reason. Then, after a few minutes, during which I think he was assessing my reliability, he relented.

"It's better that you just forget my name, and that you've ever heard of me," he said.

"Are you wanted by the police?" I asked.

"No."

"Then why won't you give me your number?"

"Because if anyone in customs or immigration opened your address book and saw my name and number, you'd probably be in trouble."

"Just having your name and number?" I queried. It may have sounded skeptical. I felt he wasn't telling me the real reason.

"I'm not wanted by police," he said, "but I am on quite a few blacklists in various countries throughout the world. I've been kicked out of quite a few."

His words intrigued me so I determined to worm the story out of him, despite the fact that he was obviously reluctant to give details.

And slowly, as our plane ploughed its way westbound across the endless Atlantic, the story emerged.

He was the son of a diplomat now stationed in Washington, who'd been in North Africa for some years. The father qualified for a diplomatic passport, which ensures immunity from local laws and from customs and immigration hassles at border points.

Because the father was entitled to this privilege, so were the sons, Foster and a brother, who had used the immunity to smuggle hash. In the process they had discovered the utter corruption of many governments, but not before getting their fingers burned on the hot stove of Interpol and other international drug agencies.

The full details of what happened would emerge later in the trip, for at this point a third person entered the conversation, a young Dutch girl who was sitting across the aisle from me. She was traveling with her little boy of three, after touring Europe and parts of the Middle East, following the traditional hashish trail with her hippie husband. They were poor and lived on next to nothing, she explained, the only money coming from selling hash they smuggled through the border points. It was a tricky procedure because, as she admitted, they themselves were stoned most of the time and looked exactly like the kind of people most likely to be smuggling dope.

I could tell this girl came from a very good family by her manner and the excellent quality not only of her Dutch, but her English, too.

She'd rebelled against the confines of her rich family, she told us, and decided to marry a poor Canadian and see something of the Middle East. They were, as the familiar phrase puts it, doing their own thing. Now they were on their way to the husband's home in Canada.

Foster and the Dutch girl, Karen, were both interesting conversationalists, and discussed the life, the mores, and the governments of the countries they had visited.

Foster said the government officials of one country—he didn't reveal which one—had come to him and his brother and asked if they would be interested in making money by smuggling hashish.

The hash was worthless to the government officials, because they couldn't get it out of the country. So they sold it to Foster for just $10 a kilo. He could do whatever he wanted with it. Which he did.

There are about 35 ounces to a kilo—and in North America the "street price" is about $70 an ounce. That's a profit of $2,440 per kilo!

So Foster and his brother were able to smuggle out a lot of "shit," as he called it. Just how he was able to do it, he kept a secret. But he made a point of never carrying any on his person.

On a few occasions he had been searched from head to toe because he looked so shabby and fitted the image of the young hippie dope smuggler. After a while, however, the fact that he was smuggling leaked out among the police agencies controlling drug traffic. Soon he was being given the full search treatment . . . including the old fingers-up-the-bum trick.

They didn't find anything, said Foster with a smile. But they stamped an N on his passport. This denoted suspicion of narcotics violations and resulted in his being given the full treatment every time he went through the border. India also made a point of banning him from that country on suspicion of drug smuggling.

The same thing had subsequently happened in England. Interpol was doing a good job of making him persona non grata on that side of the Atlantic.

Even in the States, his home turf, there had been trouble, said Foster. He even had trouble leaving the country. For when his father had heard of Foster's arrest on suspicion of dope smuggling, he'd made a deal: Release Foster, but also revoke his diplomatic passport.

That took away Foster's last vestige of protection and now he could rely on having his rectum reviewed anywhere he landed.

By this time, however, Foster and his brother had managed to salt away a million dollars in cash, and had managed to get it into the United States in safety. Now they were faced with the problem of what to do with it. The money was unearned and therefore, in the sight of the taxman, "hot." The minute they spent it lavishly, the government would want to know where it came from.

Their parents didn't believe the boys had really been involved in drug smuggling and didn't know how or whether they had acquired such a huge amount of money. According to Foster, they didn't really seem to care, either.

Between various trips on his "business," however, Foster was a serious scholar and continued the writing and research for his university thesis on the question of Papal celibacy. Foster told me that he found theology and political science exciting and interesting, and that some day he would like to be a teacher. The money, he explained, straight-faced, was just for "fucking around." He simply wanted to live well while following his teaching career: a career which just didn't pay the kind of money he needed to follow his way of life.

He'd returned to the States about six months previously, still embarrassed from being thrown out of various other countries. He'd cut his hair short and started to dress like a gentleman to allay all suspicion. But by then his name was firmly on the black list and his change of image made no difference to the hardeyed men of the nark squads.

So while he'd kept his short hair, he'd eventually dropped the business clothes and reverted to his favorite levis and cowboy boots. He'd spend the money someday, he said. After all, he'd made it to spend it.

Hours had gone by and we were approaching Montreal when Foster admitted to me he'd not had sex in three months and had become used to abstinence. However, the fact he was now sitting next to The Happy Hooker had released all those pent-up sexual feelings. He was dying, as he put it, "to get into me."

We were sitting there watching the movie *What's Up Doc?*—appropriately enough—when I decided that this charming young man deserved some relief. After all, if it had been me who'd gone three months without, I'd have been a screaming maniac. So I got a blanket and put it over us ... fortunately the cabin lights were off.

That's right. I was doing it just to keep us warm!

I had, meanwhile, lifted up the armrests.

I slipped off my panties and quickly got juiced up by the very thought of making it in a 747. My first Jumbo fuck!

I reached over and steered Foster's hands down between my legs so that he could find out for himself that Auntie Xaviera was good and ready for anything he could throw at her.

Fucking in aircraft is a highly prized pastime among the aviation set. In fact there's an organization known as the Mile-High Club for those who've gotten their rocks off above the height of a mile—an altitude of 5,280 feet. Apparently this club began in the twenties, when few people got to that height. And when they did, the plane they were flying might fall apart during a high-speed fuck.

As aviation progressed, so did the membership of the

Mile-High Club, until today, what with jumbo jets and commodious lounges, the club has ceased to be exclusive. At least no one has approached me for membership fees.

By the time I finished these thoughts I discovered that I'd moved onto Foster's lap, my back to his chest. Silly me ... fancy doing that without thinking! And lo and behold, Foster was easing his prick, now engorged with a three-month load of lovely jism, from the rear into my cunt. It was all done very gently and very quietly. To the average passenger it looked like a little mid-flight affection, though probably the stewies knew what was going on. (It takes one to know one.) The seats next to us were empty, and the girl across the aisle was either asleep or a secret voyeur.

Many people ask me how I manage to have sex in the cramped room of an airplane seat. It's quite simple if you use the sitting position. Two people having it spoon fashion take up no more room than one person stretched out.

But enough of these technicalities. Foster was deep into me, easing himself in and out slowly so that he wouldn't come too quickly.

It was a nice, gentle fuck, his cock filling me nicely while I controlled my movements by bracing my feet against the seat in front.

Neither of us wanted it to end, it was so pleasurable. So we kept going, easing off now and then when he felt a tremor of an orgasm.

If we'd been flying on to Tokyo I think we could have kept it going till then. But, of course, the stewie came up and asked us if we'd like to place our dinner orders.

She must have thought we were zombies, because we both stared at her glassy-eyed, not saying a thing. And for good reason.

While we were looking at her, Foster was beginning to come. And when I say coming, I mean *coming*.

Three months of Foster fluid started to gush inside me, first with a quick, abrupt squirt, then another, long and faster, then another ... squirt, squirt, squirt ... I could feel each one hosing my insides ... squirt, squirt, squirt ... it was going on and on! Ounces and ounces of the stuff, I thought, his prick like the berserk head of a hosepipe suddenly let loose under high pressure, the head of his tool snaking with the force of it.

Again . . . again . . . again . . .

"You would like dinner, wouldn't you?"

Gush gush gush . . .

It couldn't go on, I thought. And what was that smiling face in front of me? Gush gush gush . . .

"It's steak. With home fries. Or lobster, with drawn butter. Or . . ."

Good grief! It was still pouring out, easing off a little, perhaps, but still pumping hard. I got an awful vision of a cartoon sequence in which while he was fucking me, Foster's body started deflating until eventually I was swollen like a balloon and he was the size of a mouse.

"Maybe you'd just like a sandwich?"

Ahh . . . it was ending. At last the Foster fire hose was running out of pressure. But only comparatively. He was still coming like the average man on a good fuck.

"Maybe I should come back later," offered the stewardess.

"What?" I said.

"Would you really like dinner?"

"Yes, please," I said. "Foster, would you really like dinner?"

"What?"

"Would you like some dinner?" asked the stewie.

"Ahh . . . dinner."

"It's steak," I said. "Or lobster . . . drawn butter . . . or ahhh . . ."

"For breakfast," said Foster.

"Dinner," I repeated, still high on drawn butter.

It was all turning into a very big decision. Foster, obviously a man of action, decided to end it all decisively.

"Yes," he said.

"What?" said the stewie.

"Yes," said Foster, a little louder, but still not much above a whisper.

"He said yes," I said.

When she left, more than a little confused, I slid off Foster, wiped his prick with a silk hanky I always keep handy, then tucked it into my vagina and headed for the john.

I was in mid cleanup when I heard a knock at the door. There was no way I was going to open up in the middle of that delicate little operation, so I just didn't bother answering. When I finished I opened the door to leave and immediately got hustled back in again. By Foster, who'd been standing outside the door.

"What's shakin'?" I asked.

He was bolting the door, and as he turned he had his hand . . . guess? Exactly! Big and hard and cute as a button. A one-eyed smile button. And looking like another Hoover Dam full.

"Tut tut," I said, "so soon."

"Well, it was good, Xaviera," he said. "In the seat. But Christ, I wanted to really hump you and I couldn't in case anyone saw us move. A quiet fuck is all right once in a while, but not when you've been on the wagon for three months."

"All right," I laughed, "but don't expect these little treats on all the airlines. On some you only get coffee and cookies . . . unlike Air Hollander. Now come here."

Then I went into a little number taught me by an airplane captain I'd once known, intimately, between Paris and Rome—we'd peaked over the Dolomites.

I put down the toilet seat and kneeled on top of it, so that I was squatting with my back to Richard. The delightful thing about this little trick is that the vanity mirrors see all. As do you.

It was a nice sight, seeing my inviting tush sticking back toward Foster, and a view of his prick lancing into my curly-headed cunt. Fortunately I was relaxed and lubricated because he charged in like a bull and I took the full length of him at the first stroke.

I love watching a man's glistening prick going in and out of a cunt . . . mine or anybody else's. And in the mirror I could see every detail as he slipped in and out like mad.

At one point we hit an air pocket and I came down on him hard, and he went so far inside me I almost cried out.

The second time he came it wasn't as violent as the first. But he still poured enough come into me to make me think he had another one-month supply left over. With the two of us inside the biffy at the same time, the mopping-up operations needed a couple of contortionists. But by that time we'd had practice.

Over dinner, which Foster ate ravenously, our conversation came back to the hidden money.

"In ten years I'll have no trouble moving it," said Foster. "By that time the statute of limitations will protect me from prosecution."

"But the thought of all that money lying around and being unable to use it," I said, "must be driving you crazy."

"Don't you worry," he replied with a grin, "it's not just lying there. I've got a wealthy uncle who's investing it for me . . . what the Mafia calls 'laundering' It's growing nicely."

"Is there any reason you're going to Washington via Montreal rather than New York?"

He thought about that one for a minute.

"Well," he said, "Uncle Sam's now got computers which keep a check on people like me when they travel. If I purchased a New York ticket, the FBI would know within minutes. That'd mean a welcoming party already wondering where I got the money for travel."

Foster and his brother had planned for such contingencies by buying a farm in northern Vermont, right near the Canadian border. From Montreal he could drive to the border and almost walk over it, into his farm, without being questioned by border guards.

His life seemed terribly complicated, but I guess they're the kind of complications anyone in his twenties would love to have in exchange for a million dollars stashed away and growing daily.

As he talked, I could see below us the magnificent St. Lawrence River and the beautiful island city of Montreal—"the Paris of North America." At the airport Foster gave me a farewell kiss and headed toward his farm. I waved him goodbye sadly because I'd never see him again.

When I boarded the plane for Houston I fell asleep immediately, for the day-long travel across the Atlantic and the conversation with Foster (in more ways than one) had taken up all my energy.

TEENAGE TURN-ON

By the time I reached Mexico City I was like a damp dishrag and suffering from a bad case of jet lag. My body thought it was early morning, my stomach thought it was night, and my head was telling me it was probably high noon. And I don't drink.

And, of course, as always, that's the very time the airlines choose to screw up. One of my bags was missing.

Excuses, excuses, excuses. But the hell I raised was not in vain, for it was found an hour and a half later, and I thanked my lucky stars I spoke Spanish, otherwise I know I'd never have found my luggage.

A brief suspicious thought occurred to me. Maybe the narcotics people had known Foster was sitting next to me, and had taken their time checking out my baggage.

Anyway, the airline employees gave me a hard time with the *manana* bullshit, suggesting I go on to Acapulco right away and come back sometime later to see if it had turned up. I screamed and yelled and told them I'd payed two hundred extra to have that particular suitcase sent airfreight on the same plane, because I'd been over the baggage limit.

I think it got through to them that this Dutch pain-in-the-ass was not moving one step until that bag was found. And suddenly, when this entered their skulls, it turned up. Maybe that's the only way to do business in *manana* territory.

My intention was to stay in Acapulco for forty-five days and then go to Toronto in February, a time of year when they hold brass-monkey conventions in Canada. This jumping from hot to cold was one of the reasons I'd taken along so much baggage, for I had to carry two wardrobes.

Of course, by this time I'd missed my connection for Acapulco. When I did eventually check my baggage again

I had to pay another thirty dollars for the excess. It was eleven P.M. and I was bushed. This is the time the airlines usually pick for goof number two: the Acapulco connection was delayed for an hour.

Mexican Airlines officials took one look at me and suggested I be their guest for dinner in the airport restaurant. So I sat there trying to get my stomach to accept a sandwich and fruit juice, watching the local citizenry passing by.

My head was just about to drop onto the table with tiredness when a stewardess came and told me the Acapulco flight was about to leave. I went into the waiting room and was met by loud whistling, screaming, yelling and singing.

A young couple, just married, were leaving on the same flight for their honeymoon. They couldn't have been more than eighteen and were really sweet-looking. About two dozen of their friends were responsible for this farewell serenade. But this final flurry of activity and noise was just too much for me in my state. I was dying to get on that big silver bird and get my head down. And on a pillow this time.

But, like the airline rule of screwing up when you're bushed, so too there's another law of people: When you reach the point of not wanting to talk to anyone, that's the moment one of the many contenders for the World's Most Boring Person Award chooses to accost you.

This one was a tall, paunchy, middle-aged Texan. But not like the wealthy Houston swingers I'd known in my time. This guy was a loser. After recognizing me, he wanted to ask me a hundred and one questions, right from my place of birth to whether or not I'd fucked a fat, boring, middle-aged Texan recently.

I knew I had to get rid of him or I'd go out of my tree. So I started to throw him off by wandering around the waiting room until I located someone who might help. And immediately I spotted this tall, attractive, young man with a handsome face. Though he was well dressed, he was accompanying a teenage acne victim with a long beard, thick moustache, long greasy hair, and doggie eyes.

I stopped right in front of them and avoided the Texan's hustle to keep me moving. Desperately I started a conversation with them. In no time flat I learned they were from Toronto, and had just arrived that evening.

Thank God, they both recognized me. I whispered in their ears that I'd be forever grateful if they could accompany me to the plane and help me give this overgrown Billy the Kid the slip. Before you could say *delighted* they'd hemmed me in on both sides and walked me to the plane, where they virtually commanded the stewardess to put us on the same row.

Toronto was beginning to be a place I associated with good news, for the Texan gave up the pursuit and sat somewhere else in the plane.

The attractive, well-dressed guy was Marty and the younger semi-hippy was Terry. Both were Jewish and intent on having a good time in Acapulco. They were going there for Marty's twentieth birthday—scheduled to take place on January second. His father was the owner of a successful Toronto club, and I figured him for a rich kid who was being indulged by pappa.

This was not the case. Marty told me that he had paid for his own trip with his poker winnings: five thousand dollars of it. In fact, he had become so good that his regular partners now refused to play with him.

He'd hit jackpots that big before but had always blown them on more gambling. This time he intended to put the money to good purpose and see some of the world. Acapulco was the first step.

Marty entertained me with his story, but when it came to Terry, I couldn't help feeling that this kid was a misfit.

His father was one of the wealthiest men in Toronto—a city of many wealthy men—and heavily into the stock market. Other than his eyes, there was nothing attractive about him at all. Through his open shirt I could see skin that was blotchy and spotted with pimples about to burst. These extended up the back of his neck and it almost made me sick to look at him.

At the same time I couldn't help but feel sorry for him.

With a decent diet and the help of a dermatologist he could have cleaned up his system, and without the rash he wouldn't have been bad-looking. But in his present state there was no way I wanted to touch him, or even come close to him . . . despite those sweet eyes.

So of course I became the object of his attentions, and while he made a pass at me I could see Marty watching, listening and smiling at Tarry's naivete and stupid hamhandedness.

I had the hots for Marty . . . but I didn't show my hand. Not yet.

We eventually got to Acapulco and after the guys had diverted one final, pitiful play by the Texas ranger, we took a cab to my hotel, where they helped cart up my baggage. In return I gave them the address of three or four inexpensive hotels I'd heard about in the city.

My hotel was the Pierre Marques, and we'd hardly put down the bags and started our goodbyes when the phone rang. It was the front desk.

"Would you please ask your gentlemen friends to leave immediately."

"I beg your pardon?" I said.

"The gentlemen in your room. Would you please ask them to leave."

"When I want them to leave, I will."

"They must leave right now."

"Listen," I said, quite angry, "I'm paying sixty-five dollars a day for my room in this hotel and if I wish to have a few friends in, I will. As it happens, they were on their way out when you phoned, but if I wanted them to stay, they'd stay."

"We are glad to hear they are leaving," said the voice.

The phone went dead.

"Welcome to Acapulco," said Marty, as he and Terry took their leave. I kissed Marty lightly on the cheek and gave Terry a handshake. I know, terribly unfair and probably wounding to Terry's ego, but believe me I could no more kiss a man with skin like that than I could fly over the moon. It would be too much for me.

I started to unpack, then gave it up and slumped, dogtired, into bed. I thought about the hotel's attitude. This would definitely have to change within the next few days because . . .

I didn't remember any more, for I fell into deep, dark, delicious sleep.

But next morning, feeling that intense inner relaxation a deep sleep gives you, I looked out and was hit by the visual impact of Acapulco. The view from my balcony was spellbinding. The sea stretched to the horizon, reflecting a million variations of blue. The backdrop behind the hotel carried the silhouette of mountains in the hazy distance, and along the beach were files of palm trees edging onto sand of the finest yellow. Farther away, the manicured green of golf courses stood out like emeralds. So I forget the dumb deskman from last night.

Inside, I had a good feeling that this trip was going to be worthwhile.

The Pierre Marques—it's owned by J. Paul Getty—is one of the best, and certainly most expensive, hotels in Acapulco. Under the same management is the Princess Hotel, which is ten short minutes' walk along the beach.

During my first reconnoiter through the hotels I discovered that both were filled with a predominantly Jewish-American clientele.

There were about five times as many people at the giant Princess, which had three pools, one of them with a waterfall, and under it a bar which extended into the water. It also had a vast, sandy beach which never got too crowded, and was always hot, hot, hot, to the feet.

What struck me about the Princess was its architecture, particularly the lobby. It was open to the sky and contained miniature gardens, a waterfall, streams, and bridges all put together in a way that was breathtaking.

Both hotels were packed with kids, along with mummy and daddy, for the holiday. Most of them never left the building except to go on the beach. I found the same kind of thing in Miami and Puerto Rico. Everything they need is in the hotel—hairdressers, shops, food, drink, drugstore, entertainment—and they see little point in risking the local offerings in those departments.

As you know, I enjoy living by the pool, taking my ease and watching the passing action. And who should turn up that first day but . . . no, not Marty, the one I was hoping to see, but his friend, Terry.

It wouldn't have been fair to show my disappointment, but he could guess from my cool reaction that there was no likelihood of us tangling between the sheets. I could hardly hide my repugnance when he took off his shirt and I was confronted with this pale skin spotted with red and yellow pimples.

It was horrible, and obviously Terry was suffering from

a huge inferiority complex brought on by his skin condition. I knew I had to be diplomatic. He was easily hurt. But how do you do that with someone who gives you the creeps? I figured if I got him talking about his personal life, it'd keep the conversation neutral and save my having to refuse him.

Recently, he'd started fooling around with drugs, and this was one of the reasons his skin was in such bad shape, he said. And why he was physically so thin.

"Of course that didn't do my parents any good," said Terry, whose lovely eyes, so out of place in that body, told me more about the sad situation than his words did. "They could see me going downhill, and they were expecting something awful to happen to me. They watched me like a hawk and I could see what they were thinking. It got to me, believe me. That's why I'm all nervous and . . . well . . . fucked up."

I tried to instill some confidence in him. I told him he'd soon regain his self-esteem and physical shape if he'd dump the dope and get out in the world and organize his own life. I even hinted delicately that he could solve his physical problem with some medical advice. I think it helped.

I asked what had happened to them the night before.

"We took your advice. One of the hotels was pretty good and pretty cheap. So we had a drink in a bar and turned in."

"Where's Marty?" I asked nonchalantly.

"He's sleeping. We were up pretty late and he did all the talking to get us the hotel room. It's a bit of a dump, but for ten dollars a day for both of us I can't complain . . . considering it's right across the street from the Hilton Hotel."

"Okay," I said, "level with me. What did you do last night that meant Marty needed to sleep in today?"

"Nothing. Really. He's just spoiled and likes his sleep. I don't think he's coming over today. I told him I was going to see you and he just opened one eye and grunted. And wished me luck."

Terry paused for a moment, then added: "Why are you so interested in Marty, anyway?"

"Come on, Terry. Don't get touchy. I like you both. I just wondered what happened. Tell you what, maybe we can all get together for dinner tonight. Why don't you get Marty to give me a call when he finally wakes up."

With a grunt that sounded a little disappointed, Terry agreed and ambled off to his hotel.

I had a nap and a bath and by the time the phone rang it was seven o'clock.

"Hi!" It was Marty. Hearing his voice again turned me on.

"Hello, Marty. Whatever happened to you?"

"I was bushed by last night, so I figured to get my sleep in case I needed lots of energy tonight."

"Whatever for?"

"I've got no idea. But I might get lucky."

We joshed like this for a few minutes, sexily titillating each other without mentioning the subject. Then we agreed to meet at a cozy little restaurant once recommended to me. Although my hotel bill included two meals a day at the hotel, I didn't feel like staying in to eat there the first evening in town.

Terry, it appeared, had suffered a bad case of sunburn during his poolside conversation with me, and was in some pain.

So when we finally had dinner, it was just Marty and I, and he looked delicious in his checkered pants, wedge shoes, and brilliant white shirt. Like something out of *Great Gatsby*. There was just one thing that marred the image. He insisted, as he had on the airplane flight, on chewing gum.

So I came on just like a Yiddisher mamma.

"All right, Marty," I said, holding out a hand, "gimme the gum. You're chewing that damn stuff with your mouth open, and it's a Yankee habit that's just ruining your image as a nice, good-looking kid."

And that's just how he looked—a kid—as he reached up and took the gum out of his mouth. He put it in an ashtray and I set out for a night on the town with an escort who looked one-hundred-percent better for having an inactive jaw.

After dinner at a fashionable restaurant called Carlos y Charlie we went to Acapulco's "in" discotheques; places such as Boccaccio and Armando's Le Club, where I met dozens of acquaintances from my days in New York. It was good to be among old chums again and I kissed and hugged them, while Marty waited for me to reminisce for a while.

Eventually we made it to the dance floor, and danced for hours. Occasionally Marty was a trifle awkward and stepped on my toes. But he more than made up for it with his sweetness. After all, he was only nineteen, and his youth made me feel much younger than my years. It was delightful.

His hard, tanned body was close to mine and I could see the hair on his chest curling over the top of his open-necked shirt. I felt good and ready.

MARTY LEARNS HOW

When Marty and I got to my hotel, we arranged to sneak in without the prim desk clerk seeing us. Once in the room, we sat back and had a quiet conversation.

"How did you enjoy your day?" I asked him

"Sleeping mostly."

"Why? What had been so energetic the night before?"

"We went to a whorehouse called the Casa Rebecca."

"Aha," I said, "I suspected as much."

"On the way into town we asked the cab driver if there were any cat houses in town. He said there were a few, all government controlled. Two of them were safe, but the others didn't have medical supervision.

"The safe ones were called Rebecca's and Casa Elysia. The third one he mentioned was La Huerta, which was the largest in town."

"Why couldn't Terry tell me this?" I asked. "He said you'd just had a few drinks and gone to bed. Why did he have to lie? What's his hang-up?"

"Can't you see Terry adores you," Marty said with a laugh. "He wants to follow you around like a puppy. The last thing he wants to do is upset you, and he figures a visit to a whorehouse might do just that."

"That doesn't upset me. Not at all. In fact I'd like to know all about it . . . go there myself and see the operation."

"Well, I guess I'd better take you along there."

"Not tonight, Marty. We've got the world ahead of us. Maybe tomorrow night. But tell me . . . what was it like?"

"My chick was called Magdalena. She was as skinny as hell, with no tits. In fact, not much of anything. But she was pretty bright and intelligent and reminded me of an old girlfriend."

"You're only nineteen. How many girlfriends have you had?" I asked.

"Xaviera, please don't probe. I'm innocent. Oh, maybe not completely, but I haven't had any true love affairs. I've been to bed with a few girls, three, four. But if you want any details there's nothing I can tell you."

"Have you ever given a girl head."

"Head? What's that?"

"Have you eaten a girl?"

"Eaten her where?"

"In the pussy."

His tanned face broke into a huge smile that made his dimples ripple.

"No. Of course not."

"How would you like a blow-job? A good, old-fashioned blow-job? You know what that is, surely?"

"Yeah. I heard about that. But no girl's ever done it to me. Sucked my cock, that is."

"You're kidding. You've been in bed with four different girls and none of them gave you head?"

"The subject was never mentioned."

"The subject was . . . my God!"

"I've heard it's great, though. Some of my friends have told me I should try it. In fact, that's why I went to the whorehouse. To try it. I got all turned on by you yesterday and I needed it pretty badly. We didn't try to proposition you, 'cause you're a lady. You were tired, and the hotel was giving you a hassle when we were in your room. So that's why I went to Rebecca's.

"There were four or five girls there, but not much of a choice. Four of them were dogs and the fifth, Magdalena, wanted twenty dollars, so I took her.

"When we got to the bedroom I asked her for a blow-job, so it's strange that you should mention it tonight."

"Did she give you one?" I asked.

"No way. When she finally understood what I was asking for, she said none of the girls went down on guys. The specialty of the house was straight fucking.

"So there I was with a stiff cock. No, I lie. The thing

didn't get stiff until I lay down and she started playing with me. I closed my eyes and pretended it was you. It got big and hard before you could say *boner*.

"So I got into her right away, and do you know, she just lay there like a dead goddamn fish . . . just like the other girls in my life had done. Here I was in exotic Mexico, paying twenty dollars at the best whorehouse in town, and sticking it into a hooker who was playing dead. Not only that, she kept her bra on, and when I asked her to take it off she had the goddamn nerve to ask for another ten dollars. Fuck her. She was just a dead piece of meat."

"Easy now, boy," I said. He was getting quite bitter and I didn't want it to foul up the evening.

"Now if only I'd been with you," he said.

"Well, you are, so ease off. I'll show you how it's really done . . . not with a two-bit hustler or the four cockteasers back home. But with someone who really knows how to get it on."

I could see his prick was erect and that the time for some good honest fucking was at hand.

"Take a shower," I told him.

"Why?"

"Because I'll take one with you, and then I want you to eat me all over. For me, sex isn't complete without having head."

"But . . . er . . . I wouldn't know how to begin."

"Leave that to momma. I'll teach you all I know. Well, not *all*. But all you need to know to make many a girl grateful in the future."

I led him to the bathroom and we undressed each other. In the shower I soaped him up and he did the same for me, getting a nice foam going on my boobs. By the time he'd finished my nipples were sticking out like twin pistols.

Then I soaped his prick to a fine, hard erection. It was so good that I had to restrain myself from climbing onto him right then and there. I took the manual shower head and adjusted it to a fine needle spray, playing it up under his balls, delightfully tickling him. With the other hand I slid a ring of thumb and finger over the glistening, drum-tight skin of his prick.

When we couldn't wait any longer, we rinsed each other

down with the shower and walked into the bedroom, dripping wet, like little puppies just out of the river.

I was wet from head to toe, my hair hanging like seaweed to my shoulders, my pubic hair flat and damp. Instinctively he kissed me on the mouth while we were standing at the edge of the bed. I could feel by his darting tongue that he would be good in the cunnilingus department.

I told him to go down on his knees at the side of the bed, where the mirror would be behind him and I could see his every move. Then I lay down on the bed so that his head would be between the split in my legs, and put a pillow under my buttocks. I looked in the mirror and I could see my ass raised high, my legs hanging over the edge of the bed, and in between the wet tufts of my pubic hair, my vagina, pink and wide and glistening.

"Kiss it," I told him.

"I er ... er ..."

"Just lean forward and kiss it, like you would my mouth."

Cautiously I saw him bend down until his head obscured my cunt, and all I could see were my gaping legs and this huge head of hair in my crotch.

Then I felt his lips touch my vagina, gently, tentatively.

"Kiss hard," I said.

He kissed again. Delightfully, his tongue darted out on an exploratory trip. I felt the smooth-brutal roughness of his tongue.

Lying back, I could see his head move slowly upward until he was looking at me from my own crotch.

"That was ..."

"Yes?" I said.

"Okay."

"Okay?"

"Yes ... pretty nice."

Wow, I thought. Here I am, a woman who's used to having guys go raving mad over eating her, teaching this beginner something he's never had in his life, and all he can say is okay.

I sat up and lifted his head so that his eyes were looking into mine.

"Look," I said, "I know it's all new for you and that you're a bit nervous. So if you feel you need time to get used to it, I won't force you. Honestly."

"Hell no, I love it. You're clean as driven snow and I didn't taste anything. In fact I'd like to taste more of your cunt."

"Next time. You'll turn me on more and you'll be able to taste my juices."

"I'll just try another..."

His head started to go down again, but I pulled it up.

"No," I said. "That's fine for lesson number one. Now come up here on the bed and I'll show you what head is all about. I'm doing the directing and conducting, so take your time and try not to come in my mouth. It would be such a waste."

I started to kiss him on the neck and then worked down to his nipples which, like most teenagers', were incredibly sensitive. I sucked at them and could feel them all hard inside my mouth.

Then, kissing him all the way, I worked down toward his cock, which was on its way up to meet me.

I was about to slip it in my mouth when I stopped dead. Marty had only one ball.

I could see he sensed my hesitation, and he knew the reason for it.

"You noticed?" he asked.

"Yes."

"So what do you think of that?"

"It's... okay!"

We both broke up in an incredible burst of laughter. We rolled on the bed in one of those fits of uncontrollable idiocy that seem to go on for ever and threaten your sanity.

Then, in mid-roll, I stopped laughing and with a swoop, took his cock inside my mouth in one full blow.

Marty just about went through the ceiling from shock. Delicious shock, as he later described it, but shock nevertheless. I did everything I knew to him, let the soft underside of my tongue blanket the head; let the abrasive topside of the tongue rasp along the length of it, and let my sucking cheeks pull at it like a milking machine.

While doing this I was masturbating myself, as I knew he'd come soon and I wanted the finale to be good.

When I felt the first tremor of his orgasm I'd made sure I was close to mine.

Instantly I got the signal. I pulled his cock out of my mouth and slipped myself astride him, his cock going like an oiled piston into a cylinder, full and without hindrance on the first stab. Deep. I'd caught him just as he was coming, giving him about a dozen jerks up and down and feeling his sperm gush just as my orgasm came shuddering from the toes to burst in my head. It was a brief but enjoyable fuck for both me and Marty, and one that I hoped would be followed by many more.

We lay back, momentarily spent, and just enjoyed the silence for a few minutes as we recovered our senses. The silence was broken by Marty.

"I suppose you're wondering about it?" he said.

"What?"

"The one ball."

"No."

"Do you want to hear about it?"

"Only if you want to tell me."

"Well, about a year ago one of my balls started growing to three times its normal size. Needless to say I got to a doctor right away. I was in a state that can only be described as shitless.

"The doctor told me not to worry. He said this sometimes happened, and the testicle usually returned to its normal size or, in a few cases, shriveled up completely inside the body.

"He said no operation would be needed and while it might not look too good going through life with one ball, it wouldn't cut down on my potency. And I could still be a father. So what the hell . . . if you can do it with one ball, it's just the same as having three or four."

Following our discussion we . . . balled!

Unbelievably for a youngster, Marty managed to keep his control and go on for hours, which was just what I needed. When finally it came to an end, it was he who went limp, not his cock. He said he was exhausted.

Maybe it was because I had worked him around into so many positions. I do this with men whose cocks, like Marty's, are not that big. A man with a big cock doesn't need different positions to get a good penetration. But the medium-sized have to work around a little if I'm going to get all I want. The positions also give different kinds of friction. Pillows under the buttocks help, or doing it doggie-fashion, or with my legs on his shoulders and the man on his knees.

Marty knew only the missionary posture (and for those who don't know any missionaries, that's the straight-ahead woman-on-her-back technique), and he was working like a young stud auditioning for an Olympic screwing team.

When he finally collapsed in my arms, he apologized profusely.

"It's just too much, Xaviera," he said breathlessly. "For a guy who's only had it four times, each one a sixty-second, pump-away special, this is just too goddamn much."

In the next few weeks I really got a charge out of making a man out of this callow youth.

ACAPULCO BOLD

Two weeks just jumped—I nearly said humped—by ... but Marty and I hardly noticed. Daytime, we'd sunbathe or trip around with his friend Terry, and nighttime we'd trip around my bed—*without* his friend Terry.

Marty was more than ready to graduate summà cum laude (with emphasis on the cum) from The Hollander Acadamy of the Hump.

He also got extra gold stars for merit and proficiency in ingenuity, endurance, and enthusiasm—and the Principal's Special Award for increasing both his artistry and the size of his erection. (While many people believe that the size of a man's erection cannot change, this is not so. I have noticed, with younger men, that if they have sex regularly after a slow period, their penis gets larger, not so much in length, but in width.)

He could now average about three climaxes in two hours, and the larger hard-on, while something I'd secretly hoped for, still surprised me.

By exercising this lovely thing every day I'd brought it on beautifully, like a loving gardener cultivating his favorite petunia.

Now he was no longer a gangly, uncertain kid, but a strong, cocksure man. And he was ready to prove it any time, any place and, I suspected, with any body.

We took out a canvas boat, much like the catamaran in Nassau. We rented it for eight dollars an hour, sailed out toward the torrid sun, and drifted for hours, a cool breeze playing over us, the seagulls doing their graceful ballet overhead. In the background was the landscape of the Acapulco shoreline—the rocks, the beaches, the hotels, the playing children. It was heaven.

We took off our swimsuits and lay on the bottom of the boat and made love. Marty was now a different man. He was masterful, in control, and reacted to every nuance of my body with the understanding of a glider pilot playing the subtle currents of nature.

In the boat in the Bahamas I'd gotten fucked. With Marty it was lovemaking. Two entirely different things. In the past weeks I'd gotten used to Marty and I liked him very much indeed. My feelings toward him were similar to what I'd felt for another teenager, David, whom I described in my earlier book, *Xaviera!*

However, Marty didn't get as conceited as David. And he possessed more innocence, for David was an all-around lover and knew it. Marty was still a successful initiate and willing to listen and learn. There hadn't been anything exciting about David. He already knew it all. With Marty, however, much of the beauty was in my teaching him, and his gratitude afterward.

At this moment, lying on the bottom of the boat, this lovely guy on top of me, the bright blue for a background, the incidental music of the water and the seagulls, we had made love for half an hour. Occasionally boats floated past and looked in to see what was happening, and the sight of Marty's bare buttocks sticking up over the gunwale, my legs wrapped around him, might have been enough to make any Moby Dick reach for his harpoon.

Afterward we lay back, staring at the sky, letting the sun's heat and the breeze dry off our bodies and give us that salt-air freshness.

We lay there hand in hand, nibbling at each other's ears, occasionally rubbing coconut oil on each other's bodies as protection against the sun.

But too late. That night Marty would have a ketchup red ass.

When we got back to the beach, we dried each other down and watched the parade of Mexican peddlers—including a lot of kids—selling their wares—hats, sandals, silver rings, all kinds of souvenirs. The Mexican kids doing the selling were beautiful to behold, lovely faces with big, lustrous eyes. And they sold everything from bangles to marionettes.

Whatever the ages of the peddlers, their forté was bargaining and if you couldn't bargain, you had no business on the beach! Because it was like a fish market.

Two women with heavy Polish accents sitting close to us bargained with a gypsy woman selling dresses, the two ladies going at her at the top of their voices. They must have just come from the Warsaw flea market.

"Too expensive. Kopish. Too expensive. Somewhere else we've seen the same already. Two dollar less. Four dollar too much. We give two dollar each. Take or leave." Pause. "All right, two-fifty tops."

They eventually settled for three bucks. But they hadn't bargained enough. The next day I got the same dress for two dollars.

Marty and I had a ball watching the passing show and the characters who paraded the beaches.

There was the big, fat, loud, gambling type complete with toupee and a bad case of beer belly. He had a wife, also on the plump side, and between them they had a paper bag which contained a collection of ashtrays, papier-mâché Madonnas, marionettes, dresses, sandals, hats, silver bracelets, bikinis—you name it, they'd bought it.

So here was Beer Belly waddling over to us, bursting with pride over the stuffed turtle he'd just purchased. He was now carrying it like an Oscar Statuette.

It looked fine, but I'd been warned by some old Mexican hands that these stuffed animals don't last long. There's a lot of paper mixed in with the skin and sooner or later something will break off it; the tail, the head, the nose, the claws, whatever.

But he seemed so delighted with his turtle that we didn't have the heart to say anything. We stroked it on the head and made nice noises like you do to a newborn baby. As we admired it, he put it in various positions with some glee, shouting:

"Hey, that goddam turtle will do anything I tell it . . . just like a woman. If I tell it to lay down, it lays down. If I tell it to stand, it stands. If I tell it to pray, it stands on its head and does yoga.

"Nicest thing of all, it's housebroken. Better 'n my dog at home. And you know what," his voice dropped to a whisper, "better 'n my wife. This sonofabitch won't answer back."

A little later our friendly neighborhood turtle trainer was about to buy a marionette from a Mexican kid for three dollars when his wife leaped into the breach.

"Three dollars?" she yelled. "For that? Too damn much."

"Aw, c'mon, Gertie," he said. "You can see the kid needs it."

"You shouldn't pay more than half of that, Irving."

"It's a good marionette. Let him have his goddamn three dollars."

"No way."

"I already bargained him down a dollar."

"What did he ask originally?"

"Four dollars."

"Four dollars. The boy's *meshugana*. No more than two dollars."

"No, no, senora," said the Mexican lad, getting into the act, one he probably knew by heart. "Three dollar."

"We already *have* two male puppets, Irving," she shouted, almost like an accusation.

There was a few seconds' pause. When she spoke again it was with a difference. Now it was sweet, almost hypnotic.

"How about a girl puppet, Irving?"

The Mexican kid looked up, now having lost the thread of the psychological byplay.

"Goil, goil, goil," Gertie repeated in a heavy Brooklyn accent.

The Mexican kid smiled and smiled. The word *girl* was outside his vocabulary. It wasn't a number or a currency.

"Get off that shit, Gertie. I'll give him the three dollars and take this one. Our son will love it."

"What about our daughter? I want a puppet for our daughter. We want a goil puppet for our daughter, don't we?"

At this point she took out a woman's shirt, held it up like a skirt, kicked it in the air a few times and said, "Puppet. Goil puppet."

The kid, by this time a little past it all, said, *"No tengo. Hay salamente hombres,"* which means, roughly, "I've only got male marionettes."

They didn't understand him. They thought he was holding out on them.

Finally, after a lot of hassle, the kid ambled off, having sold two male marionettes for six bucks and congratulating himself on being Mexico's best salesman. And with problem customers no less!

Shortly after this, a pregnant native woman with a child on her back came by, begging pesos. A little later a wrinkled old man of eighty in baggy gray pants, clicking two bottles together, came along, crying, *"Aseite olio di coconut,"* selling a relief from the sun via a mixture of coconut oil and vinegar which he sold for three pesos.

"Can you imagine yourself in this heat, sweating like an animal to sell all these things," I said to Marty, paying the old man three pesos for his pitiful mixture, which I had no intention of using. While it's true that coconut oil and vinegar gives you a suntan in a hurry, try getting it off afterward.

By now it was three o'clock in the afternoon and we figured we'd better have lunch first. So he ordered huge hamburgers from the beach-side cafe and fruit cocktails from one of the Mexicans selling things on the beach.

There were literally dozens of these vendors and you could literally buy anything; scarves, ashtrays, silverware, sweaters. One tall, good-looking guy was selling slippers. So while Marty was getting our food I sauntered over to take a better look at his wares. There were two middle-aged ladies giving him a hard time over the prices.

They'd come over to his pitch and descended on his basket of slippers, grabbing like vultures.

"Whoa, easy," said the man, holding on to the basket to stop it from spilling over.

I asked the charmer, in Spanish, if I could try on a pair of his slippers. They were white and appeared to be made of leather, and he wanted six dollars for them. I offered him four. He agreed, and we were ready to close the deal when the ladies chimed in.

"Four for those? You must be out of your head."

"That's not real leather."

"Feel it. Plastic. We deal in shoes. *Those* are plastic."

"And they come from Philadelphia. That's where we sell them."

"They'll wear out."

"Shoddy."

"Overpriced."

After a while I'd had enough of their bullshit and I said quietly: "I like them. I think they're worth four dollars and that's what I'm going to pay for them."

"Two dollars tops."

"Not a penny more."

By this time I was cracking, so to please them I cut my offer to three and, after bemoaning the fate of his wife and the eight kids the extra dollar would have fed, he took my three dollars.

Later, when I put them on and started walking back to the hotel I learned that for once the *yentas* had been right. With a clip and a crack and click clack clock they started coming apart. Plastic all right.

In no time at all, I'd cased the Acapulco action and discovered that the jet set who flew in from the United States, England, France, Italy, and Canada gathered each day between four and five at the Villa Vera Hotel.

By five o'clock the crowd was composed of international celebrities, staid socialites, high-class hookers brought in by their wealthy customers, bankers, defrocked transvestites . . . you name it.

Toward the hookers I was *empatico*. Here they were, princesses for a week or two, but always on their mind the thought of returning to the big-city grind. I really felt for them. I started dropping in at the Villa Vera bar each day and met lots of former associates—interpret that as you will—most of whom began by asking me when I intended to get back to New York.

I realized that their inquiries weren't just politeness, but they all seemed genuinely happy to see me again, and those hours at the bar were often delightful. It was the Acapulco branch of Manhattan.

They all said much the same things:

"You're missing so much swinging in Fun City these days."

"Where's the action around here, Xaviera?"

"Know any girls in the neighborhood?"

"What are you doing this evening?"

I enjoyed all this. It was fun. The joys of being a famous ex-madam are various and vicarious.

But basically I stuck to Marty. He stood at my side, glowing with pride in his role as the famous lady's favored escort. He was not only getting lessons in love, but meeting far different people than he would have on his own. These might not be the people his family would have to dinner, but they were certainly an interesting new experience for young Martin.

SHOULD AULD ACQUAINTANCE

Marty and I spent our days in a hazy warmth, sailing, swimming, water-skiing, and screwing.

The lush tropical weather almost made me forget that it was December, and Christmas was approaching. And Larry would be coming soon to spend the holidays with me in Mexico.

I knew, of course, that I'd have to devote myself to Larry, and told Marty that this was the case. His first reaction was jealousy, but at the same time he was anxious to meet The Silver Fox. However, sex with Marty would then have to be a no-no because Larry was never very broadminded . . . especially when it came to good-looking nineteen-year-old boys. However, we decided that we'd at least try to work out an arrangement whereby the three of us would be able to spend plenty of time together.

At first Larry didn't choose to accept the situation, frequently becoming grumpy and threatening to pack his bags and return to New York. But after a few days he found he really liked Marty, so eventually a good time was had by all.

To be honest, however, there were plenty of times when I wouldn't have been too upset if they'd *both* split. Marty was substantially nothing more than a temporary, albeit delicious, sexual partner, and during the preceding nine months, I'd been continually trying to put my relationship with Larry into its proper perspective. More and more, it seemed that what I thought to be love was really just the mutual satisfying of needs. I had many needs during my New York days—for noncommercial sex, for security, for affection, for an escort, for a manager—and Larry had done a fabulous job in satisfying those needs for me.

Equally, Larry had needs which I was able to satisfy for him. We were good for each other, but because our affair was based on passing needs, now that I was no longer a madam and the needs had changed, so too had the affair changed. And I now felt that we had never really been in love. We had both probably wanted it to be love, which is why we may have thought it was love. But, for better or for worse, it wasn't. And things between Larry and me would never be the same.

Nevertheless, here we were together in Mexico, and while we still had sex, I recall that we didn't linger in bed, smooching and hugging, as we used to.

On Larry's first night in Acapulco, he and Marty and I took a tour of the city's red-light district.

Our taxi took us through a dark area of town, then onto narrow gravel roads and into darkest, darkest Acapulco to *la zona roja* (the red light district).

What a colorful area! Every second shack was a brothel or bar; hookers of all ages were standing in the streets, wearing hotpants or miniskirts. They seemed either fat and ugly or else skinny little underfed tarts, all with long black hair, heavy makeup, dark brown eyes, and their frequently big tits crammed into tight sweaters. A rather greasy-looking show.

Then there were the *paderotes*, or pimps, easily recognizable because they were dressed so much better than the average customer.

The district was pathetic. There was, for instance, big, fat, middle-aged *mamacita*, sitting in a rocking chair, surrounded by her dozen little grandchildren, screaming at a young sailor passing by, *"He, joven, una mamadita para cinco pesos?"*——offering him a blow-job for five pesos, which is less than fifty cents.

She reminded me of Catalina Ximinez's toothless old mother from the hilarious Patrick Dennis novel, *Genius*—but instead of cackling "mai dotter beeg starr," this one was pathetically hustling her gummy head-jobs.

I nosily peeked through the window of one shack, and to my amazement there was another old Mexican mamma —she had to be at least sixty—blowing a teenager. She was on her knees, and the kid was straddled over her rocking chair. As the chair rocked back and forth, she just knelt still, and the kid's cock rocked back and forth into her tired old mouth. And all this was happening underneath a statue of the Virgin of Guadeloupe!

There were other brothels which I looked into, and in almost every one there was a statue of the Virgin, or even Jesus Christ, standing over the bed or the ever-present rocking chair. The irony of these old whores, down on their knees in front of their religious figures—but with a cock in their mouth. Holy fuck!

The Mexican pimp, I'm told, is quite different from the typical North American one. He's a fatherly type who virtually lives with his one woman. He also often participates in setting up a family, as opposed to New York, where the pimps would never consider fathering a child with their hookers, knowing that it would mean more problems than profit.

In Acapulco, the *paderotes* generally didn't have a job, though some of them were part-time cab drivers. This enabled them to take care of the kids while mother was out hooking. By contrast, I can hardly imagine Manhattan's pimps forming a day-care center!

Our taxi driver took us on to La Huerta, Acapulco's biggest brothel. It's almost a tiny village: dozens and dozens of small rooms surround a huge outside terrace with a dance floor, a live band, a big bar, and hundreds of tables and chairs all crammed together.

La Huerta was located right in the middle of *la zona roja,* and after passing the horrible shacks, the noisy nightclubs and bars, the cheap sex shows and the dozens of tacos stands, the bustling brothel seemed like a refreshing oasis to hang your hat (or whatever else you wanted to hang).

The taxi drove past a round porch to a great parking lot with hundreds of cars. The atmosphere was carnival-like, with music screaming throughout the area—loud, vivacious rhumbas and congas. The whole scene was madcap, maddening, zany, outrageous, and fascinating.

La Huerta must have been five thousand square feet in area. Two hundred or so loud, drunken men—some Yankees, but mostly Mexicans—and about a hundred fifty girls were mingling around the dimly lit terrace. It was Christmastime, so some of the pillars were decorated and the lights, though low, were warm and colorful. The girls were all Mexican (foreigners weren't allowed to work there) and most were fairly young and considerably more attractive than the whores on the streets. Some were sitting dreamy-eyed on the balcony, others leisurely leaned against the pillars; they obviously weren't too concerned with turning tricks. Either that or they were catching a breath of fresh air between acts. Occasionally one of them would slink over to a table and ask for a cigarette or a sip of a drink.

In Mexico, anyone can go to a brothel (men, couples, children) and you don't have to screw a girl, or even buy a drink. Larry, Marty, and I were sipping our orange juice at a table, and even our cab driver had joined us. A fairly attractive hooker came over . . . she was dressed in white hotpants with a bare midriff and a top so tiny it revealed all her bosom save her nipples. She introduced herself—Juanita—and said she was nineteen and left Mexico City, her home town, to work a few nights a week at La Huerta.

When I asked her for a few details on the pimp-hooker scene, she explained that because she was new to the area she was lucky and hadn't yet been grabbed by a pimp. Sooner or later word gets around that there's a new girl in town, and the pimps move in on them with a fast, convincing tale. Then they keep a firm grip on the girls' actions, taking most of their earnings, and slapping them around if they're uncooperative. Most pimps are the same cruds everywhere! The girls are left with barely enough money to pay for their working costumes—and the seamstresses who make them, aware of how "sinfully" the girls earn their livings, charge double or triple the normal dressmaker's prices.

Juanita also told us that there was no medical control at La Huerta (which means, incidentally, the garden—I guess because of all the planting that goes on there) and that the prices ranged from five dollars to twenty dollars a shot. Cheaper than at the two other main brothels, Rebecca's and Casa Elysia, but compared to those forty-cent gum-jobs from the old *mamacitas,* that's one fuck for the price of twelve blow-jobs. However, you get what you pay for, suppose.

To round off the night, our cabbie told us we'd see a "fan-fucking-tastic" show (as Marty would call it) at El

Tropicana. We thought he meant a sex show, since the club was in the heart of the red light district. As it turned out, we saw a flamenco dancer and singer, and a funny stand-up comedian . . . but that was the only kind of stand-up. Although at first we were disappointed that it wasn't a sex show, we nevertheless enjoyed the evening's entertainment. After all, there's nothing *wrong* with good, clean entertainment, is there?

Our helpful taxi driver for the evening really had been of great assistance, not only in showing us the particulars of the red light district, but also protecting us from the pushy hookers and drunken johns. No doubt we were obvious tourists and perfect targets for pickpockets and the like.

He took us back safely to the hotel, and although we'd spent a lot of time with him, his charge was surprisingly moderate. We gave him a big tip and he invoked an entire litany of saints to protect us—at least I *think* that's what he was saying in his fast Mexican—and with exchanges of *"feliz Navidad,"* he drove off singing. Wishing merry Christmas to two and a half Jews wasn't perfectly kosher, but the thought was right, and besides, who checks out noses at Christmastime?

Whatever our ultimate relationship, Larry enjoyed our days in Acapulco, because it was such a tremendous change from the drab New York winter from which he'd just escaped. We spent most of our mornings on the beaches, sunning ourselves, as I brought him up to date on my adventures.

Our hotel was on the Revolcadero Beach section and one striking area of the Playa Revolcadero was a beautiful stretch of sea, sand, and surf across a lagoon from the little village of Puerto Marques, quite close to our hotel. It's an ancient fishing village, surrounded by swamp and jungle, and some of Johnny Weissmuller's Tarzan films had been shot there. It's a particularly quaint little village, and we enjoyed seeing it and chatting with some of the locals. Unfortunately, the beach itself is more for sunning and sightseeing than swimming. We were told it can be dangerous, so we didn't bother getting firsthand information. We had already witnessed elsewhere the recovery of a boy's body—he'd been fatally attacked by a shark—and that sad sight was more than enough to keep us cautious.

As for our hotel, it had both an Olympic-sized pool and a beautiful beach. All water sports were available—waterskiing, boating, snorkeling. And the service was superb. The only disadvantage was the distance from town. A taxi into Acapulco cost about thirty-five pesos (that's almost three bucks) and took twenty minutes. And, as an added annoyance, taxis were often difficult to find.

Larry and I were both tempted to try a parachute lift— a ten-minute flight, towed by a motorboat—costing eight dollars, but when we heard a few gruesome stories about occasional accidents, we decided to forgo the adventure.

One morning, Marty, Larry, and I rented a catamaran, one of those small sailboats with plenty of room for the three of us to stretch out. We weren't out on the water for five minutes before I took off my bikini top—I'd become quite accustomed to topless sunbathing in St. Tropez—and five minutes later I slipped off the panties, too. I felt so horny that I started playing with Larry and Marty both, and it didn't take long for Marty to sport a becoming bulge. Larry became extremely jealous, and then, when we were about a mile out from shore, he really blew his cool. I'm sure the entire beach heard every syllable.

"I realize what you're up to, Xaviera, and you can cut it out right now. You're after Marty, and you're trying to get a three-way swing going because you haven't fucked him since I got here, and now you're all horny for him.

"Well, listen to me, Marty, you get within three feet of her and I'll throw you right off this fuckin' boat!"

He ordered me to put my bikini back on, too, still screaming at the top of his lungs. "This is one day there won't be any goddamn swing. I may be a jackass to schlepp Marty around with us, but I'm sure as hell not gonna see him fuck you in mid-sea. So forget it."

Half an hour later we were back on shore. Marty and I were still superhorny and *mucho frustrato*.

Once Larry had cooled off a bit, I suggested to him that instead of returning mad to our hotel, why didn't we go to the Malibu Hotel beach and relax on the sand? I had a few connections there, as the actress said to the bishop, and I knew we'd be able to use the hotel facilities without charge. This always appealed to Larry's sense of economy.

He and Marty were both fairly relaxed by the time we got there, and we lay on the beach, under the hot sun, stretched out on brand new waterbeds. Great feeling, those rubber beds: cool in the sun, warm in the cold, plus that super motion sensation.

While we were relaxing there, lots of the regulars at the beach ambled over and said hello to me and Marty. They'd met me there before, and knew that the kid and I were having an affair. But they didn't know Larry, and as they said hello to me, they'd look at him as if to say, "Who's the old guy? Marty's father?"

This must have made Larry feel like a real outsider, so he started another quarrel, grew really furious, and finally stomped off.

He didn't find out until much later what took place between Marty and me when he left.

We went into the hotel, rode up in the elevator, found an open linen-supply room, and balled our brains out! El turno on-o! That's really what I call "running off to the sheets."

Speaking of turn-on trips, while I think of it, there was a little Mexican-Indian kid on the beach at Acapulco who, for a few pesos, offered the thrilling spectacle of turning his navel inside out.

Who knows, that could replace streaking as an international fad.

And this may be an oldie by the time you read it, but have you heard that the only difference between a streaker and a flasher . . . is four years of college!

Meanwhile, back in Acapulco . . . Larry and Xaviera, our intrepid tourists, whom you'll remember from our last jolly episode, had made up and decided to see the famous divers leaping from the cliffs at La Quebrada that night.

The young Mexicans jump 136 feet from a rock shelf to the water below. We watched the spectacle from a nightclub called La Perla in the Mirador Hotel. We were there for the eleven-thirty show, but it was so crowded that they took us to a lower floor, and we had an even better view all to ourselves. Outside the hotel, overlooking the rocks, a few thousand people had congregated to see the show, free of charge.

As the tension built, the young diver knelt before his

small altar there on the cliff, and prayed—probably to St. Christopher—for a safe trip. (Or St. Jude, the patron of hopeless cases!) As he did, other boys on a lower rock shelf ignited torches so that the diver would have a clear vision of the water below.

At the precise moment that the tide was at its highest, he made his dive, and it was over in thirty seconds. Everyone breathed a sigh of relief—the slightest miscalculation, by just a few seconds, can mean a rocky death—and applauded him heartily as he surfaced and crawled back up the side of the cliff.

Many drunken tourists, capable swimmers, and courageous fools have accidentally committed suicide over the past few years by trying to dive here, not realizing how essential perfect timing is, nor how terribly dangerous it is to plunge over a hundred feet into the very narrow cove.

The safest diving and certainly the most fun, as far as I'm concerned, is muff diving—you may not win the applause of a few thousand onlookers, but who cares? Lap before you leap!

There was so much more to be seen on Acapulco, and Larry and I worked hard to cram it in—the colorful fishing boats at Los Hornos Beach, the super surf at Pie de la Cuesta, the yacht cruises, the spectacular sunsets and the all-night discotheques. There are plenty of fine restaurants, with as good a variety of cuisine as you'll find anywhere. One night we enjoyed excellent chicken kiev, another night terrific pasta, and a third night, great spicy Mexican food. There's even a kosher restaurant on Avenue Miguel Aleman.

One thing we didn't eat was anything that had been touched by tap water or was uncooked. It sounds like an old wives' tale, but *don't* drink the water in Mexico! Unless you were brought up on it, it's unfit for human consumption.

Apparently the water supply there is in direct contact with the sewage system, and unless you've built resistance to its bacteria since childhood, it's certain to give you a good dose of Montezuma's revenge (or the Tijuana trots, if you prefer). The natives sum it up succinctly with the word *turista*.

The water looks all right, but it's safest to avoid it at all costs, and in any form. For instance, vegetables or fruit which have been washed in it and aren't protected by their own peel can infect you. An orange, for instance, is safe to eat, but lettuce and tomatoes aren't. It's a shame, because I'm a salad freak, but given the choice of no salad or Montezuma's revenge, I'd go without any day.

Our time went quickly there, and soon it was New Year's Eve. Larry and I and Marty and Terry (whose appearance was improving under the Acapulco sun) welcomed in the new year rather quietly, and in the wee hours of the morning, together in our room, Larry and I must have gotten our years mixed up, because we found ourselves in 69.

A lot of people had come to Acapulco to welcome in the new year. We went to a fabulous party, with lots of international jet-setters and celebrities—I even encountered several chicks who had worked for me during the years of my Manhattan empire. However, when I smiled in recognition and was about to say hello to one of the girls—she was from Argentina—she looked the other way and completely ignored me.

A young, handsome, well-to-do man was on her left arm, and I understood the situation. When she finally had a moment away from the man, she whispered to me, "Pleeeeease, Xavieeeeeeera, do not call me with my real name here. My name is now Rachel Goldberg, and I'm from New York. So pleeease don't tell that I'm from Argentina or that I worked for you as a callgirl . . . okaaaay?

Now it happens that this was a very sweet South American girl who never ever lost her accent, and certainly wasn't remotely Jewish, so I couldn't see how she got away calling herself Rachel Goldberg, of all things. But whatever turns her on is cool with me. I suspected she was fishing for rich husband material, and knew that this guy wouldn't bite if he knew she was a South American hooker!

Although, on the other hand, look at me. I haven't made any bones about what I've been, and except for my immigration difficulties, I'd say that honesty is still the best policy. It certainly hasn't done me any harm.

With the beginning of the new year, Larry had to return to Manhattan, and neither he nor I was too upset about parting. We were actually becoming uncomfortable with each other; we annoyed each other, petty things which formerly went unnoticed now became major issues, and our sex life lacked the old zing. It was goodbye time in more ways than one, but neither of us had the good sense to realize it there and then.

Marty and Terry had to return to Toronto, just a day after Larry left, but not before Marty and I made up for lost time with a few well-chosen fucks. What a change in that boy! He'd been an inept semivirgin when we'd first met, and now he'd become a cocksure stick artist with a very talented tool. He said he even enjoyed masturbating much more now than before he'd met me. Together we'd done things sexually that he'd never even wet-dreamed about.

I saw them off at the airport, thinking that he'd certainly have a red-hot report to write if he were ever asked for five hundred words on How I Spent my Winter Vacation.

Marty and I both live in Toronto now and we see each other from time to time. He doesn't tell me where he's been practicing, but he's still getting better and better, every time we get it on!

MY MEXICANO ROSE

Jaime and I had flirted on the beach at the Pierre Marques, but as long as Marty and Larry were around, we'd never progressed beyond that. But within a few hours of Marty's return to Toronto, Jaime very politely invited me to spend a few days in his company visiting Mexico City.

He was young, handsome, rich, and well-connected. In his late twenties, Jaime had short, curly black hair with a pretty tanned face, intense hazel eyes which seemed to bore right into your soul, lovely white teeth, and strong, fine features. We were just good friends, as the saying goes, and never became involved sexually. I'm not quite certain why—he was very attractive—but that's the way it was. His body was firm and trim, and as he escorted me around Mexico City, girls and boys both eyed him appreciatively.

Jaime was a quite successful author, and on very close terms with many of Mexico's celebrities and influential people, including cabinet ministers and other government officials. How I wished that he were on as good terms with the mandarins in Washington and Canada! I'm sure that such a "friend at court" could have eased my problems with being allowed to stay in the United States or Canada.

He was also a very knowledgeable collector of antique clocks and pocketwatches. He owned dozens of them, and took great pride in producing a valuable timepiece from his pocket each day.

What an unusual man! He was immediately likeable, sympathetic, and attentive. He wanted nothing from me, yet was anxious to make me feel welcome and pampered in his city. It was a form of generosity which I was barely accustomed to, and it pleased me greatly.

He and his friend, Eduardo—a wealthy banker, about

Jaime's age and similar in temperament—took me on a "tour de force" one night around the western hemisphere's oldest city.

We began by heading for the Plaza de Garibaldi, a city square in the shadow of the forty-four-story Torre Latino-americano—the Latin American Tower—which is Mexico City's equivalent of the Empire State Building. Since the city is at an altitude of seventy-two hundred feet, Mexicans claim it's the world's highest building.

There was music in the air as we approached the plaza, and soon enough its colorful source came into view. Mariachis, hundreds of them, sombrero after sombrero, their black costumes loaded with braid, lace, and embroidery in great extravagance. They played either trumpet, violin, *racinto* (a small guitar), *guitaron* or *guitara*.

And even today, you can hire a mariachi band, drive them to your girlfriend's house, and they'll stand beneath her window and serenade her. If she still loves you—or if she accepts your musical apology (if that's what it is)—she'll turn her lights on and off. If the lights aren't flicked, then your expression of love has fallen on deaf ears. Or perhaps she's already fallen into bed with another man, and can't be bothered reaching for the light switch!

But since this type of thing doesn't really account for most of the mariachi business, what they were doing was simple hustling. They'd pick upon a likely tourist or couple, whether on foot or in their car, and the mariachis would then surround their targets while the leader expressed his overpowering urge to entertain them with a serenade.

It was difficult, of course, to refuse. The cost per song is only fifteen pesos ($1.20) so Jaime and Eduardo ordered a serenade of welcome for me. It was lovely!

The word *mariachi*, incidentally, comes from the French word *marriage*. During the French influence on the country in the nineteenth century, musicians would play at wedding parties, and as the years went by, the practice came to be associated with romance in general.

From early morning till way past midnight, Garibaldi Square is full of visitors. Around the square are various *cantinas*—Mexico's equivalent to France's bistro or Italy's trattoria.

The mariachis gather there to quench their thirst and exchange their latest stories. If business is slow, they'll even sit around the cantina and play their music. Tequila, pulque, and mezcal are the popular drinks.

My favorite cantina was La Tenampa on the Plaza Garibaldi itself. The atmosphere was typically Mexican, but with an interesting mixture of customers. Wrinkled old Mexicans were slowly getting drunk on their favorite booze, top fashion models would strut in accompanied by wealthy young men, and clean-looking hippies and bohemian students came by with their friends.

I had a fine time at La Tenampa with Jaime and Eduardo. We were particularly intrigued by an old man with only one leg who moved around the cafe in a wheelchair. On his lap was a drawing board, and he drew a wonderful sketch of Jaime and me. There was also a Mexican-Indian man in his late sixties who carried some gadget that produced electrical shocks. He made the rounds of the tables and the deal was this: he'd administer a jolt of one hundred volts to a man; if the man stood up to it, and thus proved he was a real *machismo*, there was no cost. If the man reacted (and who wouldn't, to one hundred volts?) the charge was three pesos. You figure it out!

Bordering Plaza Garibaldi on one side is the Santa Cecilia Church, and on another is an immense market place. Jaime and Eduardo explained many of the different foods to me, and I recognized tacos, tortillas, and the chiles. There were all sorts of meats (pork seemed a favorite), vegetables and fruit, but they were displayed rather grubbily, and I'd certainly think twice before eating anything from there.

The stands at the market were called *puestos* and one of them was attended by a voluptuous, middle-aged woman who, as a young beauty, had been a great singer and performer. She was selling her different brands of coffee, and occasionally, when the mood was right, she'd read palms or burst into song. She was a true delight! We encouraged her to sing a few numbers, and soon her strong voice echoed throughout the market and everyone joined in. It was a wonderful, impromptu concert, and together with various game booths which were nearby, it gave the market a fiestalike ambience. The popular game booth was on where you could pop balloons with darts, and just like every small-town fun fair, the prize was a stuffed toy or a Disney doll.

There were other interesting markets. Similar to the Marché aux Puces in Paris, Mexico City had La Gunilla, better known as the Thief Market. Silver, chinaware, linens, jewelry, and such would be stolen by professional thieves who would sell them to merchants at La Gunilla, who in turn would sell them to the general public. Indeed, according to my two hosts, wealthy Mexicans who'd been ripped off would always check the market for their possessions, and if they found them, they'd simply have to buy them back.

Pickpockets abound in the Mexican capital. In fact, the city is full of contrasts; rich and poor live close together and terrible slum areas run adjacent to fashionable shopping streets. The city was also quite polluted, and on bad days, at that high altitude, it was almost difficult to breathe.

If tourists didn't speak a dozen or so words of Spanish, they were treated like the gringo-pox. But those who tried to express themselves in Spanish, even if they didn't succeed, were enthusiastically greeted—as long as they obviously were trying. The Mexicans were warm and generous hosts.

One day as we wandered through the city Jaime pointed out a group of peasants. They were typical newcomers, he said, having just come into the city from the outlying areas; they seemed dumbfounded and lost, staring wide-eyed, like children, not believing the opulence that they saw. I felt guilty when Jaime pointed out that the fifteen pesos I'd spent on breakfast that morning would have bought an entire peasant family's Sunday dinner.

Still, as a tourist I wanted to check out the shopping, so we went to La Zona Rosa (not to be confused with Acapulco's zona roja—the red light district), one of Mexico City's most fashionable shopping and residential areas. Prices often were exorbitant, and the quality, particularly in clothing, was often poor. If they can afford it, most smart Mexicans have their clothing fashioned in New York or Europe.

For that matter, many of Mexico's rich young men shop for more than their suits outside the country. The majority of Jaime's friends were married to girls from Sweden, Denmark, Germany, Holland, or the United States. In Mexico, blond is beautiful!

Jaime took me to Le Club Polo, an "in" discotheque just outside Mexico City, aimed at the young sophisticates. Since, as I've mentioned, we weren't having a physical affair, Jaime was very discreet when I got turned on to Pedro, and he courteously disappeared.

I'd spotted Pedro before at Armando's Le Club in Acapulco, and we'd exchanged the occasional greeting there, but this night in Mexico City, the magic seemed right and we were really digging each other, dancing for hours and hours, getting all hot and horny.

He was a lovely eighteen-year-old, just a bit under six feet, with a fantastic body, soft eyes, and almost babylike features. His chest was firm, his stomach was flat, and his ass was snug.

When we got back to my hotel room, we kissed and necked passionately, and then I rubbed body lotion on his bare broad back, meanwhile kissing his neck and earlobes. He was lying on his stomach, relaxing under my hands, and even though I hadn't come close to his groin, I suddenly felt his back arch, and his bottom twitched about six times. He was so excited, he was already creaming the sheets!

His ass was warm and tingling, and I began to gently squeeze his balls with one hand while I massaged his penis back to life with the other. Those eighteen-year-olds! They're lovely, quick rabbits, coming at the drop of a hat. But at that age they can come and come and come again.

Which is exactly what he did. We made love, properly and passionately, three times before he had to get dressed and return home. He was still going to a university, and didn't want his socialite mother to become suspicious of how he was spending (and how much he spent in me!) his evenings.

With the scent of his semen still fresh in the bed, I fell asleep, hugging my big pillow and imagining that it was Pedro, my big beautiful baby boy!

Two days later, his mother called—to my great surprise—and invited me to join her and her boyfriend, and Pedro, for dinner. Her son had tactfully mentioned only that he'd met the author of *The Happy Hooker,* knowing that his mother had read it and was a fan of mine. I'm sure she never guessed that her son would one day appear in one of my books!

I'll call her Anna. She was an extremely elegant woman in her late thirties. Her house was hung with superb art, and decorated in excellent taste. Her boyfriend was a successful young professional, and they took Pedro and me to one of the city's most fashionable Mexican restaurants, a beautiful eighteenth century hacienda.

Over *carne asada* (steak with chili and vegetables) and *chiles rellenos* (stuffed peppers), we talked about Mexico's enormous gap between the aristocracy and the peasants.

"The government today," Anna told me, "finally seems to be doing something about it—both officially and unofficially. After forty years of political stability, the country is prospering. The gross national product has increased remarkably, and plenty of money is being invested back into the land and the people."

She also explained that many of the rich and influential families had developed a sense of conscience, and were attempting their own antipoverty campaigns, raising funds from among their own class.

But the poverty remains enormous, and despite her optimism, it will take more than dilettantes' charity to bring a decent standard of living to vast portions of the country's fifty million people.

Anna was a very protective mother and though our evening was perfectly delightful and while I would have been willing to enjoy a *dessert à deux* with her son, she made certain he stayed out of my reach. And when the evening drew to a close and they drove me back to my hotel, Pedro safely sat next to mamma.

MASSAGE PARLAY

Jaime and Eduardo took me, the next afternoon, to escape the lazy Mexican heat in a Chinese bath. Unlike the gay steam baths and fancy massage parlors that can be found elsewhere, this was a simple spa in an old downtown house.

Usually men and women were segregated, but bribes seem to be a way of life in Mexico, and the attendant was easily persuaded into letting us share a sauna, shower, and steam room together. We undressed and, armed with towels, entered the hot room.

We were greeted by a huge man—he could have stepped out of a Mexican Kung Fu film, if you can imagine one—dressed only in white shorts and sneakers. His name was Emilio and he was a man of few words but lots of muscle. He generally massaged only men, and I was his first female client. The look he gave me from the corner of his dark eyes indicated that he was more than delighted with the change of pace.

However, Jaime was to be first. He lay down on his back and as Emilio began to massage his belly, I kiddingly fondled Jaime's cock. It rose in a jiffy, and Emilio didn't quite know where to look . . . at his client's stiffening member or at my bare breasts.

To save him the trouble of deciding, I chose to take a shower with Eduardo. We soaped each other under the hot shower and kissed with the water spraying us. As he held me tightly I could feel the shudders ripple through his body. His cock was by now solid hard-on, and when he'd thoroughly covered me in suds, he dropped the soap and o course I bent to pick it up. He grasped my hips from behind and, with my tush up in the air, he slipped into my juicy lucy.

With the water showering down on us, running in our eyes, ears, noses, and mouths, we had a magnificent fuck!

The hot water combined with his voluminous jism and almost poached it, I suppose—whatever, it turned thick and gooey. I was certainly in the right spot to wash it off though, so I did, and then we turned the shower to cold and both cooled down.

Then it was time for my massage. Emilio could hardly wait to get hold of me. His massage table offered a fairly decent view of the open showers, so he'd seen and heard my little adventure with Eduardo and was pretty turned on.

It was great to simply lie back and let this giant's trained fingers do their work! He oiled my body entirely and rubbed me from top to toe, and though at times it seemed that he'd break every bone in me, I loved it. When his strong hands kneaded my legs and thighs, they seemed to slow down somewhat, and then he became very gentle, his fingers almost caressing my inner thighs.

Jaime and Eduardo were having a fine time just watching the lusty look in Emilio's eyes. The big masseur had a cock's-eye view of my moist snatch, and was having trouble controlling himself. There was a thick bulge in his shorts and he was literally drooling.

The animal in him was surfacing, and his breath became louder and louder. His face was almost in my crotch and he was rubbing his groin against the table edge.

His hearty lust had also managed to make me pretty horny again and I encouraged him to take off his pants. Although the three of us were already naked, he looked guiltily at the two men, thinking they wouldn't approve. But they spoke to him in rapid Spanish, indicating their support.

They then discreetly walked away and kept watch at the doors, just to make sure no supervisor caught Emilio with his pants down. This was certainly a far cry from Andreas and his masseur.

Well, his hands were big and I was expecting a cock to match. But I wasn't prepared for the dynamite dong that finally he flipped out of his pants . . . it was so big, in fact, that he actually had difficulty pulling his pants over it!

Emilio's tool was, like his body, olive-hued, and the head was dark and glistening. It stared at me very invitingly and I was almost expecting it to wink at me. Since he wasn't circumcised—although in its rigidity the foreskin had popped back—I invited him into the shower. While he stood under the spray, I rubbed body cream into my legs and breasts, then into my pubes.

Looking at this beautiful chunk of man soaping himself under the shower really turned me on . . . the way he rubbed the lather into his hairy armpits and all over his thick, hairy chest, down to his mighty, meaty tool and around his strong ass, practically made me come! My clit had swollen to twice its normal size and I took a firm grip on myself, but stayed under control.

Then he approached me, dripping wet and superhorny. He had me on my back on the massage table, then knelt astride me and pushed his prick into my mouth. I sucked the head and flipped the skin back and forth over it. The veins down the shaft seemed alive from the blood running through them and his nuts were like two hard-boiled, extra large eggs.

What a difference between Eduardo or Pedro and this superman! They were sophomores with miniature tools compared with this guy. Whoever says that size doesn't matter just doesn't know what she's missing. I agree that it's not everything, and physically it may not make that much difference, but oooooh! just the sight of a big huge cock, let alone the feel of it, makes me writhe with pleasure.

I was hardly in a position to measure the delightful dork but I'm sure nine inches couldn't be an exaggeration. I easily went hand-over-hand three times on it. (As a comparison, the length of this paperback in your hands is seven inches, and that's pretty good length by anyone's standards). I know some people say that more than a mouthful is a waste—or more than a handful, depending on your tastes—and if it's properly used, a cock is a cock is a cock. But I'll never say no to the biggies.

Emilio then rubbed the mighty member between my tits, and the touch of his dark stiffness against the ligh pink of my erect nipples made me shiver, and goosebumps covered my body. I felt my vagina percolating and I couldn't wait for him to pound into me.

It seemed to be my day to get it from behind, but Emilio did it slightly different from Eduardo. He laid me, tummy-down, on the massage table, with my legs spread out and pussy right at the edge. Then he stood between my legs and thrust his joint deep, deep, deep into me and fucked me until I saw stars. He was jamming into me sensationally, at one point with his left hand under me, fingering my clit, and his right hand on my ass, fingering my rosy anus.

But he wasn't at all interested in getting it over with. The fun was just beginning!

Emilio turned me around then, so that I was on my back but still at the edge of the table, and he continued fucking me nipple-side-up for a bit. I could see him now when I opened my eyes, and his face was a portrait of pleasure.

Then he jumped onto the table with me, lay back, and with his giant mast pointing north he picked me up and sat me on it. I squatted astride his hips and did enough pushups to lose ten pounds.

All the while I was holding on to his strong, bull-like shoulders and it was a treat to see his eyes squinting, his mouth almost frothing with passion, perspiration beading his forehead, and streams of sweat glistening through the hair on his chest. What a man! I shut my eyes and thrust, not just up and down but also back and forth, giving my clit the stimulation it wanted. I leaned forward, still hunched on his huge cock, and kissed his eager lips, never losing the fantastic rhythm we had going for us.

Emilio was thrusting incredibly now and we were really fucking each other, when he yelled something in Spanish and jerked so violently that I bounced up off him. Believe it or not, I came down right on target, and his prick shot back into me. We repeated the trick a few more times until we were both soaking wet with perspiration from all the work and excitement. I've had enough practice so that I can time my orgasms pretty well, and we'd both managed to hold back for a while. But when I felt those distant rumblings from deep within his loins, I knew it was climax time, and we both made the best of it. I pushed my pelvic bone down as far as possible on his cock and it started pumping its load into me, thrusting and thrilling me with ejaculation after ejaculation.

It was such a far-out fuck that I could imagine the roles were reversed, that I was the man and the prick was mine. Nothing else was changed, we still looked the same—but our genitals had switched sources.

As I looked down between our legs, his pushing and pulling cock really seemed an extension of my own body.

Wow . . . what a sexual fantasy! I sometimes wish it were true.

Emilio and I were thoroughly exhausted. We supported each other to the shower. Then Emilio prepared for his next client, but I was sure that his work wouldn't seem quite as much fun for a while.

Jaime and Eduardo drove me back to my hotel and I was into my siesta as soon as I lay down on my bed.

I had to rest, for it was my final evening in Mexico City. . . .

We began our final fling at Villa Florencia, a sparkling, palacelike spot in the Zona Rosa, where we nibbled on appetizers and talked about our various future plans. Both Jaime and Eduardo were generous and outgoing, and wonderful company, but I never really got inside their heads—I was never really permitted to see into their private personalities. So our conversation was fairly light.

We took a final look at Bosque de Chapultepec, meaning Chapultepec park or forest. It was an oasis of lush greenery in the middle of the city, and the traditional home of Mexican rulers dating back to the Aztecs. The president's official home is there, along with several museums, one of them in an eighteenth-century castle which was the emperor's palace during Maximilian of Hapsburg's brief reign in the nineteenth century.

Mexico's history is colorful, and Jaime told me a few things that I'd never really absorbed before.

"For instance, Xaviera, did you know that the American state of Texas was under Mexican rule until it rebelled and joined the United States . . . in 1846, I think. Mexico was furious, of course, and it resulted in the United States invading Mexico. That's how we lost land in Arizona, New Mexico, and California. There was a fortress right here in Chapultepec!"

It was Maximilian who did much to make the capital city beautiful. In 1858, the Mexican president made enemies with the conservative element. They begged for help from Napoleon III of France, who sent Maximilian (brother of the Austrian Kaiser Franz-Josef) to rule the country and stabilize the government. He lasted only three years, though, during which time he was responsible for much handsome town-planning. He was finally executed, and the president he'd replaced was returned to power.

We continued on a final drive through the city, passing scores of monuments, Aztec ruins, impressive palaces, and churches. Eduardo pointed out the Plaza Mexico, near Avenida Insurgentes, the world's greatest bull ring. The winter season is the highlight of the bullfighting year, but neither Eduardo nor Jaime were fans, and I must say that it's a sport which has no appeal for me.

As for the prostitution scene in Mexico City, it seemed to be much on the same level as most American cities. The sleazier night spots were easy locations to hitch up with a hooker, and with my eye for talent I spotted more than a few classy callgirls cruising the best hotels. There were also the established brothels, the leader being La Bandida. The going rate, according to Jaime, was about sixty dollars in Mexico City.

When I told them I'd visited La Huerta in Acapulco, Jaime told me that I'd missed a New Year's Eve tradition named the "Night of El Burro." He described it in his carefully chosen English.

"Once a year the donkey is brought in to excite any woman from the visiting audience. If there are no volunteers, then one of the whores performs. She is placed on a table, which is pushed under the standing donkey, and while the burro is held by attendants, its penis is lowered into the woman."

Quite a show for New Year's Eve . . . certainly a change from watching Guy Lombardo on television!

For our last hour together, we returned to Jaime's apartment for music, food, and refreshment. Then they dropped me off at my hotel, and we exchanged farewells. Their hospitality had been superb, and "thank you" hardly seemed to convey my appreciation. They seemed to understand though, and rather than prolong the goodbyes, we kissed and hugged, and they drove away.

YOUR BASIC ZIHUATENEJO

Before leaving Mexico, I took time for a quick visit to Zihuatenejo (zee-wot-en-ayo). It was reached by a small plane which flew out from Mexico City whenever there were sufficient passengers on board.

It's a peaceful fishing village at the foot of southern Sierra Madre, 150 miles from Acapulco, and apparently much like Acapulco was twenty-five years ago. The banditos used to come down from the mountains to eat, drink, and swing in the town; but now they've grown more peaceful and stick to growing marijuana in the mountains. The legendary vicious mountain bandits have found it much more profitable to run their mammoth grass farms . . . they also avoid conflicts with the law, oddly enough, because the police tend to close their official eyes to the dope trade. Most of the grass ends up on the American market, though of course the famous Acapulco Gold is exported worldwide. I'm amused at the irony of it—the favorite food of the peace generation is actually responsible for bringing peace to the Mexican mountains.

Not entirely, though. The rough bandits still exist, and there are enough bullet-scarred bodies and cars (including the taxi I rode in) to prove it.

The village of Zihuatenejo has one main street, which was finally paved with cobblestones in 1973. There's a great crescent-shaped bay and beautiful sandy beaches, with none of the rampant commercialism that's to be found in Acapulco. . . . The people are friendly, and though their comforts and luxuries are minimal, they're satisfied with their lifestyle.

More and more non-Mexicans are discovering the village as a storybook retreat, and many fear that before long the idyllic spot will lose its innocence and become just another tourist trap.

I spent most of my day in Zihuatenejo with a charming television producer from New York, who was obsessed with doing public affairs programs on pollution but had become so involved in and depressed by his projects that he'd escaped to the little village for a week.

He was a strange creature with an amazing sense of humor and great zest for the bizarre. His dark, curly hair was receding, even though he wasn't yet thirty, so to protect it from the sun he kept it covered most of the time with a floppy gray Irish fisherman's hat. This earned him stares from just about everyone, but he seemed quite pleased with his little quirk of fashion.

Thomas was also an energetic drinker, and in one moment of madness that afternoon, he called for drinks all around in the small hotel bar. People seemed to emerge from nowhere for a full half hour, and he ended up paying almost seventy-five dollars. An expensive bit of magnanimity, but he seemed to enjoy doing it.

Knowing who I was, he naturally talked to me about my sexual attitudes and athletic accomplishments.

"Don't you ever enjoy your basic fuck anymore?"

"What do you mean?" I asked.

"Your basic fuck," he replied, as if in explanation. "A straight old-fashioned in-out-in-out-in-out-oh-my-god-brr-brr basic fuck. Between the sheets, with the guy on top . . . no voyeurs, no appliances, no animals, no showers. Just your basic fuck."

"Oh," I exclaimed. *"That* kind of basic fuck. Well, of course, I enjoy it. Why do you ask?"

"Well, it seems to me, Xaviera"—he pronounced i eggs-have-yaira—"darling, that in your book it's always with ten people or *en passant,* or dangling from a chandelier, or in a disused elevator in the Chrysler Building."

He was exaggerating, of course, but he got his poin across.

"You're trying to say that I only write about extraordi nary fucks in extraordinary situations with extraordinar people. Well, of course I do. Who wants to read abou 'your basic fuck'? It's so basic that it's not much fun to write about and not much fun to read about, either—it's great to *do,* and I do it all the time—but I could hardly fill a book with just basic fucks. It's my tastes for the unusual that give me a story to tell, and people want to read about the extraordinary."

"Hmmm," he said, conceding the point. "And you're telling me that everything you write about is true . . . like the scene with the dog . . . or where you had to pee on some guy?"

"Well, I'm certainly glad you've read *The Happy Hooker*," I responded. "But, yes, of course it's all true . . . listen, Thomas, I may have a vivid imagination, but it's not so vivid that I'd ever be able to invent half the kinky, crazy things I've done."

"And you've enjoyed it all?" he asked incredulously.

"Well, no, I'm not saying that. A lot of the freaky scenes were repulsive . . . either at the time or in retrospect . . . and I haven't repeated them. But on the whole (if you'll pardon the expression) I enjoy practically any kind of sexual expression. And the things I write about in my books are there because I've done them, believe me!"

He seemed convinced, and went on to a few questions about specific parts of *The Happy Hooker* that had particularly turned him on. I thought it was all building up to a big pitch for a personal test-drive on his part—and there was something in his eyes and mischievous sense of humor that would have made me say yes—but he let it be known that he was married to a wonderful woman, and that their own sex life provided him with all the satisfaction he could ask for. He was perfectly prepared to accept my sexual qualifications without going for firsthand knowledge.

His honesty was refreshing, and we understood each other. We had supper together, and he was a warm, witty companion.

We whiled away the evening, laughing and joking (He: "What's the best way to serve turkey? . . . Join the Turkish army!" Me: "What has the shortest sex life? . . . An egg—it gets laid once and it gets eaten once!") until the clean, fresh air made us so sleepy we had to call it a night.

With a chaste good-night kiss, we went to our separate bedrooms, and the next morning I flew out of Zihuatenejo to Mexico City, then via Canadian Pacific to Toronto, my new home.

XAVIERA GOES CANADIAN

From the seventy-degree temperatures of Mexico, I was plunged into twenty-degree weather in Toronto. I'd forgotten the cold and snow of a New York winter, and Toronto's are even harsher. But don't believe for a minute the myth that Canada is a snow-bound wilderness with igloos on each corner and huskies running wild in the streets.

In Eastern Canada, Toronto sees perhaps fifteen inches of snow in its coldest month, while Montreal may see twice that amount. The last of the snow has gone by mid-April, and generally isn't seen again till late October. In the west, Vancouver, which is on the Pacific Ocean, sees much less snow but has an abundant rainfall, particularly in December. In summers, the climate is equally extreme—eighty and ninety-degree temperatures are common.

Speaking of the northern myth, incidentally, it happens every year in Canada—some American tourist arrives at Montreal International Airport on a sweltering 95-degree August afternoon with a set of skis in one hand and a fur coat in the other, expecting to see a friendly lumberjack who'll direct him to a nearby ski slope. It sounds ridiculous, but it happens every year!

Canada is a big pleasant country, full of warm welcoming people, and Toronto is a remarkably friendly city of over two million. It's the capital of the country in every sense but political (the official capital is Ottawa). The bilingual nation's English-language radio and television networks, magazines, publishers, etc. are all based in Toronto. The French-language nerve center is Montreal, but since the vast majority of the country is English-speaking, Toronto is *the* place to be.

The added advantage for me, of course, is that it's just an hour's flight from New York City, and with direct-distance-dialing, my American lawyer, publishers and other business contacts were just an expensive phone call away.

So here I was at the end of January, 1973, ready to settle permanently (a month, a year, a lifetime?) in Toronto. It was almost nine months to the day since I'd left New York City, and the figure struck me as interesting. Had my nine-month swing through Europe been some form of gestation period; was I about to be born into a new life?

In a sense, yes.

During one of my previous visits to Toronto for a television appearance I had met a very engaging 39-year-old Canadian Jewish man, who reminded me a lot of my father when he was young. I'll refer to him as Paul from now on.

We must have made a favorable impression on each other because we met again—and not by chance the second time. Something new was happening to me. I was in love. I had almost given up hope of ever finding a man with whom I could share love and understanding.

Larry, the Silver Fox, knew as well as I did that our three year affair was over, but he was not willing to let it end gracefully.

He was still my manager and I guess he figured if we didn't stay together, he'd lose out on a good thing . . . for let's face it, I had become more than just a girlfriend to him—I was a gold mine, a great source of income, prestige and attention.

So Larry would come up to Toronto occasionally for one legitimate business reason or another and he would expect to spend the weekends with me. I have to admit that although my heart was not in it at all, I did spend several Saturday afternoons with him and on some occasions even had sex with him. On reflection, I guess it was a case of the proverbial "Old habits die hard."

I soon gave up Larry altogether as both a manager and a boyfriend. Particularly when he finally found out about my true feelings for Paul, someone he had met only once but never suspected to be my lover. I had kept it a secret from him until a mutual acquaintance informed Larry on one of his trips to Toronto about the involvement between Paul and me. Larry lost his cool as well as me in a screaming hysterical fight.

And while the years that Larry and I shared are full of good memories, the kindest emotion that I can sum up for him now is indifference.

If you happen to catch me on a bad day, it's *grrrrr!* And when I think of the ways Larry screwed me—and I do *not* mean sexually—I can be very vindictive.

I get angry at myself, too, for fooling myself all those years—for telling myself that I loved him, for not realizing that we were just two people who desperately needed whatever we could offer each other. I thought it was love because I wanted it to be love.

Until the real thing came along....

So I'll just say that there's nothing between Larry and me anymore. I'll always be grateful for the good times, I'll try to forget the bad times; I hope that his book is successful, and that in the years ahead he'll be able to forget me and be happy.

It was a great feeling to be free from Larry after three years and ... to be in love again. In general Paul and I aim for privacy in our love affair.

The greatest satisfaction I get out of our relationship is that our weekends and nights together provide a retreat from the usual hustle-bustle with constant phones ringing, lectures, writing, promotions and interviews that were so much part of my daily life.

In other words I worship our privacy; our romance is blooming and there's a great deal of mutual trust, respect, honesty, affection, stability, security and passion in our feelings.

It's great to be respected and loved as a person again rather than as a sex symbol. As for my own feelings: I love to be needed and need to be loved and all those needs are finally fulfilled completely by Paul.

PIPADOXI

"... and what thou art can never be destroyed."
—Emily Bronte

EDITOR'S NOTE: Xaviera's father's long suffering came to an end on October 12, 1973, at the age of seventy-one. Xaviera was in a small Canadian city at the time, on a lecture tour, when her mother broke the news to her by telephone. Alone in her hotel room, Xaviera wrote a final love letter to the one person she's loved more than anyone else in the world. "It helped ease the pain for a few minutes," she told me. She kept the letter, and here it is. Because you've shared so many of her life's experiences, we thought you may be willing to share her grief, too.

Cornwall, Ontario
October 12, 1973

My dearest Pipadoxi,

Across an ocean, in a country unfamiliar to you, I'm struggling to accept the truth that at last you're at peace forever. I can't control my tears, and my heart literally aches . . . and somehow now I feel closer than ever to you, you whom I've loved so much.

In a harsh, anonymous hotel room, with nothing to remind me of you or of home . . . not even the menorah you gave me so long ago to carry as a reminder of our Jewish ancestry . . . I was having bad dreams, a nightmare . . . intuitively I felt it coming . . . and then the phone call. . . .

"My child, it's happened," mamma said calmly. "Your father died this afternoon at four. He won't suffer anymore . . . it's best for him, poor soul."

For a moment I froze, then the tears came.

"Please don't cry, Xaviera . . . talk to me!" begged mamma.

Then I asked her how it happened. Just flesh and bones she said you were, with one attack after another. Then for twenty-four hours she never left you, till you finally slipped away in her arms. We all knew it was about to happen, of course, but the truth was so hard to accept.

And so, across the thousands of miles of telephone cable, we tried to comfort each other, until finally in grief and exhaustion, we whispered goodbye.

When I was ten, I started calling you Pipadoxi . . . and you were always the man I adored, admired, and envied. Your wit, intelligence, charm, and warmth have always been my inspiration.

You were a devoted husband, a bon vivant, a bohemian in your own way. Your many patients, for whom you worked endlessly and selflessly, by their own good health stand as monuments to your skill as a physician.

And I remember the crazy times, late at night, you and mamma dancing, or you without your reading glasses, playing the piano and missing the odd key!

There were the rough spots, too, as in every marriage, but they never lasted long. You were the first man I ever saw weeping.

Look, it's me crying now . . . tears of rage, sorrow, frustration, and relief. You, who did so much to ease the suffering of others, you suffered longest and most yourself. Poor mamma, too, she never wavered in her love for you, and devoted every moment of her life to caring for you these past years. What justice is there? You suffered so much in the concentration camp during the war . . . surely that was enough for a lifetime!

But I remember you happy . . . playing with Trippie, our dog, along the beach . . . or with me, hand in hand during our summer holidays, teaching me new languages . . . or impulsively embracing and hugging mamma in the street. And I remember you at work, rushing out of the house at any hour, in any weather, to heal the sick and comfort the infirm.

Then your first stroke, and suddenly it was you who were sick and infirm . . . and dear Pipadoxi, how you suffered these past eight years! Unable to face the reality of it, I couldn't stay in Amsterdam, and I left mamma alone to care for you. Can you ever forgive me?

Dear papa, farewell. . . . My love for you will never grow less. Wherever your spirit is now, watch over me with affection, please . . . I still desperately need your love and understanding and approval.

> Your depressed, lonely, loving daughter . . . your Xaviera.

EPILOGUE

So here we are . . . the latest installment in the adventures of Xaviera Hollander.

What makes this book different is that it's not only about me, but it's *by* me! I've been reading about myself lately in other people's books, and I'm not certain whether to be flattered or annoyed. The worst of the lot is Robin Moore's rip-off, *The Making of the Happy Hooker*.

Robin Moore's is an outright insult, frankly. Three quarters of the book is copied from the original manuscript we collaborated on for my first book. For one reason or another, they were edited out, so Moore eventually semi-juiced them up and managed to peddle them to a publisher. There's 180 pages selling for $1.50, and although I'll admit I'm prejudiced, I have to give the book a "don't bother" rating.

A recent review of the book stated, "Moore covers the same ground *The Happy Hooker* books have, but not so well."

So stick with Xaviera, and you're assured of firsthand information.

Now, back to real life: It seems I've come full circle again, and it's time to hit the road, I fear—not through my own choice, but because the government of Canada doesn't want me here. Because I've publicly and honestly admitted to being an ex-madam, that makes me a self-confessed criminal under Canadian law, so it appears that I may not be allowed to remain in the country.

Whatever happened to freedom of speech or press?

I've appealed this decision, of course, because I certainly don't think I'm a threat to Canadian peace, liberty, or morals . . . and because I truly want to live here. It's a beautiful country, both in physical terms and in terms of its people. It somehow manages to combine the best aspects of North American life with the civility and freedom of European traditions. And as Watergate uncovers more and more national disgraces, Canada appears remarkably pure and faithful by comparison.

Speaking of Watergate . . . that's the same government that so disapproved of my prostitution activities, and thought America would be a better place without me. They dared call me a whore! At least I was honest. And I paid my taxes!

Sadly, Canada doesn't want me either, although the Canadian public has been quick to come to my support. I have fond hopes that ultimately the government will change its mind, and I'll be able to become a Canadian citizen. If not, well, I'll just continue to fulfill my destiny and wander around the world looking for home.

It was never intended this way, but as I mentioned earlier, it seems I've come full circle . . . this book is ending as it began. I'm standing on the threshold of another cycle, another era. But as long as I can look backward with pride, and look forward with hope, I'm not about to stop living. And that, I think, is what counts . . . keeping it up. Any way we can.

Thank you, deeply and honestly, for your letters, your support, your kind wishes . . . there's a lot of love in this world, and sometimes some of us have no one to share it with. But I'm grateful that so many people sometimes choose me to partake in a moment of their lives. If I haven't been able to answer your letter, it doesn't mean I don't care, and I hope you'll understand.

No matter where I wander, you can always address your letters with requests for book information, my latest record, pictures, games, perfumes—or just a friendly hello—to my newly formed fan club, Xaviera Hollander's Special Collection, at Postal Box 175, Station A, Scarborough, Ontario, Canada. Or you can always drop me a line via my publishers, Warner Paperback Library, 75 Rockefeller Plaza, New York 10019, and I'm sure they'll gladly forward it to me.

Gotta go now! There's a world full of adventures still ahead, and I'm always in the mood for more . . . so thanks for your company on our trip around the world, and let's keep in touch. Toodleloo till next time!

                        Love,
                        Xaviera Hollander
                        Toronto
                        1 May 1974

READ ALL ABOUT

"THE HAPPY HOOKER"!

XAVIERA! The Continuing Adventures of "The Happy Hooker" ($1.50, 78-278) By Xaviera Hollander. Picks up "The Happy Hooker" saga and tells all about her adventures as the entire country was "hooked" by her escapades.

LETTERS TO THE HAPPY HOOKER ($1.50, 78-277) Personally selected from the thousands and thousands of letters she received, "The Happy Hooker" gives her candid comments plus glimpses into her wild life.

MY LIFE WITH XAVIERA ($1.50, 78-424) By Larry "The Silver Fox". What is it like to be the boy-friend of the most notorious woman in America? What "The Happy Hooker" didn't *dare* tell . . . Larry "The Silver Fox" *does*!

XAVIERA GOES WILD ($1.75, 59-632) Paris sizzles! St. Tropez burns! as Xaviera, "The Happy Hooker" travels around Europe where things really swing after dark.

Best of Bestsellers
Warner Paperback Library

Available wherever paperbacks are sold.

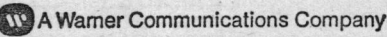 A Warner Communications Company

If you are unable to obtain these books from your local dealer, they may be ordered from the publisher.
Please allow 4 weeks for delivery.
WARNER PAPERBACK LIBRARY
P.O. Box 690
New York, N.Y. 10019

Please send me the books I have checked.
I am enclosing payment plus 15¢ per copy to cover postage and handling.
N.Y. State residents add applicable sales tax.
Name ....
Address ....
City .... State .... Zip ....
_____ Please send me your free mail order catalog

"Mean, funny, hysterical, melancholic...unique."
—*Los Angeles Times*

AFTER CLAUDE

by Iris Owens
78-427, $1.50

AFTER CLAUDE is the hilarious story of a woman cast from her lover's bed into a world that doesn't understand her . . . but that isn't because she doesn't try to explain herself—wittily, offensively, brilliantly. "Harriet tells her story like a female Lenny Bruce," says John Lahr, and "while I was reading this tale . . . I was laughing too hard to see the page."

Harriet's story of what happened before, during and after Claude "is like watching a woman depilate with an acetylene torch."
—*Newsweek*

If you are searching for true love or found it many years ago, you *must* read *After Claude*, "a very funny book by an exhilarating talent and intelligence."—*New York Times*

NOW ON SALE
WHEREVER PAPERBACKS ARE SOLD.

W A Warner Communications Company

If you are unable to obtain these books from your local dealer, they may be ordered from the publisher.
Please allow 4 weeks for delivery.

WARNER PAPERBACK LIBRARY
P.O. Box 690
New York, N.Y. 10019

Please send me _____ copy(ies) of *After Claude* (78-427, $1.50)
I am enclosing payment plus 15¢ per copy to cover postage and handling.
N.Y. State residents add applicable sales tax.

Name ....
Address ....
City .... State .... Zip ....

_____ Please send me your free mail order catalog